Some girls do...

My life as a teenager

edited by
Jacinta Tynan

ARENA
ALLEN&UNWIN

First published in 2007
This edition first published 2010

Arena Books, an imprint of
Allen & Unwin
83 Alexander Street
Crows Nest NSW 2065
Australia
Phone: (61 2) 8425 0100
Fax: (61 2) 9906 2218
Email: info@allenandunwin.com
Web: www.allenandunwin.com

Cataloguing-in-Publication details are available from:
National Library of Australia
www.librariesaustralia.nla.gov

  ISBN 978 1 74237 260 0.

Set in 12/15.5 pt Bembo by Midland Typesetters, Australia
Printed and bound in Australia by McPherson's Printing Group

10 9 8 7 6 5 4 3 2 1

Contents

Preface

Everyone tells you that your teenage years are the best years of your life. But try finding someone who really thinks that's so. They're actually the toughest years and the most confusing. Your body starts to change, friends are hard-won, your loins are full of longing but your head is not, and you're no longer sure if your parents really do know best.

It's also one of the most crucial times for a girl, when she starts to decide who she is and what she wants. The choices you make during adolescence can set the path for the rest of your life.

This book is for every woman who has been a teenager or is one now. It features true stories of the teenage years of some of Australia's top female writers, women who've battled everything from first crushes and lust to drugs, racism and sexual abuse. The 51 writers in this book have known angst, despair and not being part of the cool group, yet all of them have lived to tell the tale.

And by doing that—by donating their stories— they are helping a new generation of teenage girls. All royalties from the book are going to the SISTER2sister Program—a mentoring program connecting teenage girls from disadvantaged backgrounds (poverty, abuse, neglect) with women who are older and, in most cases, wiser. For the first time in their lives, these girls are given a role model, someone who will listen to them without judging them and, hopefully, help them to turn their lives around. To learn that whatever has happened in their past does not have to define their future. To break the cycle of destitution and abuse.

Even though I have three sisters of my own, I decided to adopt another one through the SISTER2sister Program because I'd reached a stage in my life where I thought there'd be plenty I'd be able to pass on to a teenage girl. But I failed dismally in my first task as a 'Big Sister'. My Little Sister texted me with, 'how d ya wash curtains?' I was mortified. How old did she think I was? I had to consult a book on household hints before I could reply.

There's nothing like a teenager to bring you back down to earth, which is another reason to get involved. These girls have led lives most of us—thankfully—will never know.

Imagine one girl's distress after being forced to take out a restraining order on her mother's abusive boyfriend after he threatened to kill her. How do you explain hope to two severely traumatised teenage sisters, who witnessed their father brutally murder their mother in their home? One Little Sister, whose parents are both heroin addicts, worked at a fast-food outlet to support herself through her HSC. Another moved out of her alcoholic mother's home so she could have a chance at a career.

With the support of their Big Sisters—an extra-ordinary group of women, including a gynaecologist, a magazine editor, marketing executives, mothers, a nurse, a lawyer, a mortgage broker, an aspiring pop star and a psychologist—these girls are starting again. And in the process, they remind us that dreams are still do-able, and the future is up to us.

Allen & Unwin is also donating $1 from every book sale to the SISTER2sister Program, so your purchase goes towards supporting this life-changing cause. We could have sold lamingtons to raise funds, but this way—through the words of these accomplished and inspiring writers who have shared so much of themselves with great insight, sensitivity and humour—we're also re-inforcing and celebrating the fact that you *do* come out the other side.

Enjoy. And thanks for making a difference.

Jacinta Tynan

The SISTER2sister Program's website is
www.lifechangingexperiences.org

Acknowledgements

I wasn't expecting it to be the easiest of tasks: convincing some of the country's top female authors to write for free, especially asking them to reveal intimate details about their own adolescence—an awkward era many would rather overlook. But that turned out to be the easy part. Much to my delight, most were as enthusiastic as I was about the project, leaping at the invitation to reminisce and so, in a mere twelve months, *Some girls do . . .* went to print.

It would not have been possible without:

Selwa Anthony, agent extraordinaire, who believed in the book the minute I first pitched it to her, even though I was suggesting her authors write for love. She threw her weight behind it, helping track down authors and encouraging them to contribute. Also, a huge thanks to Selena Hanet-Hutchins for her help with this endeavour.

Jude McGee, Publisher, Allen & Unwin, who 'got it'instantly and treated the book with passion and commitment.

Angela Handley, Senior Editor, Allen & Unwin, who waded through 51 stories from as many authors with great patience, interest and perfect suggestions.

Fiona Daniels, external editor, who also toiled behind the scenes doing all of the above.

Louise Thurtell and Annette Barlow, Publishers, Allen & Unwin, who suggested a stream of authors I hadn't thought of and helped source them.

Literary agents including: Sophie Hamley (Camerons Management) and Fiona Inglis (Curtis Brown) who also assisted greatly in the author search.

Those at other publishing houses who put rivalries aside for the cause, including: Alison Urquhart (Harper Collins), Gemma Rayner (Text Publishing), Sophie Higgins (ABC Books), Jane Novak (Pan Macmillan), Anyez Lindop (Penguin) and Fiona Henderson (Random House).

To the extraordinary Jessica Adams, who generously offered advice on how it's all done after she set a precedent inspiring a team of busy authors to donate their time for the best-selling Girls Night In series.

To my own private support team, my beautiful family, who is always behind me: Mum (the best mum a teenage girl could have had), Dad, Damian and Lucy, Cait and Michael, Ro, Justin and Carolina, Bubs and Tom, Dominic, Patrick and Claudia.

My friends, who encouraged me on this project and persisted with me through my absences, including: Bronwyn Curran, Fr. Jeremy Clarke SJ, Fiona MacGregor, Kelly Nestor, Elizabeth Powell, Emma Rosenberg, Lauren Rose, Ellen Stanley, Michael Tame, Sarah Wilson, Lynne Yu . . . and all the rest.

To Angelos Frangopoulos, my boss at Sky News, for rostering me around my other passions.

To the phenomenal writers who all donated their

precious time to delve deep into their own teenage experiences, many for the first time, and share their personal stories. I knew we were onto something when Nikki Gemmell responded with an enthusiastic yes. If Nikki could find the time and inclination to write a piece, even in the midst of another novel, then the others would be a cinch. Kathy Lette was next, then Jessica Adams, Belinda Alexandra . . . and there was no turning back.

Finally, but most importantly, to the team members at the SISTER2sister Program, especially its founder, my dear friend Jessica Brown, who all do extraordinary work, turning around the lives of teenage girls.

Hopefully this book will do the same.

Jacinta Tynan

Boobs

Kathy Lette

It all began with Barbie. The Breast Yearning, that is. Ever since I was a little girl, I wanted to grow those two pneumatic melons that adorned my favourite plaything. The blonde locks, long legs and small hips would come as accessories, of course; but it was the breasts I really coveted.

Looking back, it seems bizarre that I wanted to grow up to look like my doll; do little boys grow up wanting to look like a piece of Leggo? And girls, let's face it, there are logical drawbacks to a Barbie role model; a bit of moulded plastic between the legs, for starters. (Barbie manufacturers seem to think a 'clitoris' is a beach in Crete. My favourite destination is a cosy little spot which goes by the name of 'G', but that's difficult enough, even with all the right equipment.)

Well, needless to say, puberty dawned to find my mousey brown hair . . . still mousey brown (the reason blondes have more fun, by the way, is because we brunettes are too busy waxing, shaving, electrolysing and Nair hair removing). The legs? Still stunted. The hips?

Two fleshy sidecars which rode pillion with me every-where. And the breasts—an undernourished 32A.

My cup did not runneth over.

My mother's solution to my mammary angst was a 'training bra' . . . But what exactly would it train my breasts to do? Fetch slippers? Heel when called?

And if parts of your anatomy could be trained, why, I wondered, were there no training jockstraps? (For men like Mike Tyson, perhaps; men who need to be taught that there are times when a penis should roll over and play dead.)

Training gave way to stuffing. All through my teens, I was forced to fake flu as I trailed a forest of tissues.

Stuffing gave way to padding—a bra to bring out your non-existent best points.

Bosom-enlarging creams; 'I must, I must, I must increase my bust' exercises; blusher between the breasts to create the illusion of cleavage . . . To B-cup or not to B-cup, that was the constant question.

What made it worse, my best friend, Louise, was fantastically well endowed.

Out on the town together, no sooner would we latch onto a couple of hot-to-trot spunk-rats than she'd feel compelled to announce what a bore it was having such big tits. Conversation would skid to a halt. Whole rooms would fall into a cacophonous silence as every male eyeball within a ten-mile radius swivelled in her direction. It wouldn't have mattered if I'd been a nuclear scientist with more brain cells than you could shake a Nobel Prize at; a mystic guru spilling the spiritual beans on the Meaning of Life . . . The only depth in demand was in décolletage.

'Yes,' Louise would go on, plaintively, 'I'm thinking of having a breast reduction.'

'Why?' I'd hiss, resentfully. 'Aren't two the normal amount?'

Oh, I did find appreciative lovers; men who assured me, mid-grope, that 'more than a mouthful's a waste'. And I'd almost believe them . . . until, that is, I'd find the ubiquitous stash of *Penthouse* magazines beneath their beds, the centrefolds well thumbed. The first few I forgave. They'd obviously been weaned too early . . . But as the years rolled by, so did the stapled-navel-orientated boyfriends. They couldn't all have been bottle-fed, could they?

Day after despondent day I spent poring over those magazines wondering, 'Why don't I look like that woman?' And then it struck me. The truth is, that woman doesn't even look like that woman. Her body has been painted, to create hollows and shadows and curves. Her gravity-defying breasts, supported by transparent sticky tape. The photos, airbrushed to remove any wrinkle, dimple, pimple, crinkle.

It was then I got militant. I bought a 'How Dare You Presume I'd Rather Have Big Tits' T-shirt . . . I wore it at home all alone on Saturday nights, while Louise was out on the town having Wild Jungle Sex with harems of male love-slaves.

There are good things about little breasts, I told myself over and over. For example, everything stops when you do—'Jogger's Nipple' is an unknown ordeal to women like me . . . Sleeping on your stomach (something Louise could only achieve by digging two holes side by side in the sand at Bondi) . . . Limbo dancing . . . Never having to wonder why you got the job . . .

But it was pointless. I knew very well that men, all men, no matter how Politically Correct, no matter how good at doing sensitive things with snow peas, are closet Benny Hills, obsessed with the fatty tissue situated between a woman's neck and navel.

But then, overnight, my Barbie fantasy became a reality. My bosom developed with polaroid speed. Finally, I had the sort of breasts that needed their own postcode. I was up the duff. How thrilling to have a chest that looked like two tethered zeppelins ready for take-off. The pregnancy took second place to my long-awaited Barbie transmogrification. My wildest dreams had come true . . . So why wasn't I enjoying it?

The trouble was, men had stopped talking to me. Oh, their mouths opened and words came out, but it was all addressed to the third button on my blouse. This wasn't just men I knew well, but total strangers, in bank, bus and train queues. All of a sudden, everyone was looking down on me. It was as though I'd been decapitated. Four novels to my name, an 'A' score in the *Reader's Digest* 'How Good is Your Word Power?' quiz, an awareness that Filet Mignon was not an opera; in short, I was a girl who plucked her highbrows. Yet suddenly I was nothing more than a life-support system to a mammary gland.

Half an hour into this kind of conversation with my

cleavage, I'd have to glance down and say, 'Hey, when the three of you are through, lemme know, okay?'

But there was another reason I wasn't enjoying my new-found Mae West mode.

As gravity took effect, my normal sprightly gait was transformed into an angled shuffle. The Marks & Sparks lingerie lady encased my breasts in a support bra, which had the erotic appeal of an orthopaedic shoe. There were so many flaps, loops, elasticated panels and clips, you needed an engineering degree to operate it. By the time my husband got the damn thing off, it was morning. The wretched contraption also left strap indentations only surgery could remove.

But there was worse to come. After childbirth, my Barbie breasts grew to Dolly Parton proportions. Finally, I understood the real reason for bras; they're to stop an unfortunate situation from spreading. Not only was I now wheezing from the tightness of my corsetry, but there was also the constant leakage. Breastfeeding may give you the breast of a Sex Goddess, but really you are nothing more than Meals on Heels; a Kiddie Cafe; the Fountain for Youths.

It was time to face the pathetic facts. Now that I had Barbie's big breasts, I wanted to be small again. The bewildering truth is that women are conditioned never to be happy with our breasts. Females with small breasts are injecting silicone pillows which leak and cause cancer, while the women with big breasts are struggling into asthma-inducing 'minimiser' bras and going under the knife for nipple realignments.

And is it any wonder we're confused? In the past century alone, fashion has dictated that women ricochet from the ironing-board chests of the 1920s; to the over-the-shoulder-boulder-holder sweater girls of the '40s; to the Twiggy human-toothpaste-tube look of the '60s; to the Pamela Anderson aerodynamic twin engines of the '80s; to the Kate Moss bee-stings of the '90s; to the giant jugs of Jordan.

Imagine if the male anatomy was prone to such fashion whims? 'Well, boys, this season it's small penises. We want them lopped and chopped.' Then, 'Gee boys, the new look is BIG. We want them long and strong. It's penis implants and the "Wonder Y".' (The padded Wonder Y-Front for Men, can you imagine it? The slogan would read: 'No, I *Am* Just Pleased to See You.')

But men are more or less liberated from this anatomy angst. Think about it. Have you ever met a man who thinks he's ugly? Pectorially inadequate? Or even just a little bit plain? The flabbiest, chunkiest, most chunderous, aesthetically challenged bloke in the world secretly thinks of himself as an Arnold Schwarzenegger look-alike . . . Perhaps men have magic fairground mirrors which transform them, in their mind's eye, into a Greek Adonis. While a woman's mirror distorts her into a demon. Ask any woman, even a top model, and she'll tell you that she has the kind of figure which looks better in clothes. (A man actually once said this to me. Needless to say, I looked even better when I accessorised his testicles as my ear ornaments.)

Two babies down the track and my bosom has shrunk back to its usual undernourished state. I'm now using

Crone Creams and still having trouble filling out that training bra. My breasts seem to be in remission.

But if there's one thing I've learnt from all this, it's what *not* to give my little girl for her birthday. A Barbie.

KATHY LETTE ran away from Sydney's Sylvania Maximum Security High School at sixteen. She has written ten internationally best-selling novels, but mostly prides herself on having taught Julian Barnes a word and Salman Rushdie the limbo. She is now published in seventeen languages in more than 100 countries. Her latest bestseller is *How to Kill your Husband (and other Handy Household Hints)* (Simon & Schuster, 2005). Kathy says the best thing about being a writer is that you can work in your jammies all day and drink heavily on the job. She lives with her husband and two children in London, where she was recently the Savoy Hotel's Writer in Residence.

The Life Lessons of Littlewing

Bessie Bardot

One dark, stormy September night in the late 1970s, a pregnant woman rushes into Emergency with labour pains. Her robes flowing in clouds of batik cotton, long raven hair falling to her waist, she resembles a Mother Earth devotee at Woodstock. The tall bearded blond Icelandic man at her side, who looks more like John the Baptist than John the Baptist ever did, explains to the nurse that his partner will not require any anaesthesia, just Buddhist chanting, as she gives birth to this, their long-awaited 'love child'.

Sounds like something out of *Ab Fab*, doesn't it? My eccentric and irrepressible mother and I spent my early days in a hippy commune near Byron Bay. She and my father decided, no doubt in a haze of hash smoke, to name me 'Littlewing'; not so bad considering their other choice was Fanny. (But definitely a good case for banning drugs!) Not surprisingly, my back-to-nature parents were purists when it came to everything else. Soap never touched my body, I was bathed in buttermilk daily, which I'm sure explains my ruinous penchant for pampering, and when my birthday parties came around, instead of chocolate cake and fairy bread we had tofu crispbread, dark fruitcake and the obligatory lentils. All of which, at that age, I absolutely hated and unfortunately still do.

The '70s ended, and so did my parents' romance. Mum decided that she wanted a complete change, so she swapped the Krishna chanting for the life of a born-again Christian and, before long, she met another reformed hippy at Bible study. I didn't mind at first that Mum had moved on—she was happy and I still saw my dad every second week. But a year passed, and Mum and my step-father moved further into the fundamentalist church, after which 'praise the Lord' became a daily, even hourly utterance in our house. Eventually, he became a preacher and they got married. My days of dressing as a fairy and frolicking nude in nature were replaced with fire and brimstone, mind-numbing Bible studies and rules, rules, rules.

It was pretty confusing as a young kid to be told that everything you thought was right was wrong and everything that felt wrong and repressive was now right. Fortunately, my real dad still provided me with some balance; we would spend hours walking through the forest around Mullumbimby and Byron Bay, talking about everything and climbing up mango trees to poach our afternoon snack. Dad, an artist and musician, strongly believed in stimulating my mind with games, music and debates, which I loved. Life was beautiful, but little did I know it was all about to change—and I wouldn't find out why for another fifteen years.

In 1981, there were a string of memorable events. Princess Diana married Prince Charles. The first woman was nominated to serve on the Supreme Court in the US—a sign, I was informed, that society was 'going to hell in a handbasket'. Michael Jackson created the moonwalk, the 'dance of a thousand dags', and you couldn't escape the hit song 'Jessie's Girl' playing constantly on the radio, which my beautiful dad used to murder with his rendition, 'Wish that I was Bessie's girl'. I adored my dad. He took the time to really listen to me, when my mum and stepdad were too busy preaching at me. I did love my mum, but I felt suffocated by their rules. Playing cards was evil, John Farnham's music was banned. I wasn't allowed to wear pants or anything fluoro—good Christian girls wore long skirts only and drab shapeless clothes—and shows like *Young Talent Time* were hotbeds of wanton, sinful corruption that I was forbidden to watch.

My dad became my nirvana, whisking me away every two weeks from my life of starched dresses and tight plaits to an alternate reality of daisy chains, dhal and different perspectives. To my young mind, it felt like running away to the circus.

So there I was, sitting by the letterbox, waiting for Dad to pick me up for my usual visit. Minutes stretched into hours. Mum kept yelling at me to come inside to wait because the sun was melting the cupcakes I'd made for our train trip to Mullumbimby. Eventually, she took me inside. I was so confused. Where was he? He was never late. She phoned some of Dad's friends; it turned out no one had seen him for a week or more.

Two months later Mum filed a missing person's police report. Every time the phone rang or there was a knock at the door, I ran to answer it, hoping that it would be him. I kept my tears for night-time, when I could cry alone under the covers. I didn't want Mum to think I didn't love her, but I felt like my world had been stomped on. Up until my early twenties, I would look carefully at any man with a flowing beard and long hair as I passed him in the street.

I went through school as the shy girl who no one talked to. Looking back, I guess I didn't really make that much of an effort to get in with the popular girls. It felt just like home did to me—as if I hadn't been invited to the party and was really just a blow-in. As the years passed, I became extremely self-conscious, thinking up any excuse I could to hide in sick bay. In the entire twelve years of my school life, not one guy asked me out and I only had one friend. (Fortunately, not an imaginary one—although these did come in handy when dreaming about what it would be like to have a dad, a date and a day when I didn't feel like an outcast.) All the other girls at school were bubbly and confident, while I felt incredibly unsure of who I was and what I was doing there. I'll never forget feeling, as a teenager, that I was trapped in a life that wasn't mine. I used to imagine that if only Dad came back, I could have the life I was meant to live.

The day I graduated from Year 12, I thought of my dad; the day I got my licence I thought of my dad; both times I was married and many other times in between,

I wished he'd been there to give me his gentle, unique perspective and caring advice.

All I had to go on was my mum's idea of good Christian advice, which was that one day I'd meet the man I would marry, the man 'God' had chosen, and that's all I ever had to aspire to. She would tell me there was no need for a career or even to try that hard at school; marrying and setting up house was the only goal. So when my boyfriend proposed to me on my twentieth birthday, it didn't even occur to me to say no. After all, Mum must be right, right? She was a preacher's wife and spoke to God!

It wasn't until I was 23, when I was contacted after some searching by an old friend of my dad's, that I found out he had taken his own life way back in 1981. All those moments when I had felt so hurt that he didn't come for me vanished. I learnt that he had been embroiled in a custody battle for me with my stepfather and the church, and had lost. It was the classic argument—non-conformist, long-haired heathen versus churchgoing 'bastions of society'—and it completely ignored the fundamental issue of a caring father's love for his doting child. It had all become too much and he ended his life, perhaps assuming I would be better off without him now my new family and religion had won the right to remove him by law from my life.

I don't blame my stepdad and mum for what they did and the horrible results. We all make the best decisions we can with the information we have, but somehow knowing the answer to my unanswered questions—'Where was he? How could he forget about me? Didn't he wonder if I was okay?—changed me that day. And I like to think Dad got the last laugh, after all—I still love to do things differently and no one could accuse me of being a religious conformist. Though I may spare my kids the name 'love child of Littlewing'. Then again, perhaps I'll update it and go for 'Littlebling' instead! Love you, Dad!

Edited extracts from Bessie's Guide for Girls Who Want More from Life *(New Holland, 2006).*

BESSIE BARDOT is an award-winning, best-selling author of three books for girls on health, body image, career and the pitfalls of fame. She's a national radio host with Austereo, a professional speaker, TV and media regular, and CEO of Movers Shakers—Celebrity Contact Brokers. She is a regular social commentator on topics such as women's issues and relationships. Bessie is an Australia Day ambassador and has travelled to visit troops in war zones such as Baghdad, Iran and East Timor. She has been nominated for Young Entrepreneur and Business Woman of the Year awards, and lectures on personal branding, women in business, her journey as a media entrepreneur, health, wellbeing, drive, organisation and motivation, and relationships.

A Distance of a Thousand Miles

Nikki Gemmell

I

'My initiation triggered a vital force in me,' Gabriel García Márquez declared recently, describing the loss of his virginity as a teenager.

Well, well. All power to you, Señor García Márquez. Literally.

I didn't feel a vital surge when I lost mine. A vague disappointment, perhaps, a disappointment that—that was it? And hang on, it hurt. But what I felt most of all was relief. That I'd done it. That the weight of not having done it—the agitation of never having done it in my life because I'd never get a boyfriend, ever—was gone, finally.

And other women?

I rang my friend Amelia.

'Vital force? You're kidding. It was on a beach. There was a lot of sand. And we're talking everywhere, here. That's all I remember.'

Nina.

'I was drunk. I vomited. You don't want to know.'

Ah, Señor García Márquez, I suspect your feeling of empowerment may well be a particularly male phenomenon.

II

That intriguing loss of spark and voice and certainty that befalls some girls as they travel through adolescence into womanhood. Girls who were once so cheeky and flinty and bold can seem lost as soon as a man puts his arm around them. Nabokov powerfully captures the firefly ephemerality of the journey in *Lolita*. His bolshie, shiny young protagonist ends up drained by her late teens. She's pregnant, and defeated by domesticity. She's waylaid her spirit and defiance, her stroppy ability to say 'no'.

What's to blame?

Sex?

III

I'd been disciplined and focused during my secondary years, at an all-girl convent school. My zeal was for work; for English and Art; I spent my entire high school years in the cupboard known as learning. (I was a scholarship kid and grateful for it; didn't want to blow the chance.) Sex education was *The Thorn Birds* and *Scruples*. The object of desire, Nick Rhodes from Duran Duran. My nights were vivid before I fell into sleep; it was all enough.

Real boys didn't exist in my life. (And I tell you, the night of the school formal became this all-consuming problem for a year beforehand. I was eventually bailed out by a family friend of my best mate. I met him half an hour before we left for the dance and, after that night, never saw him again.)

As soon as I began university my world changed: the desire for a proper man consumed my life. Work and discipline and focus went out the window. The books I was reading were now Marguerite Duras's *The Lover* and Elizabeth Smart's *By Grand Central Station I Sat Down and Wept*. I longed for that level of intensity, vividness and passion. So much energy was spent plotting ways to get rid of the pesky condition known as virginity and obtain the holy grail: the boyfriend. And oh my Lord, the appalling things I did in pursuit of that goal. Passing out at parties? Check. Vomiting in taxis? Check. Too bleakly I often ended up drunk, with someone jackhammering away on top of me, thinking, 'This is horrible. Why did I let this happen? It's not what I ever imagined, alone, at night, in my head. What went wrong?'

Once upon a time, I was strong and principled and firm.

But now.

The grand canyon loneliness of the one-night stand. Two people connecting, but utterly failing to at the same time.

IV

Is acquiescence part of that whole female thing of wanting to be accepted, popular, one of the pack? We want to please—we give in, we say yes when we'd really like to say no. We even say yes when every bone in our body is screaming stop! Enough! More than a century ago the American writer Edith Wharton described it as a 'curtain of niceness' that befalls young women.

I'm not sure that today's teenagers are so different— no matter how much post-feminist girl power has coloured their adolescence. There was absolutely nothing assertive and empowering about the oh-so-modern teenage girl a few years back who ended up in a five-star London hotel with several very famous footballers. The whole episode was just incredibly bleak. But I can see how she got there.

She said yes when she wanted to say no.

That thoroughly iPod-age, twenty-something English celeb Abi Titmuss was notoriously exposed on video- tape as the willing participant in a sexual foursome that included a couple of strangers. It also involved full-on lesbian sex. She responded during the ensuing media inquisition: 'Most women will admit to kissing another girl, not because they enjoy it, but to entertain a man.'

Well, some girls kiss other girls because they actually love doing it, but what made me flinch was her heart- sapping phrase 'to entertain a man'.

Because I recognised it. And was well into my thirties as I read it.

I'm not proud of the times I've done something sexually that I haven't wanted to. Perhaps because I was talked into it, or made to feel frigid if I didn't, or wanted to please.

We say yes when we're screaming inside to say no.

V

My friend Zoe's nineteen years younger than me; I've watched her grow up. I was in awe of her assurance when she was eleven. When I was debating marrying a boyfriend she said, dryly, 'Nikki, you've got to wait and see what he's like when he's drunk, all right?'

Ah, such wisdom in one so young—she'll give men a run for their money, I thought.

My little Zoe fell in love at sixteen. Completely, madly, overwhelmingly. She moved in with her lover. By nineteen they'd split—and by then she'd lost her youth.

'I gave him everything,' she lamented in the messy, traumatised aftermath. 'I left school for him. I lost my self-esteem. I couldn't stand up in a room and face people, and I used to be so strong and bold about everything. And Nikki, he's the weakest person I know.'

Zoe is a large, shining spirit who'd been flattened (temporarily, thank God) by a smaller one. Why is there so often that leakage of confidence, that capitulation, as women become sexual? Virginity and chastity can seem like magic elixirs that make us calm, audacious, strong.

VI

But there are the lucky ones. Those women who, after losing their virginity, experience a transformation that's something akin to what the French writer Colette described: 'The day after that wedding night, I found that a distance of a thousand miles, abyss and discovery and irremediable metamorphosis separated me from the day before.'

But not all girls.

Zoe and Amelia and Nina and I didn't find empowerment and mystery and grace in sex until well into our twenties. We're not typical of all women, but we're representative of quite a few. I spent so many wilderness years trying to find the sex of my imagination. The only grace I can remember from any teenage sexual experience was my very first kiss; the tremulousness and scariness and utter loveliness of it is still vivid.

As for losing my virginity—like my friend Amelia, I can't remember much. There certainly wasn't the triggering of any kind of vital force within me. Quite the opposite, in fact.

Lucky you, Señor García Márquez, lucky you.

NIKKI GEMMELL is the author of the novels *Shiver*, *Cleave*, *Lovesong* and *The Bride Stripped Bare*, and a work of nonfiction, *Pleasure: An Almanac for the Heart*. She's currently working on her fifth novel. She was born in Wollongong, completed a Masters in Writing at the University of Technology, Sydney, and now lives in London.

Still Stillness

Kate Holden

The summer I finished school, there was nowhere to go.

My exams had been conducted in a heatwave, the pen slipping in my sweaty grip, but the weather had eased into a dulcet December. Sunshine was kind in Melbourne that year. I had finished school, the biggest thing I knew. Now the future spread out before me, broad and iridescent, shivering like restlessness.

In two months I would be starting university and a part-time job in a bookshop; I was reading *The Catcher in the Rye* and in the thrall of self-importance. Soon, adulthood would sweep down on me with its heavy cloak; this would be a summer I would look back on with nostalgia.

I was a nervous girl, uneasy with friends, laughing always too shrilly, I thought. The gap between my front teeth, the flash of gums in my smile. My friends loved me but I never understood why. My awe of them made me quiet when they were noisy, tentative when they offered invitations. I feared that they would fail to see the willingness beneath my graceless hesitations, and drop me, but I didn't know how to join in, shuck away the carapace of caution that held me.

Loosed from exams and school, now my friends were moving out of their parents' houses, across town. Not yet ready to take on such responsibilities, I would remain at the house in which I'd grown up, but I too was excited at the prospect of exploring new streets, claiming new territories, even as only a visitor. Fitzroy and Carlton were exotic to me, having grown up on the other side of town. There was a colourful braggadocio there, a sense that one could go out at night, that there would be voices and lights and places to be. Terrace houses and busy streets. Coffeepots on stoves and cracked old vintage cups; beaded curtains. Not like the subdued suburb where I lived, where only three restaurants opened at night and the shops were a half-hour walk away; my parents' beige laminex kitchen. Over on the other side, my friends would take me out, show me things. It would be a summer to learn a new, bolder stride.

Then, on New Year's Day of that year, 1990, the tramways union declared industrial action. The conductors, traditional stanchions of public transport, were being phased out and the union was outraged. For one day, the tram drivers took over their vehicles and ran them gleefully around town; at noon the next day, management cut the power. But by that time the drivers had churned dozens of trams into the central business district of Melbourne, and there they remained.

All along Bourke Street and Elizabeth Street, trams rested, massive and immovable, like sleeping cattle. People stared, wondered, walked past them cautiously, as if at any moment they might rattle into life and take off. But they slept, docile. No dinging bells, no trundling on the tracks. Empty seats inside gathered dust.

They were parked bumper to bumper; there was no getting past them. To cross at the intersection of Russell and Bourke, you had to walk all the way up to Spring Street, where the line of trams finished defiantly in front of Parliament House. All through January, for thirty-three days, the trams, symbols of Melbourne's affability, efficiency and eccentricity, rested in the main streets of the city, implacable as beasts.

With public transport severed for those who lived on tram lines, life changed a little. It was a quiet time of year; people cadged lifts from friends with cars, rode bikes, took up walking to work in the pleasant summer mornings. The union had public support: the public cheerfully donated to funds for the strikers' families. The only problem was for those, like me, who admired the renegade installation of trams in the genteel streets of the city, but had no other means of crossing town.

My glorious summer of social discovery fell away just as it was starting. If I wanted to, I could have asked my mother to drive me over to my friends' houses, but I wanted independence, the freedom to come and go, and without the trams that wasn't possible. This was my first season of adulthood, but it was also, I thought, the last summer of my adolescence. I relapsed into solitude, not altogether unhappily.

In the small domain of my parents' back garden, I made new plans. Time: I had nothing but time. Now was my chance to metamorphose into the literature student I would become; I would read masterpieces and write great stories late into the night. Nowhere to go, no one to see. Just me and books, me and dreams, curling around me like petals in the warm nights. For the first time in my life I bought beer, drank it sitting up in bed with a book on my lap, self-consciously adult, one sour swig after another.

Lying under a tree out the back, I felt nevertheless as if I was in haste. So many books to read, stories to dream up. On hot, lethargic afternoons I read volumes of letters between great authors and despaired at ever having such lucid intelligence, of ever having the energy to write the mass of correspondence it seemed a great writer must. Nevertheless I made an effort. A crush on a celebrity made me write fervent letters I didn't post. I sent long missives to my friends, far away on the other side of town, opened their replies with greedy hands. In the cool midnights I conjured a disaffected story about two young lovers who worked opposing shifts and never saw each other but asleep.

I made lists of all the books I read, the films I rented on video: cataloguing my life at this static moment. One day I would want to recall all of this; it might be important. The fresh morning air came through my window bringing anticipation; I dulled in afternoon to lethargy.

The trams grew dustier in the city streets; people got used to walking around them. Life went on.

I was caught in a strange stillness. Three thin wooden fence walls kept the horizon from me in the back garden; I dozed on the buffalo grass, my face resting on the pages of a book. Seventeen, I was seventeen. My own breath coming back at me, warm; the words shimmering in my mind; everything was quiet.

Something brimmed in me, but I couldn't name it.

Love, perhaps. I had no one to fall in love with, but I tended infatuations with people who weren't there; with fantasies; with my own reflection in the mirror. I gazed, mesmerised, at my soft lips, the curve of my cheek. If I stared long enough without blinking, the reflected face turned monstrous. Such a child, her awkward child's features, her perplexity at herself. The awareness that this summer wouldn't last. There was something marvellous and frightening about it all. I felt as if I should run somewhere, rush out of the house in search of magic. But there was no special place to run to, only the dry, scrubby park at the end of the road.

Out on the other side of town, my friends were having parties, claiming their domains, falling in love. When I did get a lift to see them, my skin felt slack with immaturity, tight with the habit of silence. They were conducting romances, full of drama and a kind of intimacy and bravado alien to me. Separated from them, I missed my comrades, but I also loved my solitary summer, my foolish fantasies, the pearly shell of my bedroom, and didn't mind returning to quietness.

Then the trams moved at the start of February, and a couple of weeks later I began university. The weather was baking once more. I didn't have a clue what to wear, who to be in this new world; I was too aware of my bare skin in public. My stride across campus was wobbly, my head down.

Out in the big spaces again. How strange was the camber of the world, as I walked out into it.

This piece originally appeared in shorter form in The Age.

KATE HOLDEN was born in Melbourne in 1972. She studied classics and literature at the University of Melbourne, completed a graduate diploma in professional writing and editing at the Royal Melbourne Institute of Technology (RMIT), and is currently finishing a Master of Creative Media program at RMIT. Her first book, *In My Skin: A Memoir*, was published in 2005. Kate has written a regular column for *The Age* newspaper and contributed non-fiction pieces to literary magazines. She has never had the gap between her front teeth fixed and still doesn't drive a car.

The Message

Larissa Behrendt

A knock on the door in the middle of class would get everyone's attention. When my teacher, Miss O'Sullivan, finished reading the note, she looked at me. Miss O'Sullivan was not like the other teachers in the English department who would always wear the most fashionable clothes to school each day. Miss O'Sullivan had crazy red hair and it was whispered that she was a lesbian and, even worse, a communist because she had once travelled to Russia. Because she was different, we all gave her a hard time, but she was patient with us and I secretly liked her.

Miss O'Sullivan said, 'Miss Sherwin wants to see you in her office.' Miss Sherwin was a Home Science teacher but she was also the Mistress of Girls. Already I could hear the whispering, the speculation about what it was that I might have done to be called to see her.

I followed the message bearer to A Block, where the Principal, Mistress of Girls and Master of Boys had offices. The school had been built in the late 1960s. It was made of brick, concrete and black-painted steel. I dragged my nails along the brickwork to make them shorter, both to distract me from the ominous, impending meeting and to make sure I didn't add to my woes by getting into trouble for breaching the dress code. I'd always had trouble with the dress code. My earliest memory was of having an argument with my mother about what I was going to wear, insisting on a dress when she insisted that it was more appropriate to wear a tracksuit on a bushwalk.

This was the 1980s and I wanted to be Madonna one day and Stevie Nicks the next. I loved fashion, I loved nail polish, I loved jewellery and I loved shoes, and even though my school wasn't as strict as a private school, I was often getting into trouble for embellishing my school uniform.

This was not the first time Miss Sherwin had called me out of class to go and see her, so I knew that what awaited me was a lecture.

Miss Sherwin's office was only used when she was dealing with girls who were playing up. Most of her time was spent in the common room with the other Home Science teachers. Her office was sparse—just brick walls and an empty shelf, a large desk, a chair for her and a wooden chair for her victim. There were no pictures, just a dirty window above her head. Against this, Miss Sherwin seemed to loom large, dominating the room.

She had tight white curls, an overdrawn nose and, against her wrinkled skin, her blue eyes seemed dilated. She spoke with a clipped, English-style accent even though she had never left Australia.

'Hello, Miss Sherwin,' I said and started to pick the nail polish off my nails. It was red and another breach of the dress code.

'You know I have taken a special interest in you,' she said, looking at a file filled with notes rather than at me.

'Yes, Miss Sherwin.' Lucky me.

'I see that you have signed up for your HSC classes next year: 3 Unit English, 3 Unit Maths, History, Geography, Economics and General Studies. That's a very heavy load.'

'I suppose so, Miss Sherwin.'

'Don't you think that you would be better off if you dropped one of these and did Home Science instead?'

Most of my classmates had chosen pretty much the same subjects. And I had already avoided science subjects because they were my worst. In fact, compared with the kids who had signed up for Physics and Chemistry, I thought I had already made easier choices. I had been in the top class every single year and been to a selective primary school, and while I wasn't at the top of the top class, I wasn't at the bottom either. I didn't think I was dumb. And I hated Home Science. I didn't like cooking, I hated washing up even more and my sewing was as good as my cooking (though I did make my own outfit for the Culture Club concert by taking an oversized T-shirt that I'd ripped in places and retied with ribbons, which probably looked as stupid as it sounds even if at the time I thought it was pretty special). If I was going to do something different I would have done Art.

But I didn't know what to say to Miss Sherwin. Growing up in an Aboriginal family, I'd been taught to respect my elders and not to talk back to them. In response to my silence, she said, 'I think it would be much better for you to do Home Science. You will be better at it and I can keep an eye on you. Now, what are we going to swap it with?'

I didn't want to give up any of my subjects. It was now or never. 'Miss Sherwin, I kind of like all the courses I've chosen. And I haven't done too badly at any of them so far. Science was my worst subject and I'm not doing that.'

'No. No. I can tell you, I know that girls like you will do better in Home Science. You just leave it to me and I'll fix it. I've already told you, I have taken an interest in you. You know, I am a friend of Burnum Burnum's. Lovely man. Very spiritual. He knows how interested I am in making sure that you are a good girl.'

And this was the usual content of the sermon. How Miss Sherwin had befriended an Aboriginal once and, since I was the only Aboriginal girl in the school, she thought she should give me special attention, which really just meant a lecture about how perilously close I was to ruining my life. And, fortunately for me, she had 'taken an interest' and was going to help me, whether I liked it or not. As she rambled on, I kept thinking of the work I would have to catch up later because I was missing class. Yep. Lucky me.

'You must remember what I have told you time and time again,' she continued. 'Do not get scatty with the boys. You know what I mean by that, don't you?' I nodded, too mortified that Miss Sherwin was talking about the subject of boys and doing stuff with boys to actually speak.

'I worry about you. Girls like you have a tendency to get scatty, you know? Boys might pay attention to the scatty girls, but they don't respect them.'

Miss Sherwin had constantly reinforced this message.

Girls like me, which meant Aboriginal girls like me, had a predisposition to be tramps. Sluts. Whores.

Miss Sherwin sure thought she knew a lot about what I was predisposed to, but what Miss Sherwin didn't know was that over the summer before I started high school, I had gone to visit my mother's family in Western Australia. And over that summer my grandfather, when he found me alone, would do the very things to me that Miss Sherwin thought I was inviting the boys to do. Miss Sherwin didn't know this. But neither did anyone else. I was too ashamed to say anything. I felt too disgusted and humiliated, and if I even thought about it, let alone spoke about it, I would feel like my head was spinning, like I was about to vomit, and I would start scratching myself, across my chest and arms, where my clothes would cover it—I would start scratching and scratching until the thoughts stopped, until I could think of something else . . .

And Miss Sherwin talking about scatty girls like me and how our behaviour was asking the boys to take advantage of us only made me wonder what that behaviour was. What had I done that made my grandfather think it was all right to do those things to my body, to do those things to me? And then I couldn't concentrate on anything Miss Sherwin was saying. Then I had that feeling again—my head was spinning, the bricks on the wall were closing in on me—and I started fidgeting, itching to scratch at the soft flesh on my stomach and chest.

By the time Miss Sherwin let me go back to class, it was recess and people were spilling out into the courtyards. I had to return to my classroom to get my books and bag. I wasn't crying but I was shaking. When those memories would flood back, I just didn't know how to stop them unless I could do something serious to distract myself—like the scratching. And in the middle of the playground, I couldn't scratch.

Miss O'Sullivan was still there, packing up after class, waiting for me to return for my things.

'Is everything all right?' she asked.

And instead of answering, all I could do was cry. Tears of anger. Tears of frustration. Tears of confusion. Tears of self-loathing.

'Oh Larissa,' said Miss O'Sullivan. 'You will like university so much better than this place.'

It was the first time I had ever thought about going to university. The first time that anyone had mentioned my potential. Never in all Miss Sherwin's lectures did she mention that what I might become was something exciting and wonderful; she only warned how close I was to being a disaster. And while Miss O'Sullivan's message didn't break my mood that day, it did plant a seed.

Thanks to Miss O'Sullivan, with her crazy hair and unorthodox views, I began to think about going to university and, when my HSC was over, I went on to do a law degree. I eventually went to Harvard Law School and these achievements helped me to build a life very different from the one that Miss Sherwin thought I was destined to lead. But it was decades before I learnt that I wasn't scatty, that what my grandfather did to me was not acceptable, and that what he did was not my fault.

LARISSA BEHRENDT is a Eualeyai/Kamillaroi woman and Professor of Law and Director of Research at the Jumbunna

Indigenous House of Learning at the University of Technology, Sydney. She has published on Indigenous policy and governance issues, property law, Indigenous rights, dispute resolution and Aboriginal women's issues. Larissa's book, *Achieving Social Justice: Indigenous Rights and Australia's Future* (The Federation Press), was published in 2003. She won the 2002 David Unaipon Award and a 2005 Commonwealth Writer's Prize for her novel, *Home* (UQP). Larissa is a board member of the Museum of Contemporary Art and a director of both the Sydney Writers' Festival and the Bangarra Dance Theatre.

One Sunday Afternoon

Cecilia Inglis

I am standing outside my mother's bedroom, my heart in my throat. From inside, I can hear small sounds of movement as Mum is freshening herself up and getting her face on before she makes Sunday tea.

My hand is on the knob of the half-closed door. I only have to say, 'Mum, can I come in?' and give the door a push, and I'll be in there telling her I am going to become a nun.

In the twelve months since I made the decision to enter the convent I've been very careful not to give away any clues about what I've been contemplating. I didn't want my family to know and expect me to be all goody-goody and pious. I could just imagine Mum saying to me, 'Huh—and you say you want to be a nun!' every time I got into trouble for some misdemeanour.

But now the time has come to drop the bomb, and I'm sick to my stomach with nerves. I know Mum doesn't think I am the type to make a good nun, and she'll be opposed to the idea. Bet, my sister, is already a nun, and she was always quiet: never interested in going out for a good time. Mum used to say she always thought Bet was born to be a nun. I'm nothing like Bet. Though Mum is a good Catholic parent, she'll be opposed to the idea of me entering the convent: I'm just not the type.

I've been to see Father Cronin this afternoon, and talked it all over with him. He's known how I've felt for the past year, and today he said, 'It's time to tell your mother and father. They need to know.'

I quailed. 'Don't you think it's too soon? The next intake isn't until March.'

'No,' he said. 'Now's the time. Your Leaving Certificate exam is coming up, then Christmas, and after that you'll have to be getting ready.'

My heart sank to my boots. 'My mother's going to get a shock. I don't know what to say.'

'Just tell her. Tell her you've been to see me, and I said to say you're going to Singleton next year.' He moved some papers on his desk. 'Simple.' (Singleton is the Mother House of the Sisters of Mercy, where my sister is already a nun.)

'Oh dear,' I mumbled, palms beginning to sweat at the thought.

'It'll be all right,' he said. 'No need to say any more than that. Just let her know what you're thinking.'

I've been sitting out on the back verandah in the sun with everyone, just waiting for this moment. We've got a visitor for tea tonight. Enid, who's been part of our family for years, has arrived, and they've all been talking, talking. But I've hardly heard a word. I've been peppering to get it all over with. When Mum eventually came inside, I followed her, and here we are.

I look down at my hand on the doorknob, quivering. I think perhaps it would be easier if I leave this till tomorrow and imagine myself stepping back quietly. Then—no, it will never be any easier. Better just *do* it.

I give the door a tiny push.

'Mum,' I say, 'can I come in?'

She's sitting at her dressing table, with a pot of Pond's face cream in her hand, wondering what this is about.

'Mum . . .' My voice doesn't come out right, so I start again. 'Mum—I didn't just go for a bike-ride today like I told you.' I take a big breath and blurt it out. 'I went to see Father Cronin and he told me to come home and tell you I'm entering the convent. I'm going to Singleton next year.'

She's just sitting there, looking at me. The Pond's is suspended in mid-air and her mouth is slightly open.

'Wh—what? What did you say?'

So I start again. 'I've been to see—'

She doesn't wait for me to finish. Her eyes have gone a bit funny, and she's looking hard at me. She says, 'You go to blazes!'

I back away, find my feet, and run for my life.

Looking back from a distance of fifty years, I feel for that sixteen-year-old fleeing from her mother's bedroom. She was so young; so idealistic. So sure that what she was doing was right. So vulnerable. Sixteen—sweet sixteen?—yet planning to enter the convent.

My experience of life was very limited. In our little Catholic primary school at Waratah, a Newcastle suburb, I had known boys who had been largely rough and loud and obnoxious. They had christened me 'Tojo' because of the glasses I had to wear. Even I could see why they called me that—I looked like every cartoon of a Japanese soldier that was in the paper. My glasses were of round wire, covered with black tortoiseshell, and Mum chose them because they had secure spring arms that wouldn't fall off.

I hated those glasses and the boys who called me 'Tojo Cahill' till the end of Sixth Class. Cahill, the name my grandfather had brought from Cashel, Ireland, and of which I was so proud. I was deeply offended, so I had no liaisons with, or even kind feelings towards, any of them.

The boys at the entirely innocent Saturday afternoon dance classes in town were like a different species. I went every week with my girlfriend, Carmel, and we had crushes on one or other of the instructors. They were quite spunky young men, who could also dance and, I'm sure, were as happy as roosters in a fowl yard. There were plenty of simpering young women to hold and guide around the floor.

I'd devoured lots of books with romance and sex in them, but that was hardly practical experience. I didn't know how to talk to boys. I didn't really *know* many boys. My brother Maurice had gone away to the seminary to become a priest when I was fourteen, so there weren't even any of his friends about the house anymore.

There was Frank, the Marist Brothers boy, who was a music student at the convent in Hamilton, Newcastle, where I went to high school, and he practised each afternoon after school in one of the infants' classrooms. It had been very pleasant to stay back for an English honours lesson after school, do a bit of homework, and then sneak over there when the nuns had all gone back to the convent for prayers, to have a mild flirtation. He was good-looking and friendly, and welcomed the interruption to his music practice. We'd compare teachers and lessons, swap notes and laugh a lot. Hardly experience, though.

The lady next door—Mrs Harris—was a widow with one son a bit older than me, and had a spare bedroom that she decided to rent out to a student called Peter, who was from the country. Peter was the first boy who showed interest in me, and he was close enough for me to spend time responding to such interest. That summer before I entered the convent I'd talk to him over the fence at the front gate on warm evenings. We'd sit on our opposite sides, me on our solid bricks, and he perched on Mrs Harris's post-and-rail fence, or lounging on her front lawn.

I even went bike-riding with him once. He was always asking me about the Catholic religion, so I decided to take him across to the local Redemptorist Monastery in Mayfield when they had an information night. Even then, I suspected Peter's interest in Catholicism wasn't totally genuine, but just a way of getting me interested in him. We went along anyway, as I told myself it was good to spread the faith, but it also seemed the closest thing to a date I was likely to get at that stage. I had a twitter of excitement in my tummy at the thought. I talked to my mother about it and she said, 'All right', though she must have had misgivings.

We set off on our bikes but had to walk them up the hill to the monastery. Peter changed sides so he was walking beside me. We were talking away about his family in the country when his arm slipped around me. I felt myself stiffen and my breath came in sharply. Instinctively, I knew I'd like to snuggle against him. My breath came faster, and then I remembered, I'm going to be a nun!—and I pulled away. I kept the bike between us after that, but I felt sorry to have missed the opportunity. It'd be nice to kiss a boy, I thought, before I give all that away forever.

While I was out, Mum told my father where I was and who with, and by the time I got back, Dad was in a state of high anxiety. He was so cross with me that he forbade me ever to go out with Peter again, and said I was not to 'waste time' talking to him. I was furious. He's just so unreasonable! I thought. What does he think I was doing?

Seething, I complained bitterly to Maurice, who was home on holidays from the seminary. 'Nothing happened!' I said. 'I was doing a good thing, taking Peter to the monastery to hear about Catholicism.' (I didn't mention the arm-around-me bit though.)

Maurice was very understanding and I felt he was on my side. He explained to me that fathers tend to be very protective of their daughters, and that this was partly because they remembered how randy they were as young men. Fathers just didn't trust any boys. This concept was new to me. I couldn't imagine my father, young man or not, as randy—though I *was* number seven in the family! And what did he think of me, if I wasn't to be trusted on a simple bike-ride?

Anyway, this effectively restricted any further relation-ship with Peter, though he was still interested in me and I felt flattered by that. Now that I'd told my parents I was going to enter the convent, I guessed that put an end to anything else developing.

Mum was confused by all this, and told me years later she was never sure she should have let me enter the convent. All this 'interest' in dance classes and boys didn't seem to her to be consistent with someone who said they wanted to be a nun. Bet had never been like that. She had seemed right for the convent—quiet, and not inter-ested in going out, or in boys.

'Boys' was a bit excessive, I thought, as Peter was the only boy I'd ever really talked to. We'd never held hands, sat in the back row of the pictures or kissed, like the other girls talked about. I'd never been physically close enough to any boy to kiss, and wouldn't have known how. I suspected Peter would have liked to have a try, and my heart would skip a beat when I thought about it, but that's where it stopped.

❦

The death knell to Peter's interest was sounded when Mrs Harris told him I was going to be a nun. She'd picked this up from Mum, but he was disbelieving and scoffed at the idea. She produced the final blow when she took him outside to view my calico nighties hanging on our line next door.

Old Sister John had insisted on making them for me according to the convent ten-gallon pattern in unbleached calico (think 'ten-gallon hat' for size). Mum had been trying to soften them with bleaching, boiling and hanging out in the weather. Later, during the novitiate, one of them was big enough for three of us to get into for a concert item. In spite of all the bleaching, the stiffness would still prickle me at night for months. There was no mistaking—they were strange items of clothing to be hanging on a suburban clothesline.

Peter confronted me, and there was no way I could answer his question, 'But why?'

When I said, 'I just feel I should', it sounded empty and unconvincing. He had no concept of 'vocation', with which I'd been brought up, and saw the whole idea as a waste of a life.

'Don't you want to have a boyfriend? And play around?' he asked me. 'Don't you want to get married? Have kids?'

I said, 'No, not really. The only other thing I ever really wanted was to be a journalist. If I wasn't going to be a nun, I'd like to go to Sydney University and become a writer.'

'Then why not do that? First?'

'I applied for an Exhibition [similar to a bursary that paid university fees] when I did the Leaving, and got one,' I admitted. 'I've asked them to hold it over for twelve months—just in case.' I looked at my shoes. 'But there's no "just in case".'

I could see he didn't understand the idea of giving up life and family, and I wasn't too sure about it all myself. I was just convinced I should be a nun because I '*had a vocation*' and if you had a vocation—a calling—you had to follow it, no matter the cost. It was a sort of package deal. And for life.

On the other hand, I couldn't quite imagine myself living with some of the nuns who taught me. Some were inspiring and others were stinkers. Looking back I'd have to say there was some dread, as well as the conviction it was the right thing for me to do.

My family were very Catholic—that is, Mass on Sunday, Confession every Saturday, and family Rosary every night. Besides that, I used to go to Mass on weekdays to pray for success in my Leaving Exam.

In spite of what my mother thought, I was quite a spiritual person. A spiritual person who loved life. Of course, I had a wild streak—but that came out as mischief and would do so for years, even in the Convent, where I couldn't resist sliding down the occasional banister, whispering jokes in silence times, and getting the giggles in Chapel.

Peter was saying, 'Yes—but after that? After uni? I can't believe you don't want to have a boyfriend and all that.'

'There's no "after that" in my plans.'

So that was that. I'd enter the convent unkissed, and possessed only of a conviction that I was called to be a nun, so all that side of life was not for me . . . just as study at Sydney University was a pipedream, and not for me either.

Anyway, my sixteen-year-old self reasoned, it was just as well I wasn't going to Sydney University. The nuns at school warned us and told us stories about girls losing their faith there, and the consequent hedonistic lives they led. This was laid at the door of Professor Anderson and his school of philosophy, which undermined faith.

I knew I had that wild streak tucked away inside me, and might possibly have become one of those grains of wheat who fell by the wayside, withered and died, and have given myself over to the sinful lifestyle.

Dad would be very disappointed in me if I lost my faith and led a sinful life. I wasn't too sure what this might mean, but I had heard how disgusted Mum and Dad were with the girl down the road who got pregnant and *had* to get married. I guessed that was a sinful life.

So, considering all this, at sixteen there was conviction that my decision was the right thing for me to do, but also sadness and a sense of loss for all the other things that might have been.

Edited extract from Cecilia—An Ex-Nun's Extraordinary Journey *(Penguin, 2003).*

CECILIA INGLIS is a Sydney writer who actually did enter a convent and spent thirty years as a Sister of Mercy. Since leaving the convent she has added an MA in Psychology from Sydney University to her BA as a teacher. She is now retired and lives with Bruce, her husband of twenty years. She has a family of a stepson and a stepdaughter and is 'Gran' to a girl and three boys.

Dirty Stopout

Clare Press

It's creeping slowly past 7 am, and the cruel Yorkshire half-light is not yet allowing the sun to slide fully into place and defrost the night. Steve Dunne's car coughs to a halt in Wilcox Avenue. Alex Ryland's got an MG with a roof that comes off, but Steve Dunne's car is a lime-green rust bucket filled with rancid apple cores, fag butts and naked Morrissey and The Cure tapes, some with their guts strewn over the sticky grey floor mats. The back window on the driver's side is stuck open, so he tapes up the gap to keep the wind out. It's tragic. But at least he's got a car, which is more than I can say for me. It's crap being sixteen.

The house is all lit up and ready to face the day—the loaded breakfast silences, the school run, the dash for the office, the admittance of Mrs Hoyt. She's the cleaning hag who ensures Annette doesn't have to do the dull stuff like dusting. That's *wife* stuff. And she'd never married him, thank you. Didn't seriously try to steal the man, didn't even want him, if anybody'd bothered to ask. He'd just turned up, clutching his bags, said, 'She's kicked me out,' with a shrug. No apologies, no fear of rejection. That's Annette's story, anyway. And she's not shy of telling it when she's pissed off with PMT, although she's nice enough to me. Bakes ace cakes, Annette does. And lets me bring whoever I want back to eat them, even Spencer Pile. Spencer Pile is gross. He has zits and plays bass and likes thrash-metal bands and in place of speech he grunts.

'Pole, is it?' said Dad, when I led this greasy-haired beast into the kitchen after school. 'Uh,' grunted Spencer.

Dad didn't say anything else, but he was twisted with worry inside. I could just tell.

It was the cakes, I think, that did it for Dad. And the baked crepes with ricotta and spinach, the roasts, the bechamel sauce. That's where you put a carrot and an onion and a celery stick in the milk and leave it to take on the flavours, then you shift them all out again and the milk tastes better than it would've *virgin*. That's what Annette says, but it's pretty dumb if you ask me. We all know what a virgin is and it's not a girl who's never had an onion stewing in her juices. Maybe a carrot. Or a chipolata; that's a more accurate metaphor for size in my experience. Ho ho.

Anyway, Mum can't cook to save herself. She'll say, 'Here's dinner!' and it's boil-in-the-bag Cod in Parsley Sauce or a can of Chunky Chicken with a piece of toast. She'll add a fag to her menu selection, not Silk Cut but these white minty ones called Consulate Menthol. They're dead posh; they've got a gold bit round the filter. I nick them sometimes when I'm staying over and smoke them on the back step, or in Ye Olde Coffee Shoppe, which is where we're all going these days. You can get decent cakes there, chocolate cheesecake and banoffee pie with cream, only we don't eat them as eating in public makes you fat. We just get the black coffee and sometimes Kirsty slips a square of Milky Bar in and it melts and it's delish. Kirsty is my best friend.

So anyway, Steve Dunne's car has stopped and he's grinning a bit, fiddling with the keys in the ignition, but I can tell he's not going to turn it off. He looks quite fit actually, with his wonky smile, sort of crooked and charming, a bit Harry Connick, Jr. Maybe. In jeans.

But that's only the light. And the hangover. Steve Dunne kisses like a washing machine—everyone knows that. Kirsty pashed him and she's pashed loads of boys, even Ben Darley and he's in the Upper Sixth and he kisses like a movie star. She says so and, anyway, you can just tell. I can smell the Silk Cut on Steve Dunne, mixed with Kouros, which is also delish. My first pash, Charlie McKenzie, wore Kouros. I asked for a sample once, at the fragrance counter in Debenhams, and put some on my pillow, but that was yonks ago. Right now, on Steve Dunne, the Kouros seems *a bit old hat* (that's an Annette phrase). Like, hello, times have changed! Everyone's wearing Armani now.

Steve Dunne levels his eyes to mine and ducks towards me, quite fast, as if he's scared I might escape, or he's psyching up for a rugby tackle. I can taste ten million Silk Cut and the sourness of Southern Comfort on my furry tongue. I think of the washing machine, and I duck.

'Thanks for the lift,' I say, trying to sound chirpy.

He winces. 'S'okay. See yer.'

And he's gone. His eyes are on the road, and it's time to leave, and I'll bet he tells everyone I'm frigid tomorrow. I mean today. I climb out of the car feeling like a right slag, even though I never touched Steve Dunne.

We'd just gone back to his place because his parents are in Tenerife. Loads of us. We'd danced to Nirvana and drunk a whole heap of Southern Comfort out of Mrs Dunne's best glasses. Steve made us stand out in the frozen garden to smoke, but someone had still managed to burn a hole in the good rug. Time came to go home with Kirsty and something clicked inside me and I just decided: no, I'll teach him.

'Come on! Get up!' she growled, shaking the suddenly deceitful me, feigning sleep on the Dunnes' plaid sofa. 'My dad'll kill us. It's dead late.'

I hissed at her, actually hissed. 'Just. Leave. Me.'

I set the alarm on my Casio and continued my fake doze. Some time in the shadows, I really did fall asleep. Next thing it was 6.30 am, Kirsty was gone and it was time for school. The drink pounded behind my eyes. I slipped into the bathroom, which was full of Mrs Dunne's lotions and potions, flowery ones from Crabtree & Evelyn, sad. I looked pretty scary, with waxy bits of my Rimmel Sugar Plum collected in the corners of my mouth, and some seriously slipped mascara. On Debbie Harry smudgy eyes look ace, but I just looked like a bad goth. I rubbed at the misbehaving make-up with a wet wad of Mrs Dunne's scented bog roll. Then I had a rethink, reached for the Rimmel in my pocket, and resmudged my lips. If you're going to do a thing, may as well do it right (that's Annette, too).

Back in the living room there were two more bodies, Simon Henderson and the Dunnes' dog, Nerd. Nerd is a chocolate labrador and he's as thick as Simon Henderson but much nicer. I stepped over them both, as they let out two stinky farts in tandem, and eased the front door open, my head throbbing like you wouldn't believe. The door made a *Rocky Horror Show* creak, so loud that Nerd looked up, wagged his big dumb tail. Then Steve Dunne came padding out of the kitchen in his rugby shirt and a pair of Father Christmas boxers. He didn't look embarrassed at all.

'What time do you call this?' He grinned. 'You're dead meat. Give you a lift?' Steve Dunne driving me home the morning after the night before is as bad as it gets. Way worse than walking home alone. Worse, even, than getting a taxi then making it wait while I go and get Annette to pay.

❖

So that's how I ended up in Steve Dunne's car, looking down the barrel of a major bollocking. One I engineered. One I actually welcome.

This is it! I think, my palms sticky as marmalade, the Southern Comfort bucking and rearing in my gut. It's breakfast-time and I'm just coming home! This is so it! He's going to get really riled, really blow his top. I'll be grounded for a month, or there'll be this curfew of, like, 8 pm for the rest of the year. For the rest of my life! I can feel the bile rising and I really think I might chunder. He'll take a day off work and make me miss school while we *workshop my behaviour*. Perhaps there'll be an inter-vention, with Mum and Annette and the neighbours and Mr Reed, the Headmonster. Maybe Dad will slap me, *strike* me. I can take it. People do crazy things when you push them to their limits, when emotion is involved. Like those nut-job fathers in the papers or on TV, the ones who literally pulverise their daughters to death for letting them down, because really they love them so much and it's hard, you know, to watch them grow up and feel them slipping away. They just don't know how to relate to these *women*, these *creatures* who are *so alien* to them, and every day is one more day of 'could haves' that never comes back.

I open the front door, bold as brass. And me and my Rimmel-smudged lips march into the kitchen, brazen as all hell. There he is, tea and a plate full of toast crumbs, his paper spread in front of him. He's in his dark blue suit, the one with the pinstripes, and grey socks, no shoes yet. This is it.

'If you're going to come in with the milk,' Dad says, his voice a bored drone, 'at least pick it up off the step and bring it in with you.'

I will not cry, I will not cry, I will not cry.

Then he picks up his tea and slides his eyes back to his paper.

CLARE PRESS was born in Northern England. She studied politics at Sheffield University and started out in local news, writing stories about school radio stations and lost cats. She moved to Australia in 1999 and has since worked for magazines including *Rolling Stone*, *Harper's Bazaar* and *The Monthly*. A former fashion critic for *The Australian* newspaper, she is now features director of *Vogue* Australia. She is currently writing her first non-fiction book with *Vogue* writer and television presenter Cleo Glyde.

Always First Never Lasts

Rachael Oakes-Ash

I have always been funny. Funny ha ha, not funny odd. Though when desperate to be liked, my funny ha ha has often been mistaken for odd. Like the time I breakdanced on the schoolyard stairs, scuffing my school shoes and risking detention if caught flashing my regulation royal blue granny pants to all and sundry.

To me, detention was worth the risk, as everyone was watching, everyone was laughing, and for a moment in my head I was super-popular. It never occurred to me what would happen when the dancing stopped.

At school I thought friendship was about giving so I gave and gave and gave, doing the 'pick me, pick me' two-step in the schoolyard each lunchtime. Craving the attention of those who I didn't even like, though I was yet to realise I didn't like them.

Try too hard and my desperation would be pounced upon by the cool gang who I pretended didn't matter in my world while they knew I didn't matter in theirs. Don't try at all and end up eating lunch alone in the library as though I was over-studious, not just plain lonely.

That was my first year of high school in an all-girl institution where the rich hung with the rich, the pretty with the pretty, the scholarship girls with the scholarship girls and boarders with boarders. Like stayed with like and difference was yet to be celebrated.

I wasn't rich, simply because my parents didn't have a holiday home; I was mouse brown not ash blonde; and my legs were shorter than my body, or so I thought when comparing myself with Elle, who was stuck to my fridge door.

Like most girls, I struggled between wanting to be noticed and wanting to blend into the crowd. At primary school I didn't want to be the first to get my breasts, but I was, so I strapped them down with a one-piece swim-suit under my uniform lest the boys in the playground noticed them. If anyone asked, I would tell them I was planning on swimming at lunchtime, despite the fact the school didn't have a pool. No one asked.

I didn't want to be the first girl to get my period in primary school either, but I was, carrying my surfboard-style pads to school in a brown paper bag and casing the toilet block each lunchtime should anyone see me enter the 'disabled toilet' (the only one that held a sanitary disposal unit). When my teacher pointed out a bloodstain on my uniform, I thought the eyes of every student were on me. They weren't, and I didn't know which was worse.

When, in the final year of my co-ed primary school, we went away on school camp to Canberra, the boys snuck into the girls' room and we played Spin the Bottle. If it landed on you, you had to kiss the boy who'd spun it. I imagined all the boys were praying it didn't land on Rachael and when it did, the boy in question and I said we were going to the bathroom to 'do it'.

We didn't 'do it' because neither of us knew what 'it' was, and we emerged saying we had, rubbing our lips as though we had been kissing passionately when really we'd both just stared at the chipped tiles on the floor. I retreated to my bed at home and kissed the pillow nightly, just like in the movies, turning my head from side to side and whispering soap-opera lines out loud. 'But I love you, Brad, don't leave me, stay with me all night'— and he did because he was a pillow.

My first real kiss was a long way off. I had three years of high school to get through before that. By Year 8 I had outgrown the library at lunchtime. My ability to mimic the teachers and take the general piss out of myself afforded me a regular spot with the cool chicks. The cool chicks, of course, were not to be confused with the scary chicks, who smoked durries down the back of the school and sniffed Perkins Paste every Friday. They were 'sluts' even though they had yet to hold hands with a boy on the platform at the train station.

Cool chicks had holiday homes at swanky beachside suburbs, ski instructors in winter and the natural rosy glow of the entitled. My skin was pasty and white and covered in blackheads, which I squeezed out each Sunday after scrubbing my skin with apricot kernels and oatmeal mixed up from rolled oats in my mother's pantry. Thankfully, I knew how to use my sister's blush to give the appearance of wealthy health—and how to dance for my place in the lunchtime circle.

Invitations came to weekend parties and it was

rumoured there would be boys from the school down the road. I said 'yes' though I meant 'no', scared that if I said 'no' I wouldn't be asked again. Instead, I'd disappoint at the last minute with a phone call feigning illness, or family fatality, or babysitting duties.

When I did go I'd act the clown, delighting the girls as I was no threat to the boys and ensuring the boys saw me as something to laugh at not sleep with. Post-party time was spent alone inhaling buckets of ice cream, packets of Tim Tams, frozen slabs of cake, and washing it down with laxatives. I didn't know who I hated more, me or the girls I wanted to be.

I no longer wore one-piece swimsuits under my uniform; all the girls now had breasts, though mine were safely tucked away under a layer of cultivated fat. The girls all knew how to 'do it' or at least knew what 'it' was, and knew who was doing 'it' too often and 'it' with too many others. Though none of us admitted to doing 'it' or not doing 'it'—to admit either would invite banishment from the lunchtime circle and gossip behind the hands of those we sat with.

My first kiss came on the stairs at a cool girls' party despite the fat I thought I wore as protection. Spandau Ballet's 'Gold' played in the background and the boy in question was part of the cool boys' gang, though in the outer not inner sanctum. Kissing him was enough to get *me* on the inner the next day at school.

We dated for six weeks and I developed a severe case of mentionitis, managing to drop his name into as many sentences as possible as though having a boyfriend finally made me legitimate. 'Richard says my hair is auburn, not red.' 'Richard said he likes his collars up, not down.' On days when I wasn't so sure, I'd replace it with 'What do you think Richard means when he says, "I can't see you this afternoon"—does that mean he can't see me, he doesn't want to see me, he wants to see me but can't see me, or he's seeing someone else?' Like all first loves it was destined to end and it did, though I dropped him, he didn't drop me. That's important to mention.

What goes around comes around, and my heart was ripped from my chest, thrown in a tub of boiling water, run over by a truck and fed through a cheese grater by a young man with flamboyant fashion sense and bad skin. It took nine months for it to happen, nine months in which I fell in love, discovered obsession and forgot about the size of my thighs. Who counts imaginary stretch marks when you can count the minutes since he last said he loves you.

A year older than me, in the boys' school down the road, he smoked cigarettes from a black box he kept in the back pocket of his Stuart Membrey baggy jeans. We did 'it' one night when he sneaked into my bedroom through the window after dark.

I didn't want to be the first to lose my virginity in my group. I wasn't, which meant I saved myself from being a slut. I also didn't want to be the last to lose my virginity either and I wasn't, which meant I saved myself from being frigid. It didn't stop us breaking up though he dumped me, I didn't dump him. That's important to mention.

Like all good dumpings, the timing sucked, with only four weeks till my HSC. If only I had known then that I would see him ten years later dressed in a frock and miming to Cher, his flamboyant dress sense still very much alive. I couldn't see into the future, only lament the past, convinced it was my body that had let me down. In a way it had, simply for having the wrong chromosome. I went back to counting stretch marks and monitoring my scales.

My first diet was the Israeli Army Diet, a fitting choice for a WASP living on Sydney's North Shore. I called it the 'Seven-Day War', for that's as long as I lasted. Then followed the Pritikin Diet, Jenny Craig, Weight Watchers, Scarsdale and my own Mars Bar Diet invention: three Mars Bars a day and a ton of water.

The Devastation Diet was not self-imposed, however it was my first true diet where food simply did not appeal and the kilos dropped off me as my broken heart screamed from its jagged wounds. I've always been a drama queen.

I channelled my pain into my finely crafted body, made taut by twice-daily aerobics. I dropped seven kilos in two weeks and got high on the bones jutting from my rib cage. Finally, I had the glow of the entitled and the gaze of the girls who I had gazed at for years. Now I was a real threat and they begged me to put on weight under the guise of caring, when I knew they just didn't want the competition. Eating disorders do that to you, make you deluded.

What goes down must come back up—that's the bulimic motto and was my mantra for the next eight years as I left school, started university, stopped university, started university again and fled to London, not realising my bulimia would flee with me.

Of course, I thought I'd hit the jackpot when I found myself in love with a titled Englishman. I could see myself in jodhpurs, ordering the help to pour Pimm's after the hunt. I couldn't see myself removing him soaking wet and fully clothed from a bathtub filled with water, empty beer cans on the bathroom floor. 'Lady Rachael' went down the plughole with the bathwater and I returned home.

My perception of the life I was waiting to lead was far removed from reality as I waited tables, sneaking bites from the lemon tart in the kitchen dessert fridge after closing time. When a lock appeared on the fridge door, I thought my secret had been exposed and handed in my resignation.

Years later, I would run into the barman from the same restaurant, who laughed about the lock and explained it was he and his colleagues raiding the fridge with the munchies after work that caused the lock to appear. Damn those voices inside my head.

Bulimia is a deceptive disease that relies on the fear of being discovered. To write about it now feels as though I am writing about another person. In a way I am—a person far removed from the one I have become. I couldn't accept the flaws in myself so found it nigh on impossible to accept the flaws in others. Life was supposed to be an airbrushed movie and I was the star-ring role. So I acted a role by day and binged by night, swallowing my insatiable desire to be loved with sugar and alcohol.

It was no surprise I ended up in media. The camera just replaced the eyes of the girls at school. 'Please like me, please like me' I'd will as the camera rolled. 'Pick me, pick me' were the words unsaid when the microphone switched on in the radio studio. Then the microphone and the camera switched off and I was left with myself, flaws and all.

I spent most of my adolescence (and then some) dancing around folks, begging them to like me when they already thought I was fabulous. It was me who didn't believe it. 'Please like me, please like me' may as well have been sung by me to me, only I wasn't listening.

Instead, I defined myself by my externals, believing a size-eight body, a harbourside home, a spunky boyfriend, a glamorous job, an expensive pair of shoes would bring me the happiness I thought everyone else had. When I lost the size-eight body, the harbourside home, the boyfriend, the job and then broke my heels, I knew something had to give.

Learning to accept there will always be people in this world who don't like me and always people who do, took time. Learning to like myself took longer. It happened only when I accepted my flaws and accepted that I had no control over the thoughts of others. Flaws are what make people interesting—who wants to hang out with a cardboard cutout?

Adolescence didn't finish when I was allowed to vote (and pimples aren't reserved for those whose age ends in 'teen'). There's a little adolescence in all of us. I call my inner adolescent Mary Millionaire—she's the one without limits, who after one glass of champagne demands a bottle, after a bottle shouts the whole bar. I pay her bills and send her to her room when she's come out to play too often. She goes but not before she's stamped her stiletto heels, which she charged to my credit card. She's funny that way. That's funny ha ha, not funny odd.

RACHAEL OAKES-ASH has been speaking between mouthfuls since she was a tot. One-time radio announcer, documentary maker, corporate speaker, columnist and now travel journalist, she is the author of the autobiography *Good Girls Do Swallow* and the follow-up book on female competition, *Anything She Can Do I Can Do Better*. She prefers swanky to skanky, is addicted to Skype and is a fan of the nanna nap. Her website is www.oakesash.com.

Rebels With a Cause

Eva Cox

I suppose it's appropriate for a sociologist that when I look back I see my teenage years as the starting point for a lifetime of political activism. Not only was it *my* time to change, it was also a period of much wider social change. In fact, the 'teenager' identity was only invented in the 1950s, coinciding with my entry into the category. I was thirteen in 1951, in my second year of high school, the child of newly separated parents (not very common in those days) and still finding out about Australia. I had been brought up in England, a refugee from the Nazis in Vienna, dependent on others' goodwill and generosity. We arrived here after two years in Rome, where my father was working for the United Nations. Australia offered the possibility of a new sense of belonging as we were to be reunited with my mother's family, who had migrated here before the war.

Australia was to be our long-term home so I wanted to be Australian. I spoke the language but had dark hair and dark eyes and didn't quite fit the Bondi Beach Anglo image of freckles and fair hair. I couldn't surf or do 'overarm' but swum breast stroke. My parents had accents and spoke German with my mother's relatives. We were Jewish, not Christian, ate 'continental' food and didn't delight in tinned spaghetti on toast, or lamb's fry and bacon with gravy (my first Australian breakfast). Having come from Italy with minimal cafe latte breakfasts, this was very scary.

Being a refugee in England then an English-speaking child in Italy meant I was already aware of being different, an outsider (something that was confirmed for me by the prejudice against 'reffos' at my public primary school in Bondi). Three years after arriving in the country, I was looking forward to high school, where there were quite a few other children of Jewish refugee families—I was hoping to find a group to which I could belong, to experience the comfort of being with people like myself.

While I was struggling with my own need to fit in, the culture was busy creating the rebellious teenager who wanted more than his or her parents. The 'teens' seemed to represent a new future, where the young could spend some years enjoying themselves before taking on the serious aspects of life. Meanwhile, our parents were catching up with what they saw as normality: women were back into traditional roles and babies after working in factories during the war; men returned to their jobs after being soldiers.

We were an odd generation, born just about when the war began, growing up at the beginning of a very optimistic period and determined to make our mark. Our parents had lost their youth in the depression or war and we were not going to be deprived of our growing-up pleasures and power. The first teen movies appeared in the early 1950s: *The Wild One* with Marlon Brando, *Blackboard Jungle* and its theme song, 'Rock Around the Clock', legitimating the idea of teen rebellion, followed by the ultimate troubled youth, James Dean in *Rebel Without a Cause*. The message was clear: we were not going to do what the older generation expected—but how would that play out?

The girls I mixed with added another layer of complexity to the story: their parents had lost their possessions and status in fleeing to Australia before the war. This, understandably, made them very anxious about the future, even here! For them, the most vital possession of all now was their children's education—you could take qualifications with you if you had to flee again. Education was also the way to future financial security in a new country. While most of the Anglo girls at what was then one of Sydney's few selective high schools knew they were bright, for them university was merely an interlude before the marriage that was to be their career. However, the expectations of our immigrant parents were twofold: they were prepared to educate us in professional areas so we could be secure, but they also still expected us to be good girls and get married.

Consequently, we were subjected to the pressure of doing well at school. I was often at odds with my peers as my level of commitment was much more varied than theirs. I had completed primary school in Italy and was ready to start high school at aged ten when we came to Australia, only to be put back into Fifth Class. Bored and annoyed, I stopped working hard and developed the habit of doing just enough to get through. At the same time, my parents' marriage was disintegrating and their different and conflicting approaches to life reinforced my argumentative, rather than accepting, attitude to authority and teachers.

In my first week of high school, I contradicted my new History teacher when she wrongly claimed that da Vinci's *Last Supper* was in Florence. As a recent Italian resident, I knew it was in Milan so committed the cardinal sin of being both confronting and correct. She never forgave me and I started learning that authority was not necessarily right or fair. Like my father, I raised issues, disputed facts and was vocal about what I saw as wrong. Naturally, I developed a reputation for being trouble so I was also often blamed for things that weren't my fault and picked on when I wasn't guilty. This only confirmed for me that it wasn't worth working hard to please teachers or parents, as even making an effort seemed to gain few rewards.

Blaming my father for my antics may be unfair but he believed we should all try to make the world a better place for others to share. His experiences as an activist, refugee and soldier made him a passionate reformer but a difficult person. He always had a lot to say, a characteristic I share with him. He wanted to convince people, particularly those in authority, that they were wrong and he was right, and he was also a forceful advocate for the least advantaged. I was therefore offered a model—with spikes—to follow. Not only did my absorbing of his mode of operating make my school life difficult, but it also upset my mother as she blamed his commitments for breaking up their marriage. She wanted to fit in, to become ordinary and not to challenge authority, which was not at all what my father wanted. She also wanted a quiet, obedient child and saw my getting into trouble as echoes of what made the relationships between my parents impossible.

Much of my adolescence was spent being in trouble, which failed to stop me from continuing to be concerned with problems and believing I could fix them. This didn't help much on the friendship circuits either. All my desires to find a place and group in which I could be accepted were threatened by a multitude of small differences. I was different because my family experiences made me question respectability and the expectations that girls couldn't do what boys did. I felt different and probably was, as many of my friends wanted to do well and conform to their parental aspirations.

Our small group of four or five were nearly all children of Jewish immigrants, with one local Anglo. The dynamics were strained, as they so often are in adolescence. There was jockeying for the approval of the more popular ones and sometimes exclusion of the more marginal. One member of the group was always exceedingly competitive and often needed to show power by excluding someone else. For whatever reason, I was usually the vulnerable one. So I had some miserable experiences of being excluded from desired social arrangements, being baited about my lack of financial resources and even, on a few occasions, being physically bullied by feeling her heel across my instep.

Much of this memory is mine alone. I met some school friends, including the bully, recently at an old girls fiftieth reunion, and when I raised this memory they denied it ever happened. I remember the pain of feeling an outsider at the time. I was also aware at the time that making a fuss was not acceptable and now I look back surprised at my silent acceptance of victimhood.

It was part of my learning to be me, to be a non-conformist—I probably had failed to acquire the skills to fit in and, most importantly, did not want to pretend to be something I was not. I like my passion for making a difference, for speaking up when people are bullied or hurt. I think it's important to have both the courage and skills to try to make the world a better place. Although I remember being grossly embarrassed as a teenager when my father asked me and my friends what we had done that day to improve the world, I do follow his belief that all of us are responsible for the wellbeing of others.

My outsider status is a continuing condition. I have read many studies of the processes of migration and what happens to people in those situations. New migrants have the dilemma of trying to fit in to a not very accepting culture while attempting to retain some sense of their own identity. In the 1950s we were expected to assimilate, which we tried to do, but at the same time we were encouraged to stay within our own groups for entertainment and social events. I failed to conform either within my peer group or the wider world.

If this means that I have continued my adolescent rebellions through my working life and will into retirement, it may be good to retain such passions. George Bernard Shaw once said that youth is wasted on the young. Maybe it's useful for those now young to remember that losing their passion for justice as they get older may merely be a sign of early senility, not maturity.

The relatively few rebellious teenagers of the '50s

blended into the youth revolts of the '60s, as we joined the baby boomers to take rebellion even further. The '60s and '70s were a time of almost unbounded optimism, despite the cold war and fear of nuclear war. We were effective in reforming many stuffy and toxic assumptions by expanding roles for women and creating more equity for groups such as indigenous people. By the '80s the fervour for these kinds of changes dissipated, particularly among my political contemporaries and the boomers. I have kept on while recognising these are less optimistic times and the changes people want may be harder to articulate and achieve . . . But we still need the rebels and stirrers, who may develop their consciousness and conscience from a sense of being an outsider. It's often those of us who are labelled as difficult who are the most effective at making a difference.

EVA COX was born Eva Hauser in Vienna in 1938, and was soon declared non-human and stateless by Hitler. She grew up as a refugee in England till 1946, lived in Rome till 1948, and arrived in Australia aged ten. These early experiences influenced her commitments and her rejection of injustices. Eva involves herself in many social and political issues and has worked for government and voluntary organisations in Australia. She has been an active and irrepressible advocate for creating more civil societies, is a long-term member of the Women's Electoral Lobby and an unabashed feminist. She is currently involved in projects looking at social and ethical accounting for responsible business enterprises, and lectures on social inquiry at the University of Technology in Sydney. A sociologist by trade, Eva has undertaken many research projects for the government, the private sector and community groups, and has published widely and eclectically in books, journals and newspapers. She has one daughter, lives in inner-city Sydney and wonders whether she is becoming too respectable!

The Pirate of Paradise Waters

Kate Morton

His name was Zachariasz and he was the Pirate King. Well, he wasn't a king, and he certainly wasn't a pirate, but in our high-school musical production of *The Pirates of Penzance*, he was the last word in all that was exotic and swashbuckling. For starters, he was European—he came from somewhere exotic, East of Poland—and had a surname no one could pronounce. And he was tall, practically a man, was even able to grow a proper beard (the year before, he'd played Tevye in *Fiddler on the Roof* and hadn't needed make-up).

From the day he'd turned up at our Gold Coast school Zachariasz had been the sort of guy around whom myths are fashioned. For one thing, he didn't live with his parents like the rest of us. He lived with his sister and her husband—an arrangement that seemed inestimably bohemian. There were rumours going about school that they'd moved to Australia to escape some political 'situation', though none of us had been listening well enough in Modern History to know which one.

He looked exactly like Patrick Swayze in *Dirty Dancing*. Except younger, taller and with darker hair. And he could sing. And play guitar. He was even in a band, which rehearsed on weekends in another guy's parents' garage. His hair was longer than the other boys', curling to scrape his collar, despite the rules at school that prevented such things. What cared Zachariasz for rules? He was the sort of guy who made singing in a musical cool. Even the teachers liked him.

Most importantly for me and my Year 11 friends, Zachariasz was a senior.

One day at rehearsal, the word went around: Zachariasz had his eye on someone. Someone in the cast. It was his friend, Lenny, who told us.

It was bound to be Miranda, the rest of us thought, or maybe Stacy. They were the sort of girls who usually wound up the objects of affection.

Lenny, enjoying his moment in the spotlight, the bearer of highly sought news, continued dropping hints. Larger and larger hints. Until, finally, he pointed at me.

Me?

The other girls turned to stare—appraising me afresh. Then came offers of green-eyed congratulations, which I accepted uncertainly. Was it a joke? Was Lenny going to start laughing any minute and redirect his finger to point out a far more suitable subject?

Apparently not. Unlikely though it was, Zachariasz had set his pirate's cap at me.

On learning of his intentions, I, of course, behaved like any self-respecting girl who has ever admired a god from afar. I became tongue-tied whenever he was near and avoided being alone with him. I needed time to process this stunning turn of events.

I'd admired him for ages. Who hadn't? But the possibility that such admiration would ever be returned had certainly never crossed my mind. Not for a girl like me, the Pirate King. I was neither the funniest (that was Stacy), nor the prettiest (Miranda), nor the most outgoing (Rachael). I certainly wasn't the coolest. Far from it: I was the girl who'd spent the first week of high school searching the dictionary for words like 'skeg' and 'swampy' and 'B.O.', just so I could understand what the others were talking about.

I was a knobbly-kneed kid with hair I couldn't control and a habit of doing well in Maths exams. There was nothing about me that stood out. Rather, I was shy enough never to *let* any aspect of myself stand out. When a group of us sat around in Personal Development class doing esteem exercises (in which the object was to say nice things about one another), the highlight of my haul was 'you don't say much, but you're always there'.

Luckily, I had one friend who could be counted on to see more in me than my ability to . . . well, to exist. Nicky was my sworn best friend. We'd both grown up on Tamborine Mountain and that set us apart in a way we quite accepted. We had bonded for life on the first day of school when we'd caught the bus down the goat-track to a Gold Coast school full of brown-skinned kids with sun-bleached hair. We'd spent years in each other's pockets, making up smutty poems about our teachers, and spinning elaborate fantasies about the types of lives we would surely lead some day. The kind of jobs, and clothes, and boyfriends. To the last, I'm afraid to say, we devoted an inordinate amount of imaginative energy. Though we didn't know how it would happen, we just knew that some day we'd have real boyfriends (who would, of course, adore us) and we needed to be ready.

For research, we turned to such illustrious sources as *Sixteen Candles*, *Pretty in Pink* and, our preferred text, *Dirty Dancing*. We could recite the movie, and owned the soundtrack (discs one *and* two). We'd even made a teach-yourself-how-to-Dirty-Dance manual, and alternated the roles of 'man' and 'woman' so we'd both be equipped when next we found ourselves on a family holiday at a resort where hot jive instructors did the lambada in their down-time.

Nicky already had some experience in the boyfriend department. She was a grade above me and, a few years back, had gone steady for a whole six months with Samuel, one of our friends from primary school. They hadn't got far physically—there was only so far you could take a relationship when the only time you had together was a daily bus trip up and down the mountain. Anything more than holding hands and you were likely to end up in the aisle. Worse, you might bring yourself to the notice of Mr Sheen, the Bus Nazi. He'd once been a defence force professor, but circumstances had conspired against him and he'd been forced to swap his army greens for a coach driver's uniform. He had to satisfy his pathological need for discipline by keeping us kids in line.

Nicky and Samuel had flown high in the face of such obstacles. In the glowing halcyon days of their relationship, Nicky had even received a Valentine's Day card. She'd been the envy of every other girl on the bus. So what if Samuel only waited three seconds before adding, with a nervous giggle, that his mum had purchased the card for him? And what did it matter that he'd written 'my girlfriend' and 'your boyfriend' in brackets after their respective names? Sure, it wasn't poetry, but a Valentine's Day card was still a Valentine's Day card. And who could blame a fellow for trying to stamp out confusion?

Samuel and Nicky unravelled soon after, but not before they'd shared a clumsy yet chaste kiss behind the tank stand at the Tamborine Mountain Golf Club dinner dance. Of the two of us, then, this experience made Nicky the expert in all things 'love'.

But Nicky was the first to admit that attention from the Z-man was new. It was big. This was more than just a prospective boyfriend. By attracting the likes of Zachariasz, Nicky told me, I had unwittingly struck a blow for mountain dags everywhere. Nothing either of us had been through had prepared us for this honour, but it was my responsibility, nay my *duty*, to prevail. To screw my courage to the sticking-place and make the relationship happen.

As luck would have it, an amateur theatrical group was booked to perform *The Pirates of Penzance* at the Tamborine Mountain Police Citizens Youth Club. Nicky and I bought tickets, and Zachariasz, Lenny, Stacy and Miranda decided to car-pool up the mountain to watch it with us (Zachariasz had a licence, of course, and his sister let him drive her car). We found seats (after a moment of confusion when Stacy accidentally slid in next to Zachariasz and had to be prevailed upon to let me take her place) and we all sat, watching. Not that I remember much of the performance. There was a dialogue running constantly in my mind: 'I am sitting next to Zachariasz, the Pirate King, who wants to be my boyfriend. *My* boyfriend. He may even kiss me tonight.' Repeat, ad infinitum.

He didn't. Kiss me, I mean. After the performance, the others went home and Nicky and I went back to her place. We put on her parents' CD of classic love songs, poured ourselves a glass each of Cherry Voc (it was all we could find in the liquor cabinet that wouldn't be missed) and, as Glenn Medeiros assured us that nothing was gonna change his love for us, set about decoding the evening. Analysing every last detail. The seating arrangement, the moment Zachariasz had reached across to pluck a piece of popcorn and 'accidentally' brushed my knee, almost held my hand. The way he'd engineered the walk back to the car so that he and I lingered at the back of the group just long enough to swap incredibly sophisticated insights into the performance we'd just pretended to watch.

Yep, Nicky announced. He was in love with me, there was no doubting it. Not kissing me was all part of the romance. She could read the body language. He was a real gentleman, she said, not like the other guys at school who were out for all they could get. The fact that he was taking things slowly just proved he respected me. Then we watched *Dirty Dancing* again. And *Sixteen Candles*, just for good measure.

The next two weeks passed in a flurry of flirtation. Between us, Nicky and I managed to form a composite of Zachariasz's timetable and I proceeded to turn up wherever he was—the tuckshop queue, the bubblers behind the science rooms, outside the boys' lockers—

looking oh-so-otherwise occupied. Laughing gaily with whomever happened to be there, making sure always to show my good side (damn that zit!), even, on occasion, making ostentatious application of baby oil on my newly fake-tanned legs. Yep—I was smooth. And, finally, my hard work paid off. A secret note from Zachariasz found its way into my biology book: he was having a party. His sister and her husband were away for the week and had told him to have some friends round to stay. Everyone was invited but he *really* (underlined three times) hoped I would come.

Nicky and I basked for a moment in the warm glow of success, then we began scrutinising the note. It didn't take long for us to read the subtext. We knew what those underlines meant, we knew what was coming next, we'd seen *Pretty in Pink*. Yes, ladies and gentlemen, Zachariasz was ready to make a commitment. This weekend, he was going to ask me to the prom!

Well . . . the senior formal, at any rate.

The day of the party dawned and proceeded to seep, devastatingly slowly, towards a time when it was acceptable to leave for it. Nicky had convinced her older sister, Roz, to drive us to the coast so that our parents needn't be bothered by such niggling details as precisely where we would be sleeping, whose parents would be in attendance, and why on God's green earth we wanted to be dropped off a few blocks from the party rather than let them deposit us, nice and safely, at the front door? Thankfully for us, parental concern was no match for the tyranny of distance: Rachael's house, Stacy's house, Miranda's house . . . Mermaid Beach, Main Beach, Nobby Beach . . . they all sounded so similar, after all. Our parents couldn't be blamed for getting confused sometimes.

And so, in Roz's white Mazda 121, we were spirited
to our destiny. Nicky, like the worthy best friend she was,
had made a compilation tape for our trip down the
mountain. Not only was Zachariasz going to ask me to
the formal, she insisted, tonight he would finally kiss me.
It was only proper, wasn't it, that this night of nights be
commemorated with a fitting soundtrack? 'Under the
Bridge' by the Red Hot Chili Peppers; 'Save the Best
for Last' by Vanessa Williams; 'Damn I Wish I Was Your
Lover' by Sophie B. Hawkins; 'Too Funky' by George
Michael . . . Yep, it was going to be a great night.

We made a short stop at the Southport Liquor Barn
where Roz, who was eighteen, equipped us with a six-
pack of Strongbow Sweet and a bottle of Midori (you
needed back-up, she said, in her infinite wisdom, in case
someone found your stash of Strongbows and left you
empty). Then Roz dropped us at the shopping centre
round the corner from Zachariasz's house. We were a
little early and needed to freshen up, apply the last bits of
make-up that our parents would have made us clean
off before leaving the house.

I changed into my Doc Martens and the clingy black
dress I'd ordered through *Cleo* magazine a few months
before, then brushed out my hair. Still uncontrollable—
long and triumphantly woolly—but pleasingly blonde.
The strategically applied lemon juice and vinegar
concoction had given excellent results over the past
few months.

Beneath the burning fluoro lights of the ladies' loo,
Nicky and I drew on more eyeliner, painted our lips and
sprayed ourselves liberally with *Impulse* deodorant, 'Berry

Bliss'. We stood back finally to admire the results of our labours. Smiled at each other's reflections. There was no doubting it: we looked good.

Filled with confidence, we strode down the sunburnt Gold Coast Highway and into the plush riverfront suburb of Paradise Waters. And as the sun set, and the high-rises of Surfers Paradise began to twinkle, we arrived at Zachariasz's house. The party was already in full swing, 'Smells Like Teen Spirit' pumping from the stereo inside.

We popped the tops off a couple of Strongbows and took a stroll about the pad, trying to look as cool as we possibly could.

There was no sign yet of Zachariasz so we sat for a while in the smoke-filled lounge room, where Lenny was holding court, strumming his guitar for an adoring audience of 91 Year 10 hangers-on. Through the glass sliding door, I eyed the jetty that led out into the muddy Gold Coast canal. Perhaps that's where Zachariasz would pop the question? Ask me to make his formal dreams come true? Then, if Nicky was right, he'd kiss me. My first, proper, kiss.

If I could ever find him.

'Want another one?' This was Nicky. She tilted her empty Strongbow bottle at me.

'Yeah, cool.'

We left the lounge lizards and went back to the kitchen. As Nicky opened our drinks, Lenny joined us.

'Hey,' he said to me, 'Zach was looking for you earlier. He wanted to ask you something.'

'Oh yeah?' I oozed nonchalance.

'Where is he now?' said Nicky. No nonchalance what-soever. (She may even have nudged me.)

'Dunno. Think he went to the servo. Said something about getting ciggies.'

Nicky nodded, picked up the bottle of Midori, and whispered to me. 'Better find somewhere to stash this. We'll be needing it later. To celebrate.'

'I'll do it,' I said. 'Gotta put my bag somewhere. Want me to take yours?'

I went through the lounge and into the hallway. Past the bathroom.

At the end of the hall the door was open and I could tell the room belonged to Zachariasz's married sister. That meant the closed door on my right must be his bedroom. The perfect repository for our bags. Not to mention the fact that I was curious to see where my soon-to-be-official boyfriend dwelt. Perhaps he'd even photocopied my picture from an advance copy of the musical programme; put it in a frame by his bed?

I pushed open the door.

It was dark but I sensed movement. I froze, waited for my eyes to adjust. There was a figure on the bed. I blinked. 'Stacy?' Was she unwell?

Silence.

Another face appeared from beneath the doona. My hopes and dreams and imaginings came rushing towards me. Crashed and shattered into a million sharp pieces.

'Zachariasz?'

POSTSCRIPT

They broke up: it only lasted a week. He told Rachael who told Nicky who told me he was sorry, he hadn't meant it. He'd gone into his room to get money for cigarettes and she'd followed him in. One thing just led to another. I understood, didn't I?

I didn't understand. Call me unimaginative, but I'd never understood the logistics of 'one thing led to another'. How is that, exactly? You were in the same room, fully clothed, and then, somehow, your clothes dropped off and you were having sex?

I didn't go to the senior formal that year. Neither did Zachariasz. The musical lost some of its spark, too. It seemed everyone had an opinion on Stacy-gate and, by the time we reached performance night, tensions in the cast put the dramas of the pirates to shame.

Zachariasz left school after his final exams and became an encyclopaedia salesman, door-to-door. Last I heard, he was still living in his sister's house, moonlighting as a stripper in a club in Surfers.

Stacy and I made up, sometime the following year. Her parents got a divorce (one of them cheated on the other) and she needed a friend to lean on. Someone she knew she could count on.

Nicky and I eventually both got real boyfriends (they're our husbands now). And jobs we loved. And lives, kind of like the ones we'd dreamt of.

Sadly, neither of us has ever been called upon to demonstrate our excellent dirty dancing abilities. (Yet.)

The moral of this story? Sometimes the good girl doesn't get the guy. Sometimes that's not such a bad thing.

NOTE: All names have been changed to protect the innocent. And the not so innocent.

KATE MORTON grew up on Tamborine Mountain in Queensland and now lives with her husband and young son in a 100-year-old house in Brisbane. Kate's first novel, *The Shifting Fog*, was published by Allen & Unwin in 2006. Her second, *The Forgotten Garden*, was released in 2008. Her website is www.katemorton.com.

The Language
of the Dead

Antonella Gambotto-Burke

I

I felt winged at the summit of those sixty stairs that scaled
the rock to my childhood home. We lived on Sydney's
Upper North Shore. The deep Killara basin protected
us from other suburbs (at night, no more than a necklace
of streetlights on the horizon). Even our trees were
imported. Despite the leaves—abundant, fragrant—
summers are pitiless there, and marriages fade. Christmas
is celebrated with fire: thousands of gums, those ghostly
Australian natives, explode in showers of stinking cinders,
orange and black. Decembers tear landscapes in half.
Charred driftwood washes up on beaches and ash as fine
as pure cocaine settles on surfaces by open windows.
High on those balconies, we watched the distance burn.

2

In kindergarten, I was befriended by a boy with choppy dirt-blond hair and rueful eyes. My grasp of English was negligible, if enthusiastic; he was one of the few who refused to torment me for all that set me apart. (I was a sickly child, very foreign and also asthmatic, forever entranced by words and games.) We sat together at lunchtime on those child-sized wooden picnic tables eating our egg sandwiches and sometimes leaning into each other (hot breath, stifled giggles) to reveal—through the gaping legs of his grey shorts and beneath my light cotton uniform, in a white flash—our underpants.

His smile was a feather settling.

I do not remember him as my first love—my passions were engaged by a boy who ran from me so quickly I would fall and scrape my knees—but he was the first to ask for my hand in marriage. He bought me a ring, one of those elaborate plastic numbers found in vending machine capsules (rubber spiders and worms are secreted in the same packaging) at the dreary local shopping centre. Intrigued by this tribute, I accepted.

Our engagement lasted. I remember cramming my mouth with chocolates and saving the cellophane wrappers, which I then straightened for him to crackle: glittering, wonderful. His surname followed mine in rollcall and because of this, we felt a special affinity. I remember laughing with him over the concept of bowel movements (the word *bum* had us in tears), while flatulence of any calibre was unthinkably improper and therefore marvellous. We sang:

I'm Popeye the sailor man,
I live in a caravan
with a hole in the top
where I do all my plops—
I'm Popeye the sailor man!

We were five years old. At the age of sixteen, he put his father's pistol to his head and blew his brains out.

Just before he died, I saw him sitting on the ground with his back against the brick wall behind D Block at Killara High. He was shod in desert boots. Hands limply slung over raised grey flannel knees. We were alone. As I walked past, he suddenly looked up. Our eyes met in a strange, charged moment; I know that I looked through him at the little boy he had once been. Futility informed him: it was as if he expected to be punished, pushed, abused. His voice was soft. He existed on peripheries.

I wonder what he thought as he watched me. Were we remembering that same friable opalescence, those days in which we would always be comical and sweet? It was a sphere of innocence in an existence otherwise corrupt with loss. His smile was crumpled; I smiled back. I now know that he was saying goodbye. At the heart of our every exchange over the years—there were not many; I was an outstanding English scholar and he had given up the ghost—there was a little prickle of silliness, an intimacy to which we would have been embarrassed to admit.

The memory of him still flickers, a kind of glow-worm, magical against the night.

3

I first consciously experienced grief through my maternal grandmother. Unlike my mother in every way other than a faint physiological echo about the cheekbones, she was a powerful and tender woman. Also innocently sexual in her youth. Large-breasted. A hungry laugh. She taught me to charleston. Those quick green eyes, that fine black hair, a pure complexion. Her feline mien. *Nellaaaaaaaa!* I remember her calling. *Nella!* She strides through memories in large black sunglasses and halter-neck tops, playing tennis, posing in boats, slim and lovely against the Alpine backdrops of old photographs. I loved her tremendously. She died when I was sixteen.

On her return from the city at lunchtime, she would search for me in the school playground. Sometimes she'd call my name; I'd sprint to kiss her. There would be kisses—I still miss her foaming embrace—and she would hand me a paper cup (red and white, with a smooth lip) of salty chips from town. They were lukewarm, but I devoured them. Her smile was lovely, delicate, shy. Dainty mother-of-pearl teeth. (Men were entranced.) She brimmed with love, and was Persian in her intensities. At all times, she was fragrant with Spanish talcum powder or Chanel. After hours in the kitchen, she was flushed. The heat and steam, that perfumed broth. (She could be tough: the chopping board was grooved, her knife blade thick enough.) Showcased in sandals, those toenails painted pink. I remember her walking beneath the vines, collecting sprigs of rosemary and basil in a basket, dappled by shade, leaves brushing her skin.

Born in Ferrara, that stern northern Italian city of tall elms, she is now part of its history. Ferrara is a thousand love stories and wars; it is famous throughout Italy for producing beautiful girls. These were the *vie* my grandmother strolled and on which, to the strains of an accordion and with her brothers and their friends, she danced. The middle of five children (Aurora, Giuseppe, Giuseppina, Alfredo, Antonio), she loved her older brother best. Photographs show a lean and handsome man, refined in profile, tall. He was a horseman, popular, but ended as cannon-fodder at Tripoli. She never recovered. When his name was mentioned, her eyes sparked with love or pain. Never a big talker, she did not share her grief; I saw it lodge, a kind of fishbone, in her throat. This said, her sense of propriety was not rote. She may have developed it as a courtesy to others during the war, when the maintenance of optimism is a military strategy.

I recall sensing grief as subtle, as a deeply private set of feelings tinted the palest rose or grey. My response was respectful. In grieving for her brother, my grandmother accessed a space where she existed exclusively as his sister. She grieved not only for him but for the self she was with him, for the self she was before bereavement, and for her dreams; her every hope had to be adjusted so it did not feature him. I wish I had known Beppe Mistroni, one of the two men she profoundly loved. But instead of telling me of Beppe, she told me of Ferrara during World War II: Jews stashed in attics, people machine-gunned by Nazis outside cinemas, her mother-in-law beneath the peach tree in the *cortile*, Zia Nanda—my mother's aunt, not mine—being wolf whistled as she paraded those big shapely hips, skinny little Zio Tonino running over cobblestones to a bomb shelter with my blonde mother (a bundle of straw) beneath his arm.

There was no missile more devastating for my grandmother than that telegram delivered in 1943. Zio Tonino keeps it in a drawer.

In retrospect, my awareness of these intricate feelings of my grandmother's was unusual, or perhaps it was no more than sensitivity to a woman I adored: I could not say which. She was a complex woman and I was a complex child, but we were simplified by love.

4

She died a complicated death (cancer, decay, blindness). At the time, I could not cope—how could I cope?—and wished for a gun. She held my hand when I visited. Malignancy had no place in her skin. She faded to loose rice paper, lit from within. Her breathing difficulties were extreme. I remember her gasping by two tanks of oxygen. Those tanks! I could not look at them. *So it seems to me possible that cholera . . . tuberculosis, and cancer are the celestial means of locomotion, just as steamboats, buses, and railways are the terrestrial means,* Vincent van Gogh wrote. The house echoed with her hissing breaths. She never complained.

Her death ushered the winds in. I would not face my grief. Some deaths bring families together; this death blew the family apart. There were bits of us everywhere. I was probably the worst. My consciousness cracked when she was dying, slowly at first, and then at speed. Eruption, avalanche, earthquake: this was a natural disaster.

Concentration was impossible; my consciousness was otherwise employed. The repression of grief is a full-time occupation. And I was wild. In a pink and white crinoline borrowed from the Marion Street Theatre, I played Pip's aunt in *Great Expectations* and finished in tears, sinking into my crinoline until only the crown of my head was visible. I must have looked like a rainswept camellia. The applause was torrential. Few noticed that my tears had not stopped.

5

Obeying all rules of gender, I attempted to kill myself in sissy ways. I used a little knife and little pills. I did not really want to die, but was dying to kill the pain. This urge to obliterate anguish had kicked in when my grandmother became ill. On some level, my suicidal urges were a manifestation of my desire to be close to her; if I could not be with her in life, I would join her in death. I did not want to consider a world in which she did not laugh. There was a real sense of oppression in being left behind.

The ceiling, every wall, all closed in. It was excruciating.

6

There were no religious convictions to negotiate; I was christened Roman Catholic and devolved into an atheist at thirteen. My (strident, desiccated) scripture teacher drilled a door in an eggshell; this opened to reveal a Virgin Mary miniature in sky-blue robes. I challenged her interpretation of the thing as sacred. Her eyes clouded. I was to leave and she would pray for me. As I walked out, I said that I would pray for her, too. The following week, the young priest summoned to save my soul cheerfully agreed: *You're absolutely right, there is no way of proving God exists.* His equanimity was a relief after all that hectoring. Real spiritual practice would have alarmed my poor parents.

Death was presented as both punishment and a solution to suffering. *I want to kill myself!* my volatile war-baby mother would cry. If we misbehaved, she (weirdly) hissed: *I don't want you to come to my funeral!* At other times, she was both wistful and insistent: *Promise you'll cremate my body! Scratch marks have been found in caskets—people are buried alive! They wake up in the coffin and suffocate!*

7

I will always remember the first night I wanted to die. Sixteen years old. Shivering, I lay in bed. That consciousness of darkness was very new. Sweat pricked my eyes. I could not breathe. Sentience had become fear: fear of the known, fear of the unknown. My grandmother's cancer had altered the family dynamic, and my place in it was no longer secure. The foundations of my life were slowly being washed out from under me like sand. That big knife with the wooden handle glistened with a pornographic intensity in my thoughts. Panic: I did not know how to explain this bright new urge.

That sense of isolation overwhelmed me in a sudden, wrenching twist: I wanted to die. There seemed to be no other way of exerting control. (I think of Tennyson in 1866, dreaming of folding over his face a handkerchief tenderly perfumed with chloroform.)

8

The first human corpse I saw had housed my grandmother's soul. I expected a serene mien. I expected to find her sleeping. I expected a transforming beauty, something painted by Millais. Instead, the old whore petticoats of skin. My mother, drugged and guttering, sat in the car. My father led me through the night into the hospice and then left me alone with the corpse. Her teeth were bared as if attempting to scare off pain. I stood, the light of a single desk lamp illuminating that empty room, my shoes squeaking on the linoleum, and gently slipped my finger beneath her nose. No breath at all. So this was death. As if numbed by ice, I stared.

Where had she gone?

I whispered her name. She did not answer. My index finger peeled her eyelid back from her eyeball. That staring eye was devoid of intelligence: a black and green and white marble. Holding my breath, I replaced it just as tenderly. My heart staggered, but I could not feel hers. Horror washed through me suddenly: that thin dead thing would come for me in darkness! I hurried back to the car. When my mother asked about the body, I lied. It was, I said, as if she dozed. She looked so beautiful.

My de facto husband of a few months had shoved me into the wall that morning, accusing me of sexual neglect. He was a brute; I had a taste for pain in those dead days. *Why are you always crying?* (That fist through a pink lampshade; the trash emptied onto the floor.) I swallowed another pill to calm down: sixteen years old and foundering in suppressed emotion. (My grandmother, surrendering to infinity, whispered: *There is no music in the house since you left home.*) That night I slept in her bed (my mother's instructions). Another Valium tablet or two. Unnerved, I called for my mother (I could not sleep). She joined me. As if speaking from a great distance, she said my grandmother was standing by the bed. I screamed. My father slammed into the room. *What's wrong?* My teeth were chattering. *She's gone mad!* (My mother certainly looked very relaxed as she blinked, uncomprehending, at the light.) Expertly, my father administered more pills.

Alexander, the youngest of my two brothers and then only four, searched for our grandmother. Death made no sense to him at all. *She was calling me*, he cried in a little voice, *but when I went, she wasn't there!*

9

I was tired of being brave. In the Orwellian year of 1984, I flew to London, where I worked as a rock writer for the *NME*. For years, I was most always stoned. I did not understand my grief. Memories with a respectably bohemian sheen: playing 'Blueberry Hill' on the piano with Robert Smith; snorting cocaine delivered by the erudite dealer of a member of a royal family; standing backstage at Castle Donnington in faux leopardskin with dyed wild Jaffa hair; walking through Bank in thigh-high boots and a diaphanous lace slip holding a bag stuffed with seventy thousand pounds; staying in the penthouse of a man now married to one of the world's most powerful women (a man who also liked to be photographed with his pet boa constrictor).

I shared a house with an Indian family who kept huge, flapping fish in the bathtub. I walked through fields of wheat with a man I deeply loved. I stood on Paddington station with a suitcase full of shoes. I waited in snow at night for a man I had hurt to come home. I stumbled from the bed of a director and accidentally—alarmed by the floor-to-ceiling stained-glass window of the Crucifixion, perhaps—kicked a hole in the heart of the Virgin Mary statue by the door.

the moon as a white variation/january/1986
jesus bleeding on the cross
& watching us in bed.
one eye butterfly
& the other reads the language of the dead.
(i dig this infra red.)

Living it, of course, was hell. The drugs and alcohol ensured that I was never certain of anything other than fear. I was prescribed red pills to speed me up and yellow pills to calm me down. Anne Sexton wrote of her consciousness as a war in which she planted bombs within herself. On the whole, my doctors were idiotic and irresponsible. One casually suggested (as he scribbled repeat prescriptions) that I smoke more grass. And so I did. I also smoked cigarettes until I felt hollowed, until the tip of my dry tongue adhered to my dry palate. The world just reeled. All my lovers were white-skinned, black-haired, green-eyed. I was made conscious of the meaning of this sexual preference by a therapist. She gently probed. *Who shares this colouring?* The impact of these words was deep. I had not accepted my grandmother's death: I would not, could not, let her die.

10

Years later, I took a friend's fifteen-year-old son and his best friend for a long walk along the Byron shore. We each carried our shoes. Every ripple in that temperate ocean was clear. The night was spectacular. Three shooting stars. (Mongols and Greenlanders believed that shooting stars were discarnate souls.) My grandmother's memory was now so sweet, a presence infinitely lulling. Gesturing, I said: *If our vision were less limited, we would perceive the sky as pure starlight. Out there, trillions of stars. The human eye is far too weak to discern the light emitted by most of them. And so we see only a fraction of it all—a necklace glittering against a dark backdrop. The universe as a big jewellery store, no more.* The boys looked up. They were no longer interested in words.

Edited extract from The Eclipse: A Memoir of Suicide *(Broken Ankle Books, 2004).*

ANTONELLA GAMBOTTO-BURKE is the author of four books, the most recent being *The Eclipse: A Memoir of Suicide* (exclusively available from brokenanklebooks.com), which was featured on the cover of the national paper's review section and recently translated into Finnish and Chinese. She is also a regular contributor to *The Weekend Australian*, the *South China Morning Post*, *Harper's Bazaar* and *Men's Style*, as well as writing a column for *My Child* (Australia) magazine and the core love stories of artist David Bromley's upcoming film, *I Could Be Me*. Gambotto-Burke is married to Alexander, a correspondent for *The Guardian* and very good man. They have one (perfect, darling) daughter. When not standing on her head, critiquing, or practising attachment parenting, Gambotto-Burke is at work on her fifth book. Her website is antonellagambotto.com.

Lock Up Your Sons

Emily Maguire

When I was fourteen, I was certain that I was a mis-understood genius; that I was hideously obese; that anyone over thirty was incapable of honesty or passion; that I would never sell myself into the legalised slavery of marriage; and that my parents wanted to make me so miserable I would cut my own throat, thus saving them the trouble of murdering me. The other thing I was certain about was sex. I wanted it.

Let me be clear: I did not want to have sex because the media told me I should or because my friends were doing it or I had a boyfriend who was pushing me. I wanted to have sex because my fourteen-year-old body was flooded with hormones whose entire reason for existence was to make me want to have sex. I was a young woman with brand new body parts that throbbed and swelled and moistened and ached and stopped me from sleeping at night.

In those not so long ago but pre-internet revolution days, I got my sexual information from school, my mates and the media, and the message I got from all of them was that I was a freak. Too plain to be the siren, too sexually ravenous to contemplate waiting for marriage or even a serious relationship before I had sex, I felt trapped by a body that was both unattractive and painfully, constantly aroused.

I was so desperate for guidance that I actually put my faith in Health and Development class. I spent the sessions on Nutrition and Drug Awareness daydreaming about having sex with whichever boy happened to have caught my eye on that particular day, but when we finally got around to Sexual Development I was alert and focused, waiting for the assurance that my frightening desire was normal, that it didn't mean I was turning into a hopeless slut who would be pregnant at sixteen and dead of an STD by twenty. I was seriously disappointed.

Female sexual development, according to my teacher, was an embarrassing, uncomfortable process, but one which would allow me to one day experience the miracle of motherhood. I learnt about ovulation and menstruation. I learnt that the appearance of pubic hair on a girl signals an increase in androgen levels, and that tender breasts and swollen nipples indicate a rise in oestrogen. I also learnt that testosterone was surging through my body and might cause me to feel 'strange'.

Boys would not feel strange—they would feel horny. They would be distracted by sexual thoughts and feelings. Their genitals would engorge with blood for no reason at all. They would feel a deep, low-down ache, which could only be eased by sexual release. They would have erotic dreams from which they would wake to find they had messed up their sheets and pyjamas.

I am a boy, I thought, my face hot and my thighs pressed together.

My teenage girlfriends and I talked about sex an awful lot, but none of us ever declared a personal interest in it. We giggled over the Dolly Doctor advice column, none of us admitting to feeling jealous of the girls who were close enough to doing 'it' that they were worried about contraception, none of us confessing to being in the same boat as that freaky girl who could not get to sleep at night without masturbating first.

When my best friend's boyfriend began pressuring her to have sex with him, she admitted that she was a long way from ready and was promptly dumped. The world often seems unfair when you are a fourteen-year-old misunderstood genius with large thighs, but to me this was an unprecedented injustice. While she wept over her shattered romance, I clenched my fists, my teeth, my everything, with frustration.

My friend was not ready and I respected her for knowing this and acting on it, but, dammit, I *was* ready, and there was no older boy whispering in my ear that I'd do it if I really loved him. The fabled teenage boys with one-track minds evidently went to a different school. I waited in vain for the men who coax innocent school-girls into bed; they too must have done their seducing in another town. Every day I stepped out into the world exuding sexual heat and desire, and every day I was ignored. Each time I willed someone to touch me and they didn't, I shrunk just a little.

After a year or so of this, with my body under the influence of a couple of million years of evolutionary drive, and my head full of movie clichés and chilly scientific facts, I decided that I could trust to the beastliness of men no longer. I made friends with the local thugs, a gang of boys slightly older than me with long hair and tight jeans and jobs pushing trolleys and washing cars. I did not sleep with these boys; they were my mentors.

We hung out in a pizza parlour whose owner allowed us kids to drink beer as long as we didn't throw up inside, and I listened to their stories of conquest and defeat. When the shop closed, we hit the streets and I watched these stumbling, reeking boys pick up girls. When there were no girls around, they coached me in the art of seduction. They taught me how to identify an easy target, how to convert a 'no way' into a 'maybe', a 'maybe' into a 'yes'. I learnt how to simultaneously think like a man and act like the kind of girl a man would want.

My plan was to become so good at seduction that I would never be rejected. I was willing to trade my good reputation for sexual fulfilment, but not to be seen as desperate or pathetic. This plan, of course, failed miserably. I was rejected frequently and cruelly; the boys who did accept my come-ons were usually inexperienced, clumsy and selfish; my reputation was far worse than I deserved and far harder to deal with than I had anticipated; and, more than once, I found myself way out of my depth.

This is exactly what parents fear, I know. That their daughter will fall in with a bad crowd, mess around with boys who treat her badly, be whispered about in school hallways, written about on toilet walls. That their little girl will find herself in a locked room or isolated parking spot with a man who neither knows nor cares that the girl beneath him is clever and talented and underage. That her beauty will not be appreciated, her tenderness not considered. That she will be used and cast aside, promised the world and given nothing but a reputation.

It happens. It happened to me and, honestly, it wasn't so bad. Or, I should say, it was bad but it could have been far, far worse. Far from protecting me from sex and its consequences, the just-the-bare-minimum approach to sex education left me incredibly vulnerable. Of course, I knew that I could get pregnant or worse, but I was so ashamed of my desire, and so grateful for whatever touch I was getting, that the last thing on my mind was avoiding infection or insemination. Besides, I had been taught that the only safe sex is no sex, and so there was no point bothering with protective devices that could fail anyway.

Nothing could have stopped me from acting on my desire, but I believe certain knowledge could have stopped me from taking such appalling risks and feeling so damn ashamed all the time. I wish I had known that sexual desire is neither unnatural nor harmful, and that although acting on that desire can be dangerous, it need not be. I wish I had been taught that sex in the real world—as opposed to sex as portrayed in Health class—encompasses much more than the penetration of a woman by a man. I would have liked to have been warned that sexual activity is about hands and mouths as much as it is about genitals, and that not only is it okay to say 'no', it's also okay to say 'yes' or 'not yet' or 'this but not that' or 'not without a condom'.

And as a teenage girl surrounded by images of sexually provocative women but told constantly that 'good girls don't', I wish someone had told me that I didn't have to choose between being a slut and a virgin, between sex and self-respect. I wish I'd understood that my desire, which was just as insistent as that of any boy I knew, was a positive force, that good could come from following its call.

Through sheer luck I came out of these reckless, confused years physically unscathed, and although most of my encounters during this period were disappointing and humiliating, they were compensated for by the rare but brilliant moments when I understood why I was driven to this. It was during these moments that I caught a glimpse of a person who my teachers and parents and friends either didn't see or didn't want to acknowledge. I caught a glimpse of myself as I wanted to be, as I *would* be when I finally shook off the things I had been told and embraced the things I had learnt.

EMILY MAGUIRE is a novelist, essayist, social commentator and teacher. Her articles on sex, religion and culture have appeared in a wide range of publications, including *The Observer*, *The Sydney Morning Herald* and *The Griffith Review*. Emily's debut novel, *Taming the Beast*, received Special Commendation in the 2006 Kathleen Mitchell Awards and has been translated into ten languages. Her most recent novel is *The Gospel According to Luke* (Brandl & Schlesinger, 2006).

Nudist Nights

Robbi Neal

My brothers and sister walk home from their school together. My brothers will be stepping in every puddle they can find so that they can get new shoes. I ride from my school on my bike. It is a long ride, maybe four kilometres. No one is ever home when we get there. Our mother is at work; she's a secretary.

'I have to go to work,' she says. 'I would much rather stay home and look after all of you, but someone has to pay the bills and take responsibility for this family.' Our father never gets home until dinner is ready.

I hate going home to an empty house. The others dawdle and I ride as fast as I can, so we all get home about the same time. Because I am the eldest, I get the key out from under the third pot plant from the door. I always stop to listen before I turn the key, for any noise inside the house, any creaks and groans that might be footsteps. When I can hear that the house is silent, I turn the key and we go in, but I am still scared. There could be an evil man waiting in one of the closets until we are inside with the doors closed, then he will jump out with his knife and gun and do unmentionable things to us and kill us, and my mother will come home and find our battered bodies.

I leave the front door open until I have checked in every closet and behind every door and under every bed.

Each night, I prepare the vegetables and put them on. I have to have them on by 4.30. Potatoes, carrots and frozen peas. At 6 pm my mother gets home The first thing she does is turn off the vegetables, then she cooks the chops or sausages and gets ready to serve up. At 6.25 my father gets home and kicks off his shoes. His feet always stink—you can smell them from the other end of the house. At 6.30 we eat. My father never eats the vegetables, only the meat. He says he isn't that hungry, but his car is always chokkers with takeaway food wrappers so deep you can't see the carpet.

Before my father gets home we have twenty-five minutes of peace with our mother. Twenty-five minutes of our mother being happy. She smiles and laughs and is kind to us. Sometimes, when she is in a really good mood, she brings home cream cakes to eat for afternoon tea before my father arrives, but tonight she walks in the back door and she hasn't brought us anything. I hang around her while she gets things ready for dinner. I know she doesn't like this but I do it anyway.

Sometimes she says to me, 'Are you going to be forever tied to my apron strings?'

Tonight she hasn't said that. We don't talk but I don't mind; I like standing beside her while she does things in the kitchen. Even if she doesn't talk to me.

'Your father's . . .' she says to me out of the silence. 'Your father has decided that we will all be nudists.'

I catch my breath. 'What?' I gasp. I know what a nudist is because I'd watched a *Carry On* . . . movie with Sid James on the telly on Saturday night.

'He has decided that we will all be nudists. Some nudists are very nice people,' she adds.

'Well, *I* don't have to be a nudist,' I say.

She is standing at the stove, stirring the custard she is cooking for dessert. I can see lumps floating around the top like swimmers in a whirlpool. She stops stirring, which will only make more lumps. I want to tell her this but she looks at me and says, 'In the next school holidays, we're all going to a nudist camp. Your father has booked us in.'

'But I can go to Gran's,' I say.

'This is very important to your father, he needs our support,' she growls at me. 'We are going to a quite respectable nudist camp and you will come, missy. It's a family camp and the whole family is going.'

My mother turns the heat under the custard off and walks to the fridge. She opens the door and looks in and says, 'We are also going to have nudist nights at home.'

'What?'

'Every Tuesday night is going to be nudist night. It will bring us closer together as a family. It's important to your father.'

'But you don't have to agree to this!' I wail.

She puts her hands on her hips and says in her *you better listen or else* voice, 'I am his wife. The Lord requires of me that I submit as a good and obedient wife to my husband's wishes. Someday, you will do the same with your husband. In the meantime, you will obey your parents as the Lord commands in the Ten Commandments—or would you prefer to disappoint the Lord?'

'But today is Tuesday!'

'That's why I'm telling you now.'

I am shaking. I will never submit to a husband. I want to shout it, but my voice comes out low and quiet. 'I will never submit to a husband.'

'Then you will be answering to the Lord, young lady,' says my mother, crossly.

'Do you mean I have to get naked—tonight?

'It will be good for you.'

'And I have to do it in front of strangers in the holidays?'

'They have trampolines there,' she says, as if this is really going to seal it for me—I certainly won't be able to resist jumping naked on a trampoline.

'You think I want to trampoline with no clothes on?'

What if I have my period? I think. I will have to bleed everywhere, leaving a trail like Hansel and Gretel, or I will have the tampon string dangling between my legs like a loose thread and everyone will know I've got it.

I imagine trampolining naked with my period, jumping up and down. My small breasts jiggling in front of everyone, my legs slightly apart so I can balance when I land on the mat. There is blood going everywhere, spraying everyone in sight with a fine mist of red. My father is covered in my period blood. 'Come on,' he yells in his normal foul mood, 'we're leaving!' I am smiling because for once my period has been good; it has made us leave the nudist camp. I have had about six periods so far and I hate them.

'It's very healthy,' says my mother, bringing me swiftly back to reality. 'I know a teacher who's a nudist and it's quite respectable.'

I ignore her. I feel ill all the way through dinner. My brothers and sister don't know yet what is awaiting them. I hate my father. And I hate my mother. Why can't she say no to him? I will never make my children do something so horrible just because a man wants it.

I will be fourteen years old in the school holidays. I have never seen a grown man naked. I don't want to see anyone naked, man or woman, and I don't want to be naked, full stop!

After dinner my father gets up and closes all the curtains. It is the only housework I have ever seen him do. He puts on one of his favourite records. It has songs on it like 'Oh You Great Big Beautiful Doll' and 'Deep in the Heart of Texas'. He has a satisfied look on his face—no, more than satisfied: happy, expectant.

'Rightio,' he says, 'tonight we are going to be a real family. Come on, get your gear off.'

Davie is only eight. He thinks it is fun and strips off. Wayne doesn't care about anything so he strips off too. Karyn is only ten so I guess she doesn't care either. She might as well be getting ready for the bath, so she starts to take her clothes off, and my mother and father are already naked. YUK!

My father is sitting in his chair. I try not to look at him. My mother is putting on coffee, going about business as usual, except she is not wearing any clothes. I hope she doesn't burn herself.

'What's wrong with you?' my father barks at me. 'Some kind of prude, are you? Just like that gran you love so much. Like all those bloody wowser in-laws of mine!'

I know that if I don't take my clothes off he is going to get really worked up and we'll all cop it and it will be my fault, so I slowly peel them off. I do it sitting on the couch so I can keep as hidden as possible, and when all my clothes are in a puddle on the floor I stay there on the couch, legs crossed, arms wrapped over my new, embarrassing little breasts.

My father is still scrutinising me. I imagine I am glued permanently to the couch and cannot move. I study my feet. Next, I study the gold-flocked wallpaper that my parents love.

'Come over here,' he says, 'and sit on my knee.' And he pats his hairy leg.

I don't remember once, in my entire almost fourteen years, when he has wanted to give me a hug or a kiss or even put his arm around me. And now, when I'm naked and he's naked, he wants me to sit on his knee. What if I can feel his thing?

'I'm okay,' I stammer.

'What, you can't even give your own father a hug?' he snaps. 'Karyn, come over here and give your father a hug.'

She runs over to him and clambers onto his knee. He hugs her and kisses her like a real father and then he puts her off again.

'See, it's not so hard to be nice to your own father. Your turn,' he says to me, except it's more of a command than a request and I know I am beaten, so I go over to him feeling so awful, so ashamed. I try to keep myself covered as I walk but it's hard to do.

I wish Tuesdays didn't exist. I wish my parents didn't exist. I sit on his knee. I try to imagine a piece of cardboard in between us, separating our bodies. I can't look at him. Finally, my mother comes in and says, 'Here's your coffee, Vic.'

I jump off his knee faster than you can blink as he reaches for the hot cup.

'I'm so tired,' I say to my mother. 'Can't I go to bed?'

'It's only eight o'clock. I've never seen you want to go to bed this bloody early before,' says my father. 'I don't know what's wrong with these kids, Rowena. They don't want to be a family, bloody prudes, and it's that bloody mother of yours influence, bloody Baptist wowsers!'

But my mother bundles us all off to bed and I guess they keep on being nudists for the rest of the night.

I lie there in bed, trying to imagine what a respectable nudist camp is like. I don't imagine that they will have daily devotions or an hour of songs and praises. I wonder if there will be enough bushes for me to hide behind and if there will be lots of wrinkly men like Sid James or that doctor from *Lost in Space*. I hate *Lost in Space*. It's so scary, and anyone can see that horrible Dr Smith wants to do unmentionable things to that little boy. Maybe there will be creepy old men like that guy from *Steptoe & Son*, or Alf Garnett, or the Bunker guy from *All in the Family*. The world is full of scary men.

I don't tell my friends we are going to a nudist camp. I don't have many friends at school so it isn't really a problem. David Danaher is my best friend and he asked me to go round with him. But he's shorter than me, so how can he protect me and look after me? David has that orangey blond sort of hair that flops in his face and he has even more freckles than me. We are the same age and I can say anything to him and he still smiles sweetly at me. His mother says she would like a daughter just like me; David is one of four boys. He invited me on a date to the Royal Melbourne Show but we had to go on a train and his mum picked us up from the station afterwards and that made it seem like it wasn't a real grown-up date anymore.

What I really want is a boyfriend with a car whose mother doesn't have to pick us up. Someone who is older and experienced, who will just force themselves on me so that I am powerless to resist.

David asked me if he could kiss me, but I have to save myself for my husband and the Lord. Older boys don't bother to ask, they just do it, which makes it so much easier, and more thrilling. It's better if you can't say no— even when you should. I know this because after youth group one night, Brian Lloyd just pulled me to him and kissed me.

The big problem at the moment, though, is conscription. How can I get an older boyfriend when he might get conscripted to go to Vietnam?

Even more than a boyfriend who can drive, I want a boyfriend who has long hair, and there is no way that David's parents would let him grow his hair.

When I was in the car with my parents and we were driving down the Calder Highway, we saw all these long-haired boys walking to Sunbury. They were going there for the big rock concert. Later we saw pictures of the concert on the news. The news said there were drugs at the concert and they showed naked girls. My dad leant closer to the television when the naked girls came on, even though they blanked out the rude bits.

Some of the boys were trying to hitch a ride to Sunbury. Dad said, 'Bloody hippies!' but I thought they looked ace. I would have liked to pick one up and take him home, but he would have hated my dad's records. I wanted to jump out of the car and go to Sunbury too. Their long hair made my spine feel sparkly and I sank into the back seat and imagined Clark Gable with long hair taking my face in his hands and kissing me before I could even say, 'No—I'm sorry. I'm saving myself.'

I think that I will have to settle for Brian Lloyd from youth group. He has long hair, a motorbike and he is nineteen. He asked me to go round with him when he kissed me, so when I get back from the nudist camp I will say yes.

We are at the nudist camp for the whole two weeks of the school holidays. When we arrive, my parents pull up outside the office and an old wrinkled man comes out and pokes his head through the window. I say a quick prayer of thanks to the Lord that he has his clothes on.

He tells my mother and father where everything is. He points to the toilet blocks, the tennis courts, all that stuff. Then he glances in the back, sees all us kids and, looking right at me like he knows, says, 'Kids don't have to go nudist if they don't want to. We don't force 'em. They come back to it when they're adults.'

So every day I put on as many clothes as I can. Even though it's hot I wear my jumper, just to make sure. I hide behind a bush, too. I stay hidden until dinnertime and read *Gone With the Wind*. My brothers and sister go on the trampoline. They come back with little square marks all over their naked bodies. I really want to trampoline but I don't.

I even shower with my bathers on. I have to: the showers are for men and women, and only the actual toilets are separated. I explain this to my mother.

'Of course the showers are for everyone.' My mother is exasperated with me. 'Everyone's naked anyway, silly! What would be the point of separate showers?'

Every time I see my father, like at meal times, he yells, 'I didn't bring us all the way here just so you could be a bloody prude like those bleedin' wowser relatives of yours!' So I try to sneak away as much as possible, to places where he can't find me. It's horrible and I can't wait to go home. It's disgusting to watch your parents frolic around naked all day. It's even worse when they play tennis and their bits jiggle everywhere. Each day my mother says to me, 'Come on, Robbi, join us. Don't be a prude! Enjoy yourself and stop being a misery guts.'

'It's all right, 'Ena!' snaps my father. 'She just doesn't appreciate the things we do for her! She doesn't appreciate the nature *God* has created!'

But at the end of our holiday my father seems disappointed with the nudist camp. So now we don't have to have nudist nights anymore and for our next holiday we are going to Rosebud foreshore.

Edited extract from Sunday Best *(HarperCollins Publishers, 2004).*

Robbi Neal was diagnosed with cancer in 2001. She had never written before and, thinking she was going to die, began to write about her life for her five children, the youngest was three. Her first manuscript won the 2003

Varuna-HarperCollins Manuscript Award and her book, *Sunday Best* was published shortly after and is currently into its third reprint. Since 2003, she has been the recipient of Arts Council grants; has had many feature articles and stories published in newspapers and can be heard fortnightly reviewing books on radio. She is currently working on several projects, including an adult novel and a children's story. She is cancer-free.

The Group

Liane Moriarty

On my first day of high school, I watched a tiny nun no taller than a Year 7 student slap an older girl in the playground. The nun walloped her across the shoulders and arms, veil billowing, face bright red, while the girl cowered and everyone froze to stare with avid traffic-accident interest.

The girl's sin was socks. Socks had to be long, brown and pulled up frumpily below the knees. This girl was wearing short white tennis socks. I admired her in the same 'you crazy freak' way you admire a base jumper. As an oldest daughter, I was nervous about breaking rules. My youngest sister, who was learning to crawl by the time I started Year 9, would one day not only refuse the long socks, she'd refuse the whole school, thanks very much. She went to a local public school where you didn't even have to wear the uniform. (One with boys. In the classroom. All over the place, apparently. It still seems inconceivable.)

I went to a Catholic girls high school on a busy main road in Sydney's north-west, hidden from the world behind a row of giant pine trees.

Our school uniform was a grey pleated pinafore worn over a blue shirt with a strangely comical red clip-on tie, like the one Colonel Sanders wears on the KFC cartons. There was also a shapeless grey hat and a blazer with shoulder pads. Once, I was walking home from school and a group of neighbourhood boys skateboarding in their front driveway stopped to give me long, loud wolf whistles. Then they all fell about laughing, clutching their stomachs and hooting.

That night, my dad was baffled. 'You're crying because boys whistled at you?'

'They were *sarcastic* whistles,' I explained.

'But you're so beautiful, darling!' cried my mother. 'Are you sure they weren't serious whistles?'

Mum's blissful ignorance made me roll around on my bed, writhing in agony. Could she not see the frizzy brown hair, freckles and Russian weight-lifter legs?

Luckily, my friends—'The Group'—understood. They knew nobody would ever whistle at me seriously. They said I should just walk home a different way and make sure I never, ever saw those boys again. Also, I needed to take urgent, drastic action with my hair. Everyone had a go with the hairbrush, trying to pull my hair straight. They drew pictures of suggested hairstyles in my school diary. It was the early 1980s, so Farrah Fawcett flicks were the rage. You got your flicks right and then you hair-sprayed them into solid wedges that flapped against your forehead. Flicks didn't work on me. Instead, my hair-dresser gave me a mullet—razor-short on the sides and long everywhere else. I looked like a lion.

The solution to my freckles was easy. I just needed to sunbake at length, at every opportunity. Eventually, the freckles would join together to form a beautiful golden tan. ('I *see*,' my dermatologist would say with an anguished expression when I explained this theory to him twenty years later.)

Nobody knew what to do about my legs except sympathise.

It's not clear exactly how The Group was formed in the first place. Some of the girls, like myself and Margaret, had been friends at primary school. Some were rejects from other, cooler groups. A few were a result of rescue missions, when we saw girls in 'tough' groups being pushed around. We liked to think of ourselves as kind, caring types. For example, when we ourselves decided it wasn't working out with one girl, we first held numerous secret meetings to discuss the problem, before deciding that, sadly, we really had to let her go. We gently suggested other girls who might make more suitable friends for her. She wasn't very grateful. 'Well, we *tried* to be nice,' we huffed.

In terms of social status, we considered our group squarely in the middle. Not too daggy. Not too cool. Just right.

We weren't the girls wearing short white socks smoking behind the convent, but we did at least pass Maltesers to one another whenever the Maths teacher turned around to face the board. Then we nearly choked on them, trying not to laugh, because it was so hilarious. Actually, most of Year 7 seemed to be spent trying not to laugh. It was horribly painful. Your stomach would cramp, your cheeks fill with air, your head nearly explode.

We never skipped a whole day of school, but sometimes, if it was very hot, we skipped a lesson and sneaked out to Maree's house down the road. We tore off our uniforms and swam in her pool in our underwear, before running back to school with soggy uniforms and wet hair. It was wildly exhilarating. Later, we would try to impress boyfriends with this outrageous tale, but they were never especially impressed. They just wanted to hear more specific details about the underwear.

It's true we weren't the girls getting drunk on bourbon during the Year 7 school musical performance of *Pedro the Fisherman*. (I was delighted and horrified to hear that someone was drunk and felt that meant I was a real teenager dealing with really worrying teenage issues. Did those poor girls have a *drinking problem*? I sang the lyrics about Pedro and his fishing with a distraught expression on my face, hoping that the audience would wonder what was torturing that poor thirteen-year-old girl. Nobody in my family even mentioned it.)

We missed the bourbon in Year 7, but by Year 10 we had discovered champagne. One Sunday, we went bike-riding in Centennial Park and took bottles of Seaview and chocolate biscuits. The chocolate biscuits melted and the bubbles and the sunshine went gloriously to our heads. Weak with giggles, we deliriously zigzagged the bikes around the park, before smearing the melted chocolate biscuits over one another's face and falling asleep in a sticky mess under the shade of a Moreton Bay fig.

We went through various stages. For a while, we thought it was sublimely funny to randomly hit one another with the flat of the palm over the back of the head while shouting, 'BOOFHEAD!' It could happen at any time and it really hurt.

When we were sixteen, we joined a Catholic youth group movement and became excessively loving and devout. We wore wooden crosses around our necks and went away on weekend retreats. We sat in shadowy halls, breathing incense, holding hands, swaying and singing hymns, crying and feeling intense . . . something. We hugged and kissed and wrote five-page letters to each other, expressing our love and friendship.

Then we got over all that and tried to pretend it never happened.

Of course, boys and how to attract them was a constant preoccupation.

We used to practise something called the Sultry Look. It worked best on the beach. You had to walk a few paces ahead of the others, nonchalantly swinging your sandals in one hand, and then stop, turn around with a hand on one hip, pout and give the Look. You were normally greeted with gales of laughter, so you knew you had more work to do.

In Year 8, Margaret told me that when boys kissed you they put their tongue in your mouth. I was appalled and told my mum, who agreed it was an outrageous lie and not to worry, darling, she was just being silly.

A few years later, I got my first kiss in a public telephone box, while my first boyfriend was calling his mum to come and pick us up after our first date. It was exquisite, and the whole time he was kissing me I was already planning exactly how I would describe it to The Group.

His name was Rafael and I met him at the snow. Margaret and I were on a week's skiing trip run by the Department of Sport and Recreation. I'm not sure how I snared him. Perhaps I gave him a successful Sultry Look at the ski lifts. Raffy was tall and fair and wore copious amounts of Ménage aftershave, which I found unbearably erotic. He was also a Polish refugee, so you'd think it would have been interesting to chat about his life in Poland and how he felt about coming to Australia. Unfortunately, it never really occurred to me to talk to him. All we did was kiss. We kissed on the train. We kissed on the ferry. We kissed on the beach. We ate kebabs and had garlicky kisses. Sometimes, on the way home in the train, he would stop kissing me long enough to head-butt the side of the carriage, to demonstrate the strength of his skull. I was impressed. As soon as I got home, I was on the phone for hours to my friends, giving them every detail of every kiss and masculine head-butt. You talked to girls. You kissed boys. That was the way it worked.

(I did, however, have a mortifying secret about Raffy. He was younger than me. He was sixteen, while I was seventeen. Boyfriends were meant to be at least two years older than you. The older, the better. So the relationship fizzled after a few months. I couldn't handle the humiliation.)

The Group didn't dissolve after the HSC. We still did everything together—from having our hair streaked to going to the Family Planning Centre to get prescriptions for the Pill.

As the years went by, we backpacked around Europe together, we were bridesmaids at one another's weddings and godparents to one another's children. Margaret and I met our husbands, who were also friends, at the local RSL disco. We divorced them within a few weeks of each other. We took off our rings on the way to Jackie's wedding and sang 'I Will Survive' on the dancefloor.

Today, we meet up for dinners and step classes ('Anything the problem, *ladies*?' says the instructor when we're laughing instead of concentrating on 'connecting with our abdominals'; we haven't matured much since Year 7) and facials and an annual Christmas party. Rachel says once the men die, we'll all move into a retirement home together. The men say thanks very much.

We've been good Catholic girls and given birth to seventeen beautiful, noisy children between us. I'm the only one who hasn't yet contributed a baby, but as my fortieth birthday approaches, I'm still giving it my best shot. Last week, over sushi and champagne, three friends offered to be surrogate mothers if that would help. It made me cry.

The world has changed in so many ways since 1984, but I can still rely on The Group; their friendship is the loveliest thing I've kept from my teenage years.

LIANE MORIARTY is an advertising copywriter turned author who has written two novels: *Three Wishes* and *The Last Anniversary* (Pan Macmillan). Both were published in Australia, the US, UK and Europe. Her first children's book, *The Space Brigade and the Problem with Princess Petronella*, has just been published.

Death to Disco

Jessica Adams

The best thing about becoming a prefect at Brooks High School in 1979 was definitely the blazer. It may have come with weird military-style stripes on the sleeves, but it also had wide lapels—and at the age of fifteen, all I ever wanted was a place to stick my punk rock badges.

They weren't all punk, of course. There was a Snoopy brooch in there as well (although his eyes had been partly rubbed off in the washing machine, which did make him look a little bit like Johnny Rotten).

Alongside my weird, myopic Snoopy, I also had a homemade shrunken Twisties brooch. Like every other Australian girl in the '70s, I found out how to make them in *Dolly* magazine.

You shoved an empty packet of Twisties (or a Polly Waffle wrapper), under the grill for five minutes, waited for it to shrivel into a tiny heap, then stuck a safety pin in the back and wore it as a brooch. *Dolly* always said 'Ask your parents' permission first', of course, but nobody ever did.

Mum: 'Whoo, I can smell something awful. (Fanning nose.) What are you doing in there?'

Me: 'Nothing. I don't know. (Muttering darkly.) I saw it in *Dolly*.'

Never mind the shrivelled Twisties brooch, though— or the plumes of acrid smoke in my parents' kitchen. The best places on my Brooks High School prefect blazer lapels were reserved for my punk rock and new wave badges.

I had The Damned, The Buzzcocks, The Stranglers and even the Sex Pistols. But best of all, I also had a gigantic yellow badge bearing the legend DEATH TO DISCO.

In the late '70s and early '80s you were either into disco, or into new wave. Disco girls had flicky hair like Olivia Newton-John, and used to sit on boys' knees on the bus, and giggle. Disco girls put Pot O'Gloss on their eyes, and cheeks, and lips—and they smoked Alpine Lights on the beach in summer.

New wavers like me never sat on anybody's knee (there were too many sharp safety pins sticking out of our black leggings). And, to the best of my knowledge, we never did summer at all, staging a kind of stubborn boycott of the sun, and everything it stood for, from October to February.

In the late '70s, temperatures above twenty degrees were definitely a disco thing—the summer belonged to KC and the Sunshine Band. The hot weather was about Farrah Fawcett-Majors-strength suntans, cute little pink bikinis, and everyone doing the dopey 'Nutbush City Limits' dance in unison on the volleyball court at the beach. As a defiant punky/ska/new wave person, I wanted none of it.

Instead, my summer-loathing, Clash-loving tribe were pale, spotty and white. We used to sit in our bedrooms every day of the school holidays, reading *NME* (even though it was always three months out of date, because it came on the boat from England). We deliberately drank hot tea on the hottest of days, pretending that nothing weird was going on with the weather. And—most of all—we didn't do suntans.

There's a photograph of me taken in the school holidays where I'm so white, I look as if I've been dipped in typing correction fluid.

The biggest difference of all between new wave girls and disco girls, though, wasn't our view of summer—it was our opinion of Sting.

The disco girls and KISS fans at school thought that he was disgusting and weird, and that The Police couldn't sing—but new wave girls worshipped him. On the very few occasions I actually saw Sting on *Countdown*, I think I may even have knocked my tea over.

Sting may be in the Dad Rock category these days, but in 1979 he had dyed blond hair (outrageous!), was alternative and exciting, and sang songs about prostitutes.

I still remember that fateful night in Mowbray Heights, Tasmania, when a real policeman (he was a volunteer DJ at the local Blue Light Disco) put the other, musical, Police men on the turntable.

At last! Sting!

Penny Grainger and I immediately leapt up and raced onto the dancefloor—only to find that everyone else had evacuated.

Can life hold any greater humiliation than suddenly finding yourself stranded on the dancefloor, with someone from your own netball team, for three long minutes?

The song was 'Walking on the Moon' (The Police's only Australian hit). I can still remember how I danced to it, with 100 of my fellow Brooks High School students perched on wooden chairs in a circle around the edge of the disco, staring and pointing.

This was the dance I did:

Shuffle round clockwise, head down, trying not to bump into Penny Grainger coming the other way. Shuffle round anti-clockwise, jerking head vigorously as if *really into the music*—but still trying hard not to bump into Penny Grainger. Cough a lot, to give the impression that you might be drunk, or on drugs—which might explain the fact that you have just got up to dance to The Police with the Goal Defence on your own netball team. Then shuffle round clockwise again, head down, until the song (At last! At last! We're not really lesbians, you know!) finishes.

Here's what I used to wear to the Blue Light Disco in 1979:

A flat tweed cap
A thermal underwear spencer (bra sadly
    unnecessary)
A checked Miller shirt with mother-of-pearl stud
    buttons
For some weird reason, a velour windcheater
Baggy brown tweed trousers
Big grey school knickers that showed through the
    brown tweed trousers
Leather braces to hold the trousers up
My mother's 'good' striped green T-shirt from work
Brown leather clogs
Toe socks

The badges from my prefect's blazer, carefully
    transferred to the braces

And on my face? Tiny bits of Yardley Oatmeal face mask,
which I never scrubbed off properly. It used to set on my
chin like concrete.

Perhaps because of the concrete oatmeal chin (or the
big grey knickers), nobody ever danced with me at the
Blue Light Disco, and absolutely nothing ever happened
to me there (except I once saw a wild girl from Year 10
shaking up a Coca-Cola with two Disprin in it and
sculling it down, because someone had told her it was
exactly like dropping acid).

When the disco was over, I used to go home, open up
the strange vinyl-covered wooden box that passed for a
record player in our house, and put on The Clash. It
might have been mono, but it was the real thing.

Fast-forward to 1993. Nirvana are in Sydney, and I am
interviewing Kurt Cobain.

'Which album changed your life, Kurt?'

'*Give 'Em Enough Rope* by The Clash.'

'Me too! Me too!'

'After I heard it, I went straight out and bought myself
some combat pants.'

'Me too! Me too!'

(Well, not exactly—but I could hardly tell Kurt
Cobain about the tweed pants and the clogs.)

I told Kurt I had to borrow my copy of *Give 'Em
Enough Rope* from the Launceston Public Library, because

none of the shops in our town sold it. He sympathised. Seattle, too, was a musical wasteland in the '70s, he said. You couldn't buy any decent punk records there either, and all you ever heard on the radio was the Eagles—or disco.

I still have the tape of that interview with Kurt, and have been meaning to get it to Frances Bean, his daughter, for years—just so she can hear how funny he was, how kind he was, and how sane he was, particularly now that he has gone and is unable to defend himself against the rubbish that has been written about him.

When I finished my story on Kurt Cobain and Nirvana, I sold it to a magazine in London called *Select*. They ran it on the cover—and overnight I found myself becoming a proper rock journalist.

Select editor in London: 'Who else have you interviewed?'

Me: 'Mental As Anything.'

Select editor: 'Who?'

Mental As Anything were my first band, and I still love them. I interviewed them when I was seventeen, together with my old friends from Brooks High School, Jane Pirkis and Karen Dick.

In exchange for giving us backstage access after the Mentals' concert at the Princess Theatre, the promoter made Jane stick advertising fliers for his other concerts under the windscreen wipers of every parked car in the centre of Launceston. Meanwhile, Karen had a camera, so she became the official interview photographer.

I just made up the questions—and wrote down notes

on the back of my hand, to remind me who was who. (GREEDY is the TALL ONE and MARTIN is the SPUNKY ONE.)

When we finally went backstage to meet them, Mental As Anything had the longest, pointiest, sharpest shoes we had ever seen. They were crazy shoes—like the brogues that Ratty wore in *The Wind in The Willows*.

'Oh my God! Take a photo of their shoes, Karen.'

I've still got the photos—and strangely, after all these years, Reg Mombassa still remembers the gig, and the interview.

On tour, Mental As Anything used to feed themselves in their hotel room by boiling the electric jug and throwing in a packet of instant noodles.

Wow! Scoop! I wrote up the story about the noodles for the school magazine, with Karen Dick's photographs, and then, when the first copies came back from the printer, photocopied the story and sent it to *RAM*.

Any teenage girl at the end of the '70s and beginning of the '80s who liked music used to buy *RAM*.

'What's that about, sheep shearing?' said the boys at school.

'Shut up. It's short for *Rock Australia Magazine*.'

RAM told me they didn't want my Mental As Anything interview, because they had enough of those already from proper journalists, but they did tell me to enter their writers' competition. Because I may have been the only Tasmanian entrant in the *RAM* Writers' Contest, I ended up winning the Tasmanian section the week I entered university.

'Do some more stuff for us,' *RAM* said.

And so I doubled up on every interview I did for

Togatus, the University of Tasmania's student newspaper, by sending carefully photocopied versions to *RAM* and waiting, with fingers crossed, to see if anything would ever make it into the magazine.

When a US war ship docked in Hobart, I interviewed Peter Garrett, who was there to speak at a rally with the People for Nuclear Disarmament. Peter had a queue of journalists and TV crews waiting to talk to him, but he let me in first, ahead of Channel Nine and the ABC, because I was from a student newspaper.

Hurrah! And he even autographed my copy of *Red Sails in the Sunset*.

Afterwards, I got a lift in the car with him, and he offered me some of his vegetarian spaghetti. He was the first vegetarian I had ever met. He was also the first man I had ever met who *deliberately* shaved his head.

I interviewed Bob Brown as well. He wasn't a rock star, but he seemed like one, with his cool sideburns, and his brilliant blue eyes, and his 5000-watt charisma. He was so magnetic that even women who knew he was gay still developed huge crushes on him.

Meetings like those, when I was nineteen years old, with people like Peter Garrett and Bob Brown, changed me forever.

I also tried to interview The Church, in The Sound Lounge at The University of Tasmania (it sounds like some fabulously groovy retro nightclub, I know, but it was actually a smelly room with two beanbags, a record player and an old Austen Tayshus poster).

Because there were some gorgeous modelly blonde women in The Sound Lounge when I arrived, the only member of the band who could actually be bothered talking to me was the keyboard player—who wasn't even in the band at all, he was just hired to go on tour with them. He was nice, though, and he had strange pointy glasses with see-through plastic frames.

Wow! Pointy glasses! It was like Mental As Anything and their shoes all over again.

'Where did you get your glasses?'

'Sydney.'

Fast-forward to the launch of *The Delinquents*, Kylie Minogue's first feature film, in the late '80s. I am interviewing her in her room at the InterContinental Hotel, while she perches on a sofa.

'Where did you get your gloves, Kylie?'

'London.'

When I finally became a music magazine editor, looking after a free Sydney weekly called *On the Street*, teenagers would arrive on work experience from Dubbo and sidle into my office, hoping to find out the magic secret that would get them into the business, too.

'Hey, Jessica. (Shuffle, shuffle.) Can I ask you something? Did you do a course to be a writer, or what?'

'Nah. (Airy shrug of the shoulders.) Don't worry about that. If you're doing interviews, just ask everyone where they bought their clothes. Or their shoes.'

Here's a useful tip I didn't pass on to the work experience students, although I probably should have done: if you get locked out of your house, just before an important phone interview, don't worry—just borrow a gas bill and a pencil from your next-door-neighbour and write it all down on that.

I did this with Depeche Mode. They couldn't believe it.

Here's another tip I should have passed on to budding journalists: when you do finally get a tape-recorder, for God's sake, don't mix up the pause button and the play button.

To this day, I will never actually know what Bob Geldof said to me, in his hotel room at The Ritz Carlton.

When I went to interview Elvis Costello, I was so nervous, I took two tape-recorders, just to be sure.

'Is this for radio?' he asked, pointing to the two tape-recorders, side by side, on the table.

'No, I just thought that if one of them went wrong, the other one might still be working.'

'Right.' (Sympathetic nod).

❧

When Kurt Cobain died, they printed his date of birth in the newspaper, and I drew up his horoscope. He was born with the Sun in sensitive Pisces, a water sign. Jeff Buckley was a water sign, too—an intense, passionate Scorpio.

Astrology, my other first teenage love, eventually replaced music as a career for me—and in the end, I had no choice. By the '90s, I hated music so much, I just had to get out.

The revival of disco (aargh!) and the new boom in stupid doof-doof dance tracks were the main reasons for my rapid exit. *Death to disco!* I never forgot, you see . . . And then there were my traumatic memories of dancing around my handbag with Penny Grainger.

House? Hip Hop? Actually *dancing* to music? Blah!

By this time, too, the music industry promoters were getting richer, and ruder, and the phone calls to my office were becoming nastier, because everyone was doing so much cocaine.

Most of all, though, I had to get out of music because all the Kurt Cobains, Jeff Buckleys and Michael Hutchences were disappearing fast—and all the Debbie Harrys, Siouxsie Siouxs and Chrissie Hyndes were vanishing, too. Women were becoming bimbos again, and an army of misogynistic rappers arrived, just to make things worse.

Britney *Spears?* Are you serious? Paris *Simpson?* Are you losing your *mind?* Eminen?

That's the great thing about being over forty. You get to moan all about the youth of today and their appalling taste in music.

When punk rock broke in 1976, people who were twenty years older than us hated that as well, and the 'in my days' came thick and fast.

'In my day, they knew how to play their instruments.'

'In my day, they knew how to sing.'

'The Rolling Stones were doing that in 1965.'

'Those punk ladies are all so hard and ugly.'

'They call him Johnny Rotten because he is.'

'Debbie Harry looks like a hooker.'

'Chrissie Hynde dresses like a man.'

'Patti Smith's got hairy armpits. She should call herself Hairy Patti.'

Fast forward again, to the early 21st century. I caught the train this morning from the country to the city, and there were three girls and two boys singing 'Whip It' by Devo—and 'Am I Ever Gonna See Your Face Again' by The Angels (with the requisite alternative chorus, of course). One of the girls was even wearing a tin army hat and a gigantic Kurt Cobain T-shirt. They were about fourteen years old. The more things change . . .

In the meantime, I have an iPod in my pocket that will not only deliver all my old favourites like The Damned, and XTC, and The Jam, and The Stranglers, and The Slits, and The Buzzcocks, and The Go-Betweens and The Saints—it will also shuffle these ancient, wonderful songs around in a strangely unpredictable way, so they suddenly turn up next to The Hives, and The Vines, and The White Stripes, Lily Allen and Babyshambles.

And, even better, these days I don't actually have to write about *any of it*, thanks to the arrival of the blog—and YouTube.

It's enough to make me feel fifteen again—even if I have lost all my badges.

Jessica Adams is the astrologer for international editions of *Vogue* and *Cosmopolitan*, and *The Australian Women's Weekly*. She is the author of five novels, including the bestsellers

Single White E-Mail, *I'm A Believer* and *Cool For Cats*. She has been a team editor on six books in aid of the charity War Child, including *Girls' Night In* and *Kids' Night In*, raising $2.5 million for children in war zones around the world. Jessica's website is www.jessicaadams.com.

The Bush Doctrine

Lisa Pryor

'Leafy' was a word regularly used to describe the neighbourhood I grew up in. In real estate ads and newspaper
articles, leafy was always the word used. It meant the
streets were lined with jacarandas, eucalypts and poplars.
Residents were forever sweeping fallen leaves and
dropped blossoms from driveways and decks. Leafy meant
other things, too. It meant life was supposed to pass
quietly, tastefully, conservatively and politely. And, mostly,
it did.

My family's steep and rambling backyard in Roseville
was something slightly wilder than leafy. It sprouted
gnarled lemons, loquats, grapefruits and strawberries
when we could be bothered tending them. There were
nasturtiums to suck, a banana tree covered in cobwebs, a
pungent tobacco tree and plums that served as ammuni-
tion for neighbourhood wars. Lemongrass and parsley
grew madly in the herb garden behind the shed.

As a child of the '80s, I spent a lot of time in this
backyard, engaging in wholesome after-school pursuits
like handball with my little brother and our friends from

the street, during the brief intervals when we were not lounging inside on the pink velour couch or the cork tiles, eating muesli bars, glued to afternoon television shows like *Wombat, Now You See It* and *C'mon Kids*.

As a teenager of the '90s, I saw the backyard take on a different role in our lives. In the face of wave after wave of parties, it lost its innocence. On the night of my sixteenth birthday party, the paling fence along the side was breached by dozens of gatecrashers bypassing the parental command post on the front verandah, where my mum and dad waited to tick names off the invitation list and police the most obvious transgressions of the no-alcohol rule. Among the maidenhair ferns and behind the pool, beer bottles were chucked, ciggies were stubbed out and homemade bongs fashioned from shampoo bottles and bits of garden hose were put to use.

It was at that birthday party in November 1994, the wildest night I had ever known—where the police came five times, where older boys car-surfed down our dippy street and where, out the back, we danced to techno music in baggy pants and stripy tops—that I acquired my Year 10 formal partner.

Late in the night, this boy and I became acquainted in the spa, where the water churned with half-eaten chunks of pavlova, and bits of my birthday cake, which kids had chucked in because it was funny.

Sebastian, as I will call him, was a good-looking party boy. He was tall with curly brown hair. Not only that, he was cool. He went to a private school in Sydney's eastern suburbs, an exotic land far away, which my friends and I had recently discovered, extending our geographical knowledge all the way from Wahroonga to Vaucluse. As my parents cleaned up inside, Sebastian and I ended the night of my party pashing in that spa where, not so many years before, I had engaged in more innocent pursuits like duck-diving for weighted rings and running in circles until I was dizzy.

A few days later I called and invited him to the upcoming formal. When Sebastian told me, at some stage during our brief conversation, that he did work experience at a gym, alarm bells should have rung. Building muscle was his greatest ambition. But I was sixteen and he was cute, and at the time that was enough for me.

The formal was something that kept the adolescent minds of my friends and I occupied for months. At our private girls school we had many lunch hours in which to contemplate such things as we ate salad rolls and doughnuts on the balconies and lawns. In a world filled with clarinet lessons, shopping and playing hockey badly, it was exciting to think there might be something darker, saucier and a bit more glamorous than the lives we led in blue-checked tunics. We spent months speculating about the shenanigans we might commit when we were out of school uniform, like bored prisoners who turn their thoughts to the havoc they might wreak on the outside.

During our hours of speculation, we contemplated which boy we might take, where the after-party should be, how we would smuggle alcohol in. We recounted tussles with our mothers over what we should wear and how much was a ridiculous amount to spend on something you would only wear for one night. I can remember the kinds of fights we'd have, the unreasonable things our mothers would say, uncomprehending. It might be: 'I can tell you right now, you would look much better in the green. But I wouldn't dare—I'd get my head bitten off.' Or: 'Wouldn't you rather spend the money on something you'd get more use out of? Like rollerblades or a new music stand?' As if.

The formal finally took place a couple of weeks after my sixteenth birthday party. On Saturday, 26 November 1994, to be precise. I know this because I have the invitation here in front of me, stuck in an old scrapbook crinkly with too much glue.

The first sign that the night might be a disaster came early, before the sun had even set. When I arrived with my mum at the pre-formal party at a friend's house, girls and their partners were already crunching their way down the gravel driveway past the tennis court, mingling on the sandstone terrace and posing for photographs snapped by the various mothers who buzzed around in linen shorts, as younger siblings watched on and died of boredom.

In those photographs, which I still have now, some of us look our best. Others do not. Sausage arms hang out of spaghetti straps. Starched symmetrical ringlets frame pimply faces. Evening purses are clasped unconvincingly. My dress, a black floor-length number worn by my mum in the '70s and rescued from the attic smelling only slightly of mothballs and mould, did not look too bad. My shoes were another story. High-heeled sneakers peeped out from the bottom of my dress, black with white racing stripes and a chunky white plastic heel. I fancied myself as a bit of a raver at the time, though I had never, you know, been to an actual rave.

As the clock passed five, more and more friends arrived but there was no sign of Sebastian. I started to get nervous. You can see my nerves in the photos, each one slightly darker than the last, as the late afternoon light fades. Early on I look slightly worried and a little teary. Later on, as it heads towards full-blown evening, I look downright hostile.

We waited and waited. I remember the crowd growing and then thinning. Seven o'clock approached and the stragglers could not wait for us any longer. In hired limos and family station wagons, they left for the formal. I was abandoned to the darkness and the mozzies, along with my mum and a friend who was waiting for Sebastian's mate, who also hadn't showed.

Then came a miracle. Just when it looked like we would be going to the formal alone, a taxi rolled up the drive. Out stepped Sebastian and his mate.

'Our cricket match ran late,' Sebastian told us.

There was no apology. Obligingly Sebastian, smartly dressed in a tuxedo and burgundy waistcoat, posed with me for the obligatory couple shot. In that photo, we stand stiffly and wear fake smiles. My smile is marred not only by its artificialness but also by a scabby cold sore that I had artfully painted over with lipstick.

We piled in Mum's hatchback and raced to the school gymnasium. There, we danced and dined on the same sprung parquetry floor where we sat cross-legged and prayed during twice-weekly assemblies, where we jumped rope during PE, dressed in royal-blue tracksuit pants and fluffy yellow jumpers. For a few sweet hours, it seemed like the night was back on track. Sebastian and I were even friendly to each other as midnight approached.

The memorable bits of our teenage lives always

seemed to happen outside, in backyards and parks, and so it was with this night. When the last dance was danced we headed off to another friend's backyard for after-party mischief.

Baby boomers have mythologised the back seat of the car as the place of sexual conquest, where bodies were explored and virginity was lost, hampered only marginally by gear sticks, sticky vinyl seats and cold metal seat-belt fasteners.

For my generation, shrubbery could be awarded such a hallowed place. Bushes, along with local parks, dewy deckchairs and trampolines, are the lovers' lanes of the unlicensed. It was in these semi-public spots that teenagers who were not old enough to drive enjoyed or endured early sexual experiences, only marginally hampered by twigs, pebbles and the asthma-inducing smell of cut grass.

There was no shortage of such shrubbery at the after-party, which was held in a large backyard with a pool, tennis court and many shady corners. After quickly downing a small cup of what I think was Jim Beam and Coke, I forgot Sebastian's failures earlier in the evening. Wanting to revive our tryst of two weeks ago, and not wanting to miss out on a pash on my formal night, I wandered down the side of the house with him, towards the bushes.

We lay down in our formal attire and kissed. In hindsight, it was probably enthusiastic but wildly unco-ordinated, although I lacked the life experience to judge him harshly for it. At least I would have gossip to share come Monday morning, as we hung around the locker room eating finger buns and waiting for the bell to ring.

And at least he didn't seem to notice the scabbiness of my lip.

Then I felt Sebastian's hand creep up my skirt and into my underpants. I dutifully moved his hand down my leg. His hand crept back up my leg. I moved it down again. I realised a pattern was emerging. Every time his hand crept up, I'd move it down. Well, more or less.

My group of friends didn't do hands-inside-the-underpants at that point. By the end of summer, head jobs had been deemed acceptable among the more advanced girls in the group, but for the moment, things were strictly hands-over-clothes only. With us, as I'm sure with many groups of girls, how far you went was determined by the rules of your friends as much as the persistence of the boy. And so I toed the official line and kept moving his fingers away from my underpants.

And that was when Sebastian got up and left. Not only did he leave the shrubbery, he left the party altogether. A short time later, from a distance, I saw his sullen face in the back of a taxi as it pulled off, back to the other side of the Harbour Bridge. He didn't even bother saying goodbye. Let alone 'Thank you so much for the invitation—and a lovely evening'. I think that was the last time I ever saw him.

Sebastian was a loser, but he didn't ruin my night. Not only did he give me an anecdote, he also gave me something that has stayed with me through the years, even now that I am a grown-up, who can drink in a pub rather than a backyard, and have sex in a proper bed rather than a garden bed. He inoculated me against tossers, prancers, cads and bounders.

And I just hope, all these years later, that I gave him something, too. Something that will stay with him for the rest of his life. Cold sores.

LISA PRYOR is a journalist and writer with seven years of hands-on experience as a teenager. For the last five years she has been a journalist at *The Sydney Morning Herald*, where she has learnt the key journalistic skills of writing, shorthand, cynicism and occasional substance abuse. She now writes a weekly column in the *Herald*, where she tries to start off funny then make a serious point at the end. In 2006, she was a Walkley Award finalist in the category of investigative reporting, with her colleague Debra Jopson, for a series of reports about suspected war criminals living freely in Australia. The story also won Debra and Lisa a Human Rights Award from the Human Rights and Equal Opportunity Commission. More importantly, Lisa won the NSW Lawn Bowls Association's award for Best General Bowls Article in 2002. In her spare time, Lisa enjoys indulging her inner gay man by whipping up cakes and singing along to musicals. She also writes satirical articles for *The Chaser*. She has been a *Chaser* shareholder for seven years but is yet to receive a dividend. She studied law at the University of Sydney, leaving her with a degree, some regrets and material for a book which will be published later this year about neurotic high-achievers who fight to get into prestigious university courses only to end up trapped in corporate jobs they don't particularly like. Lisa lives in Sydney and is married to a nerd she met through debating.

The Adolescent Detective

Diane Armstrong

When I was twelve years old, I accused three of my class-mates of plotting murder. I'd been watching them for months, overheard their suspicious conversations, and knew beyond a shadow of a doubt that they were about to strike.

As a result of a steady diet of Enid Blyton novels and weekly magazines such as *The School Friend* and *Girls' Crystal*, I knew that mysteries lurked behind every doorway just waiting to be solved. All you had to do to match the enviable exploits of the heroines of these stories, was keep your eyes open. By being vigilant, I'd be sure to recognise the signs of evildoing.

When I wasn't devouring girls' own adventure tales, I was glued to the wireless every evening, following the investigations of inscrutable detective Charlie Chan and reporter Randy Stone, whose *Night Beat* series always began with the thrilling words: 'Stories start in many different ways . . .' I couldn't wait for my own story to start.

As a result of my insatiable appetite for mysteries, I cast suspicious glances at everyone I knew in the hope of discovering that they were *up to no good*. For some time, I'd had my eye on Mr Wood, who lived two doors away and came home from work every day clutching a bulbous brown leather bag whose contents I was eager to investigate.

One afternoon, just as I was trying to figure out some way of distracting him so that I could spirit away the bag and look inside, there was a knock on our door and there was Mr Wood asking for my father. The fact that he was holding his bag confirmed my suspicions. Obviously its contents were so incriminating that he couldn't risk letting it out of his sight. I hovered around, waiting for my chance to snoop. Luck was on my side because a few minutes later, Mr Wood opened the bag to remove something. I craned forward to see what he kept hidden in there when he removed a strange-looking object that reminded me of a torture instrument I'd seen at the movie matinee the previous week.

'Why are you staring like that?' my father wanted to know. 'Mr Wood's a plumber. He's come to fix our bathroom tap.'

That revelation was a big disappointment but I had no time to dwell on it because I knew there was a world of criminals out there who would get away with their nefarious schemes if I didn't redouble my efforts.

From the stories I'd read, I had a foolproof method of identifying the 'baddies'. The men always had moustaches and carried Malacca canes, while the women walked stealthily and sneered a lot. Baddies huddled together, fell silent as soon as an outsider appeared, curled their top lip in a distinctive way when they talked, and communicated in a secret code.

And that's how I came to identify the plotters in my class. While the rest of us peeled the foil tops off our half-pint bottles of sun-warmed milk, ate vegemite and lettuce sandwiches and played skippings, this trio never joined in. They always clustered in a remote corner of the playground, whispering and giggling in a suspicious way. I was quite convinced that they had selected Maureen, another classmate, as their victim because whenever they passed her, they would chant 'Pop goes my eardrum' and give each other that conspiratorial look. This was obviously in some code that indicated something evil was afoot.

They had to be stopped.

Waverley Public School in the innocent 1950s might not have appeared a likely venue for murder and mayhem, and to most people the girls in question probably seemed quite normal, but as any self-respecting detective knew, appearances were deceptive and the culprit was always the last person you'd suspect.

By now, I was convinced that the trio were about to kidnap and kill our playmate, but knew I had to tread warily and restrain myself from exposing them before I'd amassed sufficient evidence. So I followed them around for several months, keeping a careful distance, as Randy Stone or Charlie Chan would have done. I dogged their footsteps as they walked home from school, eavesdropped on their conversations and snooped around for clues. It wasn't just Maureen's life that was at stake: I knew that my own life would be in peril if they discovered I was on their trail. Then things began to escalate. Maureen looked very pale and I detected fear in her eyes whenever she looked in their direction. As for the plotters, they were always scribbling on bits of paper which they hid whenever anyone approached. I was sure they were sending her poison pen letters.

Fired up in my role of sleuth and saviour, I mulled over the best way to deal with this dangerous situation. First, I tried to alert the victim. Maureen was a big girl with an easygoing personality, but when I cornered her in the playground and said I knew what was going on and offered to help her get away from the plotters, she gave me a startled look, backed away and avoided me from that moment on. I understood. She was obviously terrified in case her tormentors found out she'd been talking.

Next, I sidled up to the conspirators. 'Some people know what you're up to and you won't get away with it,' I whispered, but this only made them hold their sides and shriek with raucous laughter. I knew it was time to take action.

In my very best writing, dipping the nib carefully in the inkwell so it didn't make blots on the page I'd torn out of my exercise book, I wrote a letter to the Headmistress. There was a dastardly plot afoot, I told her. One of the girls was in deadly danger, and it was imperative that she took prompt action to foil the plan of the three plotters in my class.

It's strange to come face to face with the adolescent I once was, and try to understand why I lived in constant hope of discovering mysteries, solving crimes, and rescuing someone in trouble like the heroines in the books I loved. At the time, I had been in Australia for about three years. After surviving the Holocaust, my parents and I had migrated here from Poland, unable to speak a word of English. While I was honing my skills as an amateur detective, my parents were struggling to rebuild their lives. My father had to study dentistry all over again, this time in a foreign language, while my mother sat up late at night hemming piles of skirts, coats and jackets to support the three of us. Unlike me, they'd had more than enough excitement in their lives and were grateful for a quiet existence in a suburban Sydney backstreet of identical semi-detached cottages and kind-hearted neighbours. They regarded my insatiable appetite for mysteries with amused indulgence but I wasn't discouraged. In all the books I read, the parents were always sceptical but in the end they had to eat humble pie because their children were always right.

When you consider that from the moment I was born our lives had dangled over an abyss, and that tension, fear and anxiety had surrounded me throughout my early childhood, you wouldn't think I'd have needed to manufacture plots and introduce more turmoil into my life. But it could be that when you've grown up with turbulence, you become bored when things are quiet, and long for excitement. Or perhaps like so many only children I simply had an overactive imagination and confused fantasy with reality. In some misguided way I might even have been trying to put the world to rights but ended up becoming Diane Quixote, tilting at imaginary windmills.

After sending my letter to the Headmistress, I waited

on tenterhooks for her response. Several days later, I was summoned into her office and invited to sit down. Miss Child was a short, plump woman with a round pink face and a pink scalp with soft white hair that reminded me of cotton wool. I can still hear her slightly bemused but kindly voice as she said in her no-nonsense manner, 'Now, Diane, what's all this deep and dark mystery?'

Glancing towards the door to make sure I wasn't being overheard, I sat forward and eagerly launched into what was probably the most outrageous story she had ever heard. To her eternal credit, Miss Child didn't burst out laughing. She didn't make fun of me or let on that she doubted my interpretation of events. And if she began to entertain serious misgivings about having recently appointed me as school captain, she gave no indication of it. With a solemn nod, she thanked me for bringing the matter to her attention and promised to look into it.

The suspects continued to sneer and whisper, especially when they looked in my direction, and a stricken look always appeared on Maureen's face whenever she saw me coming, but I stopped worrying about her now that I had reported the matter to a higher authority. Besides, I had a new mystery to solve: the girl next door had a visitor who was supposed to be her uncle, but I knew better. He had a neat moustache, a supercilious expression and carried a walking stick, and as every reader of *Girls' Crystal* knew, these were the signs of an impostor who was up to no good . . .

When I confided these suspicions to my mother, she shook her head and said that I read too many mystery stories. 'You should write books yourself,' she told me.

Forty years later, I took her advice.

DIANE ARMSTRONG was born in Poland and migrated to Australia with her parents in 1948. She is an award-winning author and journalist. Over 3000 of her articles have appeared in major national and international publications. Her prizes include the Pluma de Plata, awarded by the Mexican government for the best article written about Mexico, and the George Munster Award for Independent Journalism. Diane's first book, *Mosaic: A Chronicle of Five Generations*, was published in Australia and the USA, to critical acclaim from Nobel prize-winner Elie Wiesel and the late Joseph Heller. It was short-listed for the Victorian Premier's Literary Award for Non-Fiction and for the National Biography Award. Her second book, *The Voyage of Their Life*, became a bestseller and was nominated for the NSW Premier's Literary Award. *Winter Journey*, her first novel, was short-listed for the Commonwealth Writers' Literary award. Diane is currently working on her second novel, *Nocturne*.

New School

Sofie Laguna

Nobody ever asked how I felt about it. I was scared. My family had decided to move from our beach suburb in the city to a farm in the country. I had to leave my school and all my friends. I was thirteen.

My school was a girls school and I was always in the plays at the end of the year. Once it was *The Wizard of Oz*—I wore orange and silver striped pantaloons and sang 'Ding-Dong, the Witch is Dead' with all my friends on the stage singing loudly beside me. I was a relay runner, too—I'd see the next runner waiting for me up ahead, I'd race towards her, carrying the blue baton, she'd be holding her hand out, ready, and I'd pass that blue baton hard. At my school the teacher gave the poems that I wrote gold stars. I wrote poems about colours—'What is yellow? Yellow is the middle of an egg'—and thunderstorms—'The lightning cracked across the sky like an angry whip'.

My best friend was Amanda Lamb; she had round curly handwriting and front teeth that stuck out. Every Thursday I wrote plays for Amanda Lamb and me to put on for the class; we made everybody laugh. Thursday was a good day. I kept the scared feelings inside.

I was going to be starting Year 8 at a Catholic school called Elm Court while my big brother, Stefan, would be at a different campus for older kids. I'd never been to a Catholic school before, but my parents thought it might be better than the local high school.

We had to buy our uniforms from a shop called Whytes. While Mum was in the supermarket, Stefan and I lay across the back seat of the car looking across the road at Whytes. The sky was grey over the wide empty street. 'You Can Face the World When Dressed by Whytes' read the sign.

❧

Elm Court had boys in it. I hadn't been to a school with boys in it since Second Class. I didn't know what boys did in a class. I'd never thought about it before. It was the first morning and the boys were making a lot of noise; they were shouting and throwing bits of paper and rubbers and fruit peel. When the teacher walked in the room I stood up at my desk.

Nobody else was standing so I sat down fast, hoping that nobody noticed. Mr Napper shouted at the class until it went quiet.

Mr Napper taught Economics. I didn't know what Economics was. I liked English and History—I liked learning about the Industrial Revolution, about how the washerwomen tipped their dirty water from the upstairs windows onto the English streets below and if you walked underneath at the wrong time you'd be soaked.

There was a black and white illustration of a wet angry man in *Modern English History*. I didn't understand what Mr Napper was saying. The words on the page in front of me made no sense. They floated around me, away from me. The other kids in the room understood. They looked down at their books and nodded and answered questions. I heard numbers and looked at a graph and then the graph stood up, left the page and waved from the window ledge.

At recess everyone raced out onto the black hard ground. They ran to squares marked with chalk and hit a tennis ball. I didn't know which square to get into. At my old school we played volleyball in the car park every morning. I'd get to school early to hit the ball as hard as I could to Cathy Day, grinning on the other side of the net. At Elm Court I ran into one of the squares but I didn't know the rules of the game. I didn't know which direction to hit the ball. The other kids ran past me, sun shining bright over their heads.

At lunchtime I pulled my lunch out of my bag. Mum had made Vita-Weats with thick cheese and salami. It was the first time my mother had ever made lunch for me— I always ordered. The Vita-Weats looked lumpy, with butter squeezing through the holes and the heavy smell of salami hot in my school bag. I walked to the bin and, with a quick flick, threw the lot out.

It didn't take long to work out that at this school the boys were more important than the girls. They were louder and did better at Maths and they played football. They were the leaders and you wanted them to like you. You had to wear your uniform very short because that made them like you more. At my old school you sat cross-legged on the floor. You didn't think about how sitting cross-legged pushed your thighs out, making them look wider, because you were listening to the teacher or talking to your friend or reading. At Elm Court you had to sit with your legs stretched out in front of you, one placed over the other at just the right angle so that both legs looked long and slim.

The girls went round in a circle pointing at our legs and saying, 'You do, you do, you do,' and when they got to my legs they said, 'Yuk, you don't.'

They meant I didn't shave my legs. I stared down at the fine blonde hairs. I didn't even know hair grew on legs. I had never thought about it. There it was and it was wrong.

For the first couple of days I was a novelty to the other girls. Everything I said they repeated and laughed. 'Fancy that,' they said, 'fancy that, fancy that!' The more they repeated it, the harder and louder their laughter became. Then they stopped laughing and turned away from me. As the weeks went by the boys began to tease me, too; they made a circle around me and shouted, 'Diamonds, diamonds!' I didn't understand what diamonds meant. Diamonds wasn't a rude word—why were they saying it?

Someone explained to me that they were referring to my breasts; diamonds were precious but hard to find. I didn't have any breasts.

At lunchtimes I didn't know where to go, I didn't have anyone to be with. I panicked as I walked alone along the concrete path. I didn't have any reason to be there. Everybody would be able to see I had no friends. How could I pretend this wasn't happening? The minutes of being alone would never end. I smiled and kept walking.

Elm Court had nuns in it. The most I'd ever seen of nuns was in *The Sound of Music*. Those nuns were nice; the Reverend Mother never minded when Maria sang 'The hills are alive!' before clattering across the stone floor of the abbey, late for prayers. The nuns at Elm Court weren't like the Reverend Mother. They looked at you with pinched-up eyes, suspicious. They wore chains around their middle and rocked along up the school corridors in black lace-up shoes. One nun was called Sister Ignatius. She had long grey hair; you could see the strands under her habit. She was as big as a car. She stood on the stage at assembly in her black dress and accused us of *rumour*. She said the word over and over. She shouted about the evil and sin of rumour. Rumour rumour rumour. She said rumour was a bad sin and that you went to hell for it. The rumour was that a boy had been caught on top of a girl in a tent at school camp. Somebody saw their moving silhouette.

I felt guilty—but I didn't start the rumour, did I? Maybe even if you just heard the rumour you were guilty.

We had to do a lot of Bible study. At my old school we'd learnt about the different religions; I liked the Japanese one, Shinto, because in Shinto, nature was God. I could imagine praying to mountains and waterfalls.

In Bible studies at Elm Court I had to say the word 'psalms' out loud. I had never said it before and I didn't know that you don't say the 'p'. Everybody laughed at me.

At Elm Court the other kids believed in God. Religion wasn't just fairytales from *The Children's Picture Bible*—Lot's wife looking glamorous in stone, Moses floating through the rushes in his basket, Jesus transforming earthenware jugs of water into wine. Here you had to eat the living flesh, you had to drink the blood from the goblet. Christ looked down with blood dripping from his sore feet, his crown hurt him, you had to thank him for dying for you. All the kids were quiet during Mass, even the boys.

It was the only time—they hung their heads and thanked Jesus for how he died. The Jesus statue hanging from the cross looked sad. Under his eyes was dark, the blood was draining from all the holes in him.

It was Saturday and I was in the cattle yards, helping my father bring in the cows. While we worked I felt a tight fist with words curled inside stuck in my throat. I'd never spoken to my parents before about what was going on at school. That day I couldn't stop the fist from opening and the words from coming out. 'Dad, I have no friends.' My father looked confused, helpless.

I'd never spoken like this to him before. 'But you're really fun, Sofie,' he said. I walked into the hayshed, full with bales stacked high. My brothers and sisters and I liked to climb the stacks and build tunnels inside. I sat on a bale that had fallen loose. Rain fell heavily on the corrugated-iron roof. Hay prickled the back of my legs through my jeans. I held on to the edges and cried.

At school I stopped learning. When the nuns spoke

I didn't understand them. I looked at their black dresses and their covered heads and watched their mouths moving up down up down. All I wanted to do was get home to my horse and Annabelle the dog and to my diary where I began every entry 'Dear Diary'. Sometimes on the weekends a friend would come up from my old life. Emily, or Nina. We would laugh as we bottle-fed the poddy calves or rode the donkeys down to the dam without saddles or bridles. I was funny and I forgot to worry; I was in life again. Not outside of it, watching myself.

At lunchtimes boys took girls into the bushes that lined the oval. What did they do in there, I wondered? I pictured a bush cave with a roof of leaves.

It would be cool in there, you could hide; the sun would make leaf shapes on the dirt floor. I wished you could go into the bushes by yourself, or to read. I wished you didn't have to go in there with a boy while the other kids shouted and chanted outside, waiting for you to come out with red marks on your neck.

At home on the farm all the paddocks were lined with trees. They were called tree belts. When you went into the tree belt you could hear the trees creaking over your head as they rocked in the wind. Beyond the belt you could see the bright green of the open paddocks. Fallen trees made small homes to climb into, with branches for walls and roofs. You could imagine living a different life in there, with clothes made of leaves, and food that you hunted. I sat and listened to the creaking of the trees, then

I lay on my back and looked up at the branches waving at me. Above me the sky was blue. My back stayed on the cool earth as I was drawn up to the sky. I thought about the centre of the earth and how there was a core of hot lava somewhere underneath me while above me there was this open space. When I sat up again I noticed that the trees were the width of an adult body. I wondered what it might feel like to hold one. I put my arms around a tree; the bark scratched my cheeks. The tree was cool and still in my tight arms.

I didn't understand why nobody wanted to be my friend. What was wrong with me? Boys circled me every lunchtime; one was called Stiffy. Everybody said it over and over. Stiffy Stiffy Stiffy. I knew that it was something to do with the red marks on girls' necks and going into the bushes but I wasn't sure. I wasn't sure about anything.

A lot of my friends were in the plays I wrote, not just Amanda Lamb. We did a comedy version of *Romeo and Juliet*. Everybody laughed as Brigid Wheel sang, 'I am the Friar!' dressed in a sack and a shower cap. I was so used to joining in that when the Elm Court gym teacher came round with the list for the swimming carnival, I said yes, I'd race. My mother bought me a dark green swimming costume from Whytes so I could face the carnival in the school colour. I'd never swum competitively before. At my old school I was a runner, a school champion. I'd hear the gun go off and I'd say to myself 'first'. My legs were separate from my body. I would look down as I was racing and watch the thick muscles moving in my thighs. I'd notice how fast my legs were going. When I arrived at the carnival I found out that only the really good swimmers swam; everybody else just watched from the side and cheered. It was too late; I had to race.

I stood on the block beside the other swimmers. I didn't have any goggles. I didn't know you needed them. When the gun went off I dived into the water, but I couldn't see anything. I couldn't see the black line on the pool floor that kept you straight. I swam as fast as I could, I swam off the sides, I ran into the other swimmers, I was panicking. I heard shouting when I turned my head out of the water to take a breath. My eyes filled with pool water. When I touched the wall at the other end I stood up. My new costume was pulled to the side. I straightened it fast; I didn't know where I was for a moment. I wasn't sure what had happened. I didn't know about the goggles. As I walked back to where I'd been sitting I heard a boy say, 'There's the dog who fucked that one up.' Was it me he meant? Was there anyone else he might mean?

When I got home I didn't tell anyone about the race. Nobody asked. It was my secret; I was the dog who fucked that one up.

Not telling anyone what was going on was the problem. I kept all the big feelings inside. I'm sure my brothers and sisters did the same. I didn't grow up in a family where you could tell, so I wasn't used to the idea. You always had to pretend to yourself that you were handling everything. In my family you sank or swam. I wrote.

SOFIE LAGUNA was born in 1968 in Sydney. She studied to be a lawyer, but what she really wanted to do was act. Sofie trained as an actor at the Victorian College of the Arts and is now an author, actor and playwright. Her books have been named Honour Books and Notable Books in the Children's Book Council of Australia Book of the Year Awards and have been short-listed in the Queensland Premier's Literary Awards. She has been published in the US and the UK and in translation in Europe and Asia. Her novels include *Bird and Sugar Boy* (Penguin, 2006) and *One Foot Wrong* (Allen & Unwin, 2008).

This Much
I Know ...

Sarah Wilson

You learn lessons when you're a teenager. You realise this later. These are some of mine . . .

The salty, dusty smell of baking skin. From lunch spent propped against the science building, legs out in front, school uniform rolled up to my scungies. And coconut oil. And Body Shop Dewberry Perfume Oil impregnating the cuff of my sloppy joe.

The taste of bourbon and menthol cigarettes. Mushed beer labels I've been peeling off wet bottles all night rolled up under my nails. We drink in the alleyway behind the Youth Café, and it tastes painful.

The excitement of boy deodorant. And the feeling on my neck of Year 9 Bad Boy's breath the time we're picked to demonstrate the barn dance. (Did everyone do barn dancing for PE when it rained?)

The thrill of being asked to the Year 10 formal by one of the bad boys. And the excitement of it, mixed with the incongruity, is way too much. Life seems too big. Too expansive to grasp in a snapshot statement: Sarah and Stuart are going to the formal together. Should I let him off the hook because he was drunk when he asked? But I've been watching the bad boys for two years and I'm fascinated by their fearlessness and the way they move effortlessly with one another, supporting one another's dumb-ass antics. They're everything I'm not. I'm a square. For some reason I sense they notice me. The curse of the bad boys.

Willing the phone to ring. Or a car to come up the long driveway. Wishing Something Would Happen. Dad moves us to the country just outside Canberra when I'm eight, to a property on a rocky hill where it snows in winter. It's because he thinks capitalism is coming to an end. He builds the house from a cyclone-proof kit home he bought from someone in Darwin. At least that's what he said once. I hang on to these explanations. We have goats for milk and meat, ducks for eggs, an orchard and a vegetable garden, two dams, solar panels on the tin roof and a pot-belly stove that heats the house all year. Dad builds most things from recycled stuff, like concrete from footpaths that the council digs up back in town, and railway sleepers. He collects logs and rocks for building and galvanised iron and Peugeot 404s that sit on bricks in the 'junkyard', because he wants us to have a self-sustaining existence. Everything can be recycled. Bath water, sewerage, tin cans, the fat from the roast. And goat manure and compost, which he stores in 44-gallon drums, just in case. (When we move back into town years later, the manure and the compost and the corrugated iron and the rocks come with us, just in case.) There are no curtains, no carpet, the walls aren't painted. Do we really need them, kids? Dad says. The summer holidays are dusty and barren and Mum goes into town once a week to visit Grandma and go to hardware shops and the Tip Top bread factory, where she tells them she's a pig farmer to get day-old bread at ten cents a loaf. 'I'm not lying, am I?' says Mum, who has never lied in her life. Anyway, so I'm bored. 'Uh-oh, watch out, Sarah's bored,' Mum groans. I want contact from the outside world to break the dreariness.

The anticipation of Something More Exciting. I have a longing for something I know will come eventually. It's a rumbling in my gut which never leaves. My teens, as far as I'm concerned, are to be endured. They are preparation for The Rest of My Life. But I might as well make the most of it. So I'm thirteen and I start up my own business. I make dollhouse furniture and accessories and novelty jewellery out of Fimo modelling clay. I set up a production line with two of my brothers, who I've recruited to massage the clay to a consistency that allows me to mould it into cockatoo brooches and gumnut necklaces (Australiana sells well). I also make Australiana-inspired gift tags, wrapped in packs of five, which I sell to an Australiana-geared gift shop. And library bags painted with trains and clowns and sunbaking elephants, which I sell to a boutique toy shop in one of the expensive suburbs in Canberra where mums in Volvos buy them for their kids. Mum drives me into town once a fortnight to drop off the gear. I get $7 a bag. Minted.

The smell of baby goats. When they are born early, and

it's still frosty outside, the goats are allowed to come inside and sit in front of the fire with us. They smell like bush flowers dipped in ocean spray. And they lick our hands.

The smell of bushfires. It's an exciting smell. Sitting up a tree and the wind stops and there's a silence and heat that crackles. I still climb trees most days. Up in a tree it feels like you have the perspective to see What Life is Really About.

The seemingly urgent potency of Jim Morrison's poetry. I lie awake trying to understand it. Why can't I get it? In my journal I write poems about how much life sucks. Now it's dripping with nonsensical metaphors. Tadpoles who have frontal lobotomies to get in touch with absurdness. That kind of thing.

That scene in Stand By Me *when the narrator, Gordie, discovers stillness.* It's his turn to keep watch on his mates overnight. In the morning he's sitting on the train tracks and a deer approaches and just stands there in the soft light and stares. Gordie recounts how he wanted to race back to the guys and tell them about it—the still moment. But he realised that some things just don't need to be shared. You can keep them quietly to yourself. And then they're special.

Knowing that God is everywhere. And nowhere. I have to find out what keeps all the people in church on Sundays so convinced. I turn around in Mass and watch them getting into it. I go on a mission. Every Sunday, Mum and Dad drop me off at different churches and groups—Baptist, Buddhist, Anglican. None make sense.

❧

The art of camping. No one has holidays like my family. I know this. Every year, Dad takes a map of NSW, closes his eyes and points. Jindabyne, Dubbo, Kiama, Cootamundra. That's where we're going this year, kids. Mum, Dad, one of the boys and the baby in the front of the Ford Falcon XC, which Dad has panel-beaten and spray-painted metallic blue. Me, my sister and the rest of the boys in the back. We can't fit all our shoulders across the back seat so we sit tilted to one side. And then we swap directions. We slide off one another's sweat and sing advertising jingles. Red Rooster, Red Rooster, Barbecue Chicken. It's a deliriousness that I actively avoid later in life because it brings back an instant headache. Dad's converted the trailer into a little cabin with a welded metal frame and a foam mattress and the boys sleep in there. It always rains and Dad is up all night digging trenches around the tent with the pickaxe. Mum makes Hungarian goulash in a cast-iron pot. Who has goulash camping? I just want to die when other teenagers walk past our tent in fun groups on their way to the toilets, drenched in Impulse. (Years later I become a Person Who'd Rather Sleep in a Tent Any Day.)

The art of teflon attitude. I have a lazy eye and have to wear an eye patch. Over the top of my plastic-rimmed pink glasses. I'm not the kind of kid who wears my Clarks lace-ups as I leave the house and then swaps them for Adidas three-stripes once out of Mum's sight. And I don't hoick the hem of my uniform twenty centimetres higher with safety pins once I get to the bus stop. And then unpin it before I get home. I'm not sure why I don't. I don't think it occurs to me. So I wear the eye patch every day for eighteen months. But I hold my head high and very consciously create an air of not caring. My mum says that It Will Make Me Stronger. 'Do you respect the kids who are teasing you?' she asks. I guess I don't. And the Air of Not Caring becomes part of me.

An awareness that women's bodies are a moveable feast. It happens the day Mum takes me to Just Jeans on Quean-beyan High Street to buy my first ever pair of jeans that don't have an elasticised waist. I have just turned four-teen. We walk into the shop and the sales assistant turns to Mum and says, 'And so what size is he?' I look like my brothers, my Little Athletics shorts perched on non-hips. No draping, no clinging. So I go home knowing I have to fix the situation. I stuff crumpled wads of tissues in the outside edge of the seams on the front pockets. I then wash them and dry them in the sun so the wet tissues cake into the seam, creating a centimetre of extra hippage on each side.

And other fashion patchworking . . . Grandad works at St Vinnies, tearing the clothing they couldn't sell at the charity shops into grease rags for mechanics. When he sees a good sloppy joe or tracksuit or pastel spray jacket, he brings it home for us. We dress in the gear Vinnies rejected. I love it. I wear the oversized men's T-shirts layered like they do it in the Cherry Lane catalogues, the sleeves rolled over each other. I cut off the jersey track-suits at the hems and roll them at the cuff and at the waist and wear them with boots and slouchy socks. I ask Grandad to bring home anything in grey fleece. Like in *Flashdance*.

The trick to putting on weight fast. I start modelling at sixteen. I get called to castings and ride there on my bike straight from school, swinging through the city where I apply make-up using samples at the David Jones counters. Modelling isn't for me. I have unstable feet and not a modicum of sexiness. I do it for two years and then escape overseas. But I can't help myself, and visit a few London agencies. Agents look at my skin up close with a fluorescent light and measure me and tell me to lose five kilos over Christmas and then they'll cut off my hair and get me a wardrobe and send me to Japan for quick work. So I go to Yorkshire and eat pudding and put on fifteen kilos. Which makes my decision for me.

A story can last a lifetime. Everyone has a story. A girl can hang on to hers. She can still be the kid from the broke family for decades. The stories go around and around and create new neural synapses. And it can become real. If she lets it.

SARAH WILSON is the editor of *Cosmopolitan* magazine. In her career as a journalist, she has worked as a writer and restaurant reviewer for the *Sunday Magazine*, as well as columnist for the *Herald Sun*. Sarah has extensive experience writing celebrity profiles and covering social issues, and a broad background in women's health, politics and social policy, developing a profile as a commentator on young women's issues over the course of her career. She has also worked in television and radio, and did a stint at the

Press Gallery in Canberra. Sarah is currently also the weekly fashion editor on Channel Nine's *Today* show and a columnist for *Men's Style* magazine.

Football Groupie

Libby-Jane Charleston

I was always a magnet for trouble. Being tall and blonde had something to do with it. Sometimes, the air around me was so thick with it, if you punched it you could swear you really hit something. As a teenager, I'd been sweet and innocent. I didn't smoke, didn't drink, didn't stay out late, didn't wear make-up, didn't have a boyfriend, didn't like music that rocked harder than Duran Duran, didn't even wear a bikini. When a guy kissed me at a Bachelors and Spinsters Ball and asked me, 'Are you on?' I was so frightened that I ran and hid in a shearing shed, peering through holes in the wall, until I could see he'd moved on to a girl with auburn hair and endless legs wearing pink boots. It wasn't until I turned eighteen that the trouble started. And it started with famous footballers.

My friends and I liked to go to the pub in Claremont, which later became famous for the Perth serial killer's victims; girls who were last seen drinking there who went missing, two found murdered, one never seen again, dead or alive. These days, it has an eerie night-time glow, a near-invisible warning sign. But back then, it was bright and fun. Full of hope, full of footballers.

Number 16

My friend Katie dragged me to all the football games at Subiaco Oval because she was obsessed with the West Coast Eagles. Her life's ambition was to meet one. Her dreams didn't extend as far as actually going out with one. She wasn't interested in football. She didn't understand the rules. Neither did I. But I agreed to come along to every home game because she was my friend and needed my 'support'. (Years later she still needed my support when she caught her fiancé lying in the arms of a 17-year-old girl. She was a cancer survivor and apparently that was part of the attraction.)

Katie liked to watch the entire football match through her father's binoculars. Her father, Aaron, was a retired sailor with a frightening temper who once whacked a boy over the head with Katie's bicycle, breaking his cheekbone. I can't remember why; perhaps he saw them kissing.

'Ooh, I like Number 3,' said Katie. 'Which one do you like best? Pick one! Here, have a look.'

All I could see was a group of men running around in too-tight shorts. What was it Warwick Capper used to say? Size-ten bum in size-eight shorts. They all looked the same to me and most of them had mullets. These men didn't really interest me. They were 'older men', even though the oldest footballers were only in their mid-twenties. All I wanted was a boy my own age; a school-leaver, a university student, anybody under twenty.

While Katie's eyes were glued to the match, mine were wandering sideways to the teenagers shouting abuse: 'Pull your finger out, you big fairy, and kick the fucking ball!' They were potential boyfriend material. Not the frighteningly muscular men on the field.

'Number 16. He can be mine,' I said, feigning seriousness.

Afterwards, she dragged me to the Claremont pub.

'All the footballers hang out here,' she said, ordering me a wine and orange. I would never drink full-strength wine. 'Why don't you just drink wine by itself?' asked Katie.

'Because I want guys to think I'm drinking orange juice. If they know you're drinking wine, they'll take advantage of you,' I said.

'They'll take advantage of you anyway. You might as well just drink.'

We hadn't been standing at the bar for more than ten minutes when Katie nudged me. 'Oh my God, there's Number 16,' she said, more excited than I was.

'Who?' I asked.

'Your footballer. The one you picked.'

I turned around, caught his eye and he walked over and asked, 'Can I buy you a drink?'

It was that easy.

'I've already got one,' I said, lifting my wine and orange, feeling every inch of my eighteen years, tugging at my denim skirt.

'Why don't I buy you another one?'

Then he told me I had sexy eyes and that I looked like Jerry Hall.

'Ha,' I said. 'That's only because I'm tall and blonde,' and he said, 'Right you are.'

'I wouldn't want to be with Mick Jagger, though,' I said.

'Why not? He's rich and famous.'

'He's too old for me.'

'*I'm* too old for you,' he said.

Number 16 asked for my phone number. He told me he'd like to take me out for a drink during the week and I said yes because I had absolutely no idea how to turn down a date. Two nights later, he took me to the Newport Arms in Fremantle, where he ordered two glasses of red wine and neither of us spoke until our glasses were half empty.

'I'm a bit nervous,' he said.

'Why?'

'I don't want to muck this up.'

'Muck what up?' I asked.

'Tonight.'

'Why?'

'Because you're the second most beautiful woman I've ever seen,' he said.

I wanted to ask who was the most beautiful but I was worried about sounding vain. Maybe he was talking about Jerry Hall? Or maybe he was talking about his last girlfriend because, after three more drinks, he started rambling about a girl called Sharon whom he had loved like crazy but she got into modelling and posed in the *Daily News* as a Page Three girl. He said his family were so embarrassed that they insisted he break up with her.

'I must be the only bloke in the world who dumped a girl because she was a Page Three girl. She wasn't even topless! She was wearing a one-piece,' he said, looking traumatised.

'I wear a one-piece,' I volunteered. 'I'm too shy to wear a bikini,' and he nodded and smiled but he wasn't looking at me. I saw a tear in his eye and I knew our date was over.

'Shall we skip dinner?' I asked and he said, 'Dinner? We were just having a drink. I never said anything about dinner.' Then, from out of nowhere, the coolest girl in my year at high school pulled up a chair at the next table. Jennifer, who had rarely lowered herself to speak to me during our school years, was suddenly by my side.

'My God, you're with a West Coast Eagle!' and Number 16 said, 'Do you want my autograph?' and she said, 'No, it's okay. I've already got Chris Mainwaring's autograph. If you've got one, you've got them all.' Without even saying hello to me, Jennifer had summed up my entire evening.

Number 44

Two weeks later, I was back at Subiaco Oval with Katie, clutching our lukewarm meat pies, shivering in the sea breeze. I was a little embarrassed sitting next to Katie because she was wearing a balaclava in the hope she'd be unrecognisable if the television cameras got a shot of her. She was lying low because she'd been grounded by her father for stealing $10 from his wallet and she knew he was at the pub watching the game on TV. She looked ridiculous. The balaclava was bright orange.

'But if the TV cameras get a shot of me, with you

sitting next to me, wearing his balaclava, he'll know it's you!' I said.

That week, we were joined by Katie's elder sister, Elizabeth, who was also grounded because she'd wagged a day of school to follow Spandau Ballet from the Hilton Hotel to the airport, screaming all the way. Elizabeth said the taxi driver, whom she'd hired to drive her and her friends around the city, stalking the band, told them, 'I would not be this hysterical if my wife left me.'

'Check out Number 44! He looks amazing,' said Katie, and even I had to admit he was pretty good-looking. About six-foot-seven.

'Wow. He looks tall,' I said.

'That's okay. You're tall. He'd be perfect for you.'

We went to the pub again and the moment Number 44 walked in, Katie whispered, 'Hey, you won't believe it. He's here.' I looked at him, he looked at me. The usual thing. He came over, offered to buy me a drink and, when he returned with my glass, he said, 'I'd really like to take you home with me.'

'No thanks,' I said, horrified. 'I'm not into one-night stands,' and he said, 'Hey, we'd do it more than once!'

He asked for my phone number and I told him but he said, 'My memory is terrible. Just tell me your surname and I'll look it up in the book. I'm dreadful with numbers. I can't even remember my girlfriend's birthday.'

'Oh, you have a girlfriend?' I asked, crushed.

'Um. Not really. She's my ex. We've broken up.'

'Okay. How come?'

'She was too suffocating. An emotional ball and chain around my neck,' he said.

'Ha. Funny, that's how my mother describes *me*,' I laughed.

'See? I always go after the same kinda girl. I never learn from my mistakes,' he said.

'You're calling me a mistake and we haven't even kissed yet?' He kissed my cheek. 'Yes, we have.'

He asked me for my surname and I said 'Charleston' loudly, slowly, three times, so he wouldn't forget. Three days later, when I was starting to worry that he'd never call me, I got home late at night to find a sign on my door, penned by my sister, who had written in huge letters: 'Number 44 phoned!!'

The next morning I called him but his father, who sounded elderly and foreign, answered, saying, 'He is at his fiancée's house.' Fiancée! But that didn't put me off. I called the next day and the next, and each time his father said, 'He's at his fiancée's house.' Then finally Number 44 returned my call and suggested we meet back at the Claremont Hotel, where he was catching up with some friends.

I turned up fifteen minutes early, which proved a good move. Sitting on the bar stool, looking towards the other end of the bar, was Number 44, hand in hand with another woman—his fiancée? I went over and said, 'Hey. How's it going?' and he looked at me blankly before turning to the woman. 'Must be a fan.'

I was so upset I didn't know what to do. Maybe he had wanted to use me to make his girlfriend jealous? Or maybe he was always going to meet me, but she decided to join him at the last minute? His girlfriend was drinking a cocktail; the pink umbrella and sliced pineapple poked her in the face every time she took a sip.

'Do you want my autograph?' asked Number 44.

'No thanks,' I said, turning on my heel. 'I've already got Chris Mainwaring's. If you've got one, you've got them all.'

I caught the next train home, where I lay on the couch and dialled Number 44's home number. His father said, 'He's at his fiancée's house,' like a tape recording, and without the slightest irritation, as though I was one of 100 girls who'd called that night.

Number 31

Saturday, Katie and I were at the oval again and Elizabeth joined us, but she was quickly bored. 'Footballers are idiots. What happens when they're too old to kick a ball? I prefer rock stars,' she said, flicking her hair in my face as she told us about the Simple Minds concert. Afterwards, she'd waited for two hours outside the Entertainment Centre stage door and eventually the drummer, Charlie, had appeared and she'd walked with him as he signed an autograph. 'Then he said, "Why don't you come up to my hotel for a drink?" So I went up in the lift with him and in his room, sitting on his bed, was Jim Kerr and the keyboard player, and they all said hello to me and we sat down and watched the tennis,' said Elizabeth.

'Who was playing?' I asked.

'Boris Becker.'

Then Katie put the binoculars in my hands and said, 'I've found another one for you. Check out Number 31.'

'Oh, I'm bored with footballers too. They're sleazy. They have too many girls on at the one time.'

'You're still sore about Number 44,' said Katie as the siren blew. 'Let's go to the pub.'

The pub was only half full and, of course, Number 31 walked in, but this time I didn't catch his eye because he had a girl on his arm. Okay, so he was taken. But I kept looking at him and we locked eyes a few times. Then, just as I was leaving, there was a tap on my shoulder and he whispered, 'Tell me your phone number *quick*,' and I said my number, even though I felt a bit sorry for the girl he'd arrived with. Still, it wasn't my fault if her boyfriend preferred me. The next morning he called me and said, 'I *have* to see you.'

'Okay,' I said and so began a very brief flirtation with a handsome giant who ended up telling me one of the most memorable things I've ever heard a man say about a woman.

He arranged to pick me up at my house at 7 pm but by the time I exited the bathroom at 6.45, he was already there, chatting to my parents in the lounge room. I was appalled! My parents were asking him about last week's game. My mother couldn't believe I was going out with a West Coast Eagle. She thought it was my first time. She'd be horrified if I admitted this guy was my third brush with AFL fame. We said goodbye to my parents, but not before my mother asked him what colour his siblings' eyes are (already fantasising about blue-eyed grandchildren). 'Blue,' he said, 'just like mine,' eyes literally twinkling.

We went to the Brewery and had two glasses of wine with a bowl of Twisties. He was very open, talking about his father, who was dying of cancer. He had the look of a child trying not to cry. 'He smokes twenty cigarettes a day. My brothers and I tell him over and over that his habit is killing him. But he won't believe us.'

'My mum says anything that's repeated 100 times becomes meaningless,' I said, feeling very wise.

'Really? What about "I love you?"' he asked.

He also told me that he felt like a failure; that his father's dream was that he would follow in his footsteps and become a doctor.

'But I could never be a doctor. I've got zero brains but lots of compassion,' he said. The rest of the night was uneventful. He offered to drive me home but I said I'd prefer to catch the train, and he must have thought I wasn't interested in him because I never heard from him again.

Still, all was not lost. On the train, I sat opposite a guy who smiled at me and then started a conversation about surfing in Bali. His name was Michael and he became my first proper boyfriend, who, six years later, phoned me from London on the eve of my wedding, crying, 'I can't believe you're getting married,' to which I replied, 'But *you* broke up with *me!*'

I would cross paths with my favourite footballer one more time. As a TV reporter, I was sent out to cover a story about a hit-and-run car accident, and standing by the side of the road was Number 31. It was a stormy afternoon in the city and there he was in a nice suit, holding an umbrella over the body of a pedestrian who had been hit by a car. I noticed a wedding ring. I caught his eye but he didn't recognise me and, when an ambulance arrived, I watched him help the paramedics gently lift the injured man onto the stretcher. Zero brains, plenty of compassion.

And the most memorable thing I've heard a man say about a woman? Number 31 told me, 'The first time you see a woman, you see a flower. But when you look again, you see a jungle.'

NOTE: Footballers' numbers have been changed to protect their identity!

LIBBY-JANE CHARLESTON is an award-winning short-story writer who was an internationally known news anchor based in Hong Kong. She began her career as one of Australia's youngest ever newspaper columnists; she's also been a Beijing correspondent, a finance news reporter and anchor, a catwalk model and radio show host. She has worked on-camera for every TV network in Australia. Her short story 'Redheads' was published in *Great Australian Bites*, an anthology of Australian humour. Her unpublished novel, *Light Sweet Crude*, was written as her Master of Arts thesis, completed five days before she gave birth to twins. (She is the mother of three boys.) She has also written two (as-yet unpublished) children's books and is working on a second book of fiction, plus a non-fiction book about people who never made it in Hollywood. After Number 31, Libby-Jane gave up footballers for ever and has been happily married to an architect for the past fifteen years.

The Island of
Lost Souls

Kathy Buchanan

*'There are things known, and there are
things unknown, and in betweeen are the doors.'*
Jim Morrison, 1943–71

All I could think was . . . America, here I come! It was
1988 and my dream was about to come true. I'd just
graduated from an all-girl private school in Brisbane and
was excitedly waiting to fly to the USA on a year's
exchange student program.

Until this point, the highlight of my social calendar
had been hooking up with the cool kids who hung out
on Friday afternoons at the city mall. There was a special
spot where teens—most of whom attended single-sex
schools—intermingled and flirted by standing in a self-
conscious circle around their school bags while the really
wild ones pashed for hours behind Donut King.

Yes, after enduring the desolate social Siberia of Brisbane's outer suburbs, my life was about to take off in the sweet Land of Liberty. After all, I knew what was waiting for me, right? I'd been raised on a strict TV diet of *Happy Days*, *The Brady Bunch* and Mickey Mouse, and my favourite movie was John Hughes's *Pretty in Pink*. I figured that if Molly Ringwald could capture the heart of a hottie like Andrew McCarthy then the sky was the limit.

Visions happily danced around my head of Sean Penn as the über-cool stoned surfer Jeff Spicoli in the movie *Fast Times at Ridgemont High*. Spicoli was such an awesome dude—he had a double cheese and sausage pizza delivered in the middle of Mr Hand's high-school History class. My life was a million miles away from all the excitement of those spunky American stoners and studs . . . but not for long.

Okay, so I was going to a nondescript, never heard of it before, small city in Ohio, not gritty New York or glamorous Hollywood. But I still couldn't wait to be greeted with warm chocolate-chip cookies every day after school by my loving host mother and have fun hanging out with my younger host sister. I was also dying to wear my cool new wardrobe to school instead of the strict uniform I was used to. But most of all, I was longing to go out on lots of 'dates' with local guys who loved the Violent Femmes and The Doors as much as I did.

It wasn't that I didn't love my normal life in Australia. But let's face it, apart from a few movies, netball matches and sleepovers with friends, the odd free Mental As Anything concert in the park, school dances, the excitement of annual Brisbane Ekka, random parties and pashes, and endlessly wandering around the local Kmart on Saturday afternoons, I wasn't exactly grabbing life by its horns.

As far as I was concerned, everything was ahead of me and this was going to be the most exciting year of my teens. Like Liesl von Trapp in *The Sound of Music*, I was sixteen going on seventeen and I was ready to take on the world (or at least a small corner of the Bible Belt in Ohio that I'd planned to make my very own). I was going to cheer along at high-school football games, make fantastic friends from around the world, explore this amazing new country, possibly even fall in love . . . and I couldn't wait.

Little did I know that within hours of landing in The Buckeye State on a freezing cold mid-January afternoon, an eerie presence was about to enter my life. Being the youngest of four kids, I'd always secretly wanted a cute little sister. And when I saw Emma's blonde curls and big blue eyes, I was delighted—she was the embodiment of Cindy Brady. But when I tried to hug my eleven-year-old host sister at the airport, she seemed . . . *well*, not terribly excited to meet me.

I got the feeling that something wasn't quite right. For starters, she didn't really talk to me on the drive back from the airport—although she did announce proudly that she was on something called the Honour Roll, which was apparently a status symbol for all the smart kids, and in the Chess Club. As her parents looked on fondly, I quickly realised that Em was perfectly happy with her single-child status and was doing her best to pretend I didn't exist.

Determined to forge a friendly new bond, despite my misgivings, soon after arriving in my new home I forced a massive smile and sat down to chat and play with Emma and her treasured collection of My Little Ponies in the lounge room. She had a massive toy box full of animals who she told me had names such as Crystal Princess, Cherry Blossom and Merriweather Pony. Just when I thought maybe I'd judged her unfairly, Em carefully waited until her mother's back was turned and hissed at me softly, 'I'm only going to tell you this once. Don't *ever* touch my ponies again!'

Shocked but telling myself that perhaps she was just having a bad hair day, I tried to push down the feeling of overwhelming fear and dread. I decided to change tactics. I gave her a lovingly chosen 'we're going to be great friends' gift of a toy koala and cool T-shirt. When I passed the beautifully wrapped offerings over, she didn't even look up. After an awkward minute in which you could have cut the tension with a knife, my host mother tried her best to cover by quickly opening them and exclaiming loudly how wonderful they both were.

It's not even retro cool to admit now, but I was feeling really scared and alone on my first night in a new country and in a new house, on a suburban American street where the homes all looked alike and were painted various shades of pastel. So I tried to sing myself softly to sleep, to take my mind off my horrendous jet lag and the sick feeling that Em obviously wasn't as keen to have a big sister as I'd hoped.

I was listening to my favourite mix tape entitled 'Kathy B's Party Tape '87', which included, among some truly good music, that classic hit by the titian-haired teen pop princess Tiffany, 'I Think We're Alone Now'. I used to think it was hysterical to make fun of how truly B.A.D. the song was with my pals. But that night tears were falling while I was curled up holding a pillow for comfort and crying softly in an unfamiliar bed. For some reason I rewound the song and listened to it again and again and again. I'd only been away from home a day or so and I already missed my family, friends and Freddo Frogs.

As I'd been carefully instructed by my new host parents when I said goodnight, I'd remembered not to make any noise so was listening to my stereo via those massive 1980s headphones. But my host father knocked on the door in his dressing gown anyway, partly opening it to ask me politely to please quieten it down, and through my teary eyes I could see Em standing behind him, smirking delightedly.

Apparently, my angelic host sister was having *dreadful trouble* getting to sleep due to my barely audible warbling and muffled tears. I apologised, turned off the stereo, blushing ferociously, shoved my face in the lumpy pillow and silently cried myself to sleep.

It was the end of a long and difficult day and my mind was racing. I couldn't help wondering if I'd been brought halfway around the world to try to befriend and repro- gram this lonely little girl. Perhaps my host parents had decided that having me there was cheaper than sending Em to weekly therapy sessions. But the reality was that she wasn't at all interested in altering her behaviour and no matter how much I tried, she certainly didn't like me.

Let me set the scene for her heinous habits, which she kicked off from the get-go. Em did all the classic brat-packer stunts like not pass on messages so I'd get in trouble for not calling when I was going to be late (when I had). Then she pretended it was me who ate all the cookies and finished off a six-pack of soda before dinner, and told me school started at 7.45 am instead of 7.15 so I was late on my first day and got detention. I naively thought the worst day was when $20 went missing from my host mother's wallet and I was grounded for a week and labelled a petty thief. I didn't do it, but how could I prove it? After all, as Em loved to keep pointing out, Australia was founded by convicts . . .

Evil Em also took great pleasure in branding me as a 'social butterfly', which in this particular house was *clearly* not considered to be a good thing. When, within weeks of arriving, I excitedly told my host family I'd been asked to the prom by my new boyfriend, it was as though I'd done a massive, loud and smelly fart at the dinner table, and they never let me forget it.

In the days before email, texting and instant messaging, and when international phone calls cost the equivalent of a sample sale Collette Dinnigan dress, I sometimes felt isolated and alone living in a tiny room in a new town, next to Evil Em, who was clearly not getting crowned Miss Congeniality any time soon.

Luckily, there was a fantastic bright side to all of this. I quickly gained a group of truly fabulous friends—a bunch of other exchange students from diverse places like France, Japan and Chile—and an American best friend who saved my sanity, took me shopping at the mall and cruising the local streets in her broken-down red Honda after school. In so many ways, I was living my American dream and loving it. I was going on dates, wearing trendy tight stone-washed Guess jeans, my favourite frosted watermelon lip-gloss and my hot-pink Converse High-Tops. I was hanging out with friends, going to the drive-in, eating burgers, 3 Musketeers chocolate bars and drinking A&W Root Beer. I even surprised myself by developing a passion for heavy-metal bands like Bon Jovi, men with bum-fluff facial hair and mullets. *Note: anything becomes attractive if you are surrounded by it long enough!*

I was going to Friday night football games, studying American history and had to ask for a hall pass when I needed to go to the bathroom in the middle of class (exactly like in the movies). And yes, I even had a gorgeous American boyfriend who had a diamond stud earring and who I liked to think looked a bit like Judd Nelson in *The Breakfast Club*. The problem was that like most seventeen-year-old guys, he was a true rebel without a cause, with more style than substance, and was much more interested in making out than helping me to find a way to deal with my demonic little host sister who was determined to make my home life a living hell.

I learnt two very important things during my time as Emma's big sis.

Lesson 1: That playing board games with your host family is not a fun way to spend Friday and Saturday nights (no matter how many times they tell you it is).

Lesson 2: That you should always trust your gut instinct.

Emma extracted her final revenge on me on the most exciting night of the year—the prom. The theme was

'California Dreaming' and I'd been looking forward to it for months. I'd even saved up to buy a pretty last-season on-sale cream lace dress, which clung to my newly formed curves in all the right places.

I normally had a strict midnight curfew on weekends but on this one special occasion I'd been told I could stay out all night as it was common knowledge that's what everyone did—going to an after-prom party at the local YMCA, innocently hanging out with friends, and then bonding over blueberry pancakes and black coffee the next morning. And that's exactly what I did. But when I elatedly arrived back 'home' after our early breakfast there was a tersely written note taped to my bedroom door. My heart sank as I read the words: 'You are in BIG TROUBLE young lady and we'll deal with you when we get back from church.'

Evil Em had been at it again. I learnt later that she'd lied and told my host parents she'd heard me arranging to spend the night in a hotel with my boyfriend. No amount of denying it did any good—Em had done such a thorough job convincing everyone I was a fallen woman that the truth didn't stand a chance. Apparently, in the course of history, there were several slovenly women who could never be forgiven—Mary Magdalene, Madame Bovary, Madonna and, er, me. Two days later, I was run out of town as a Scarlet Woman, when really I was just a fairly harmless teenager who'd—admittedly to the dismay of my boyfriend—never gone further than third base.

As my lifesaver and lovely best friend helped me hurriedly pack all my belongings into her beaten-up car, I mustered all the pride I could to appear gracious and say a genuine thank-you and goodbye to my host parents. After all, just because I was being unfairly relocated, disgraced and thrown out of town to spend the last six months of my exchange in a different county, I figured there was no reason not to be polite.

I heaved a genuinely huge sigh of relief as I turned to walk away and took one last look back, before getting ready to start afresh with a fabulous new family whom I instantly loved and who made up tenfold for Emma and her demonic streak. And sure enough, there was Em, standing there all alone at the window, her single-child status reclaimed, holding on tightly to her favourite My Little Pony and sweetly waving goodbye.

NOTE: Name has been changed to protect the guilty.

KATHY BUCHANAN is a journalist and the author of *Charm School: The Modern Girl's Complete Handbook of Etiquette*, *Happy Endings* and *Quit for Chicks* (Penguin). Her fiction has appeared in *New Woman* magazine and she is currently working on her first novel. Kathy's website is www. kathyb.net.

Finding My Voice

Melinda Hutchings

I remember distinctly the day I made the decision to go on a diet. I had been experimenting with diets on and off for about six months when I decided that this would be the one where I would succeed in losing weight. I had always been slim, never overweight, but I felt it was time to take control of my life.

I was only fourteen years old and felt I had reached a stage where nothing I did was good enough. I was constantly pushing myself to the limit to exceed my goals and I felt like a failure. I remember feeling lost and depressed, wondering what life was all about. Would I always push myself so hard? Would there always be so much pressure to succeed, to be the best? I was at an all-girl private school in Sydney where the environment was highly competitive and to get noticed, you had to be a frontrunner. So I'd immersed myself completely in school life—I did debating, athletics, gymnastics, softball, netball, volleyball, and I was extremely academically driven. I used to lock myself away from the world in my bedroom, buried in textbooks. It left me little time for an active social life—I had a handful of good friends but was always comparing myself with others and wondering if I would ever be as good or as pretty as they were.

It was a Sunday in March when I made the decision that would cost me the next three years of my life. I was studying in my bedroom, as always. I put down my textbook and fronted my reflection in the mirror. I felt fat and disgusting, and I turned away.

And so I embarked on my starvation diet.

The first week was easy—no one suspected a thing. I felt oh-so clever when, at the family dinner table, I shovelled food into my napkin using the water jug as my shield. Every night, when the dinner ritual was over, I retired to my bedroom to do five hundred sit-ups.

After the first week, I felt elated when I got on the scales and had lost weight. It excited me—I enjoyed the feeling of power; the ultimate control. I began to wear baggy clothing and, every opportunity I had, would walk or run to my destination. I avoided all situations where there was food. For a while, life seemed great and I enjoyed my secret. Anyone who knew me would never have suspected that I wasn't eating because, outwardly, I seemed happy and together.

And then I began to feel tired and weak, and one day at school I fainted in the bathroom. I was taken to sick bay and remember lying in bed in a large, empty room, shaking with fear. I didn't feel like myself anymore. My mind was telling me to do things, telling me I was fat and ugly and a failure. It was the first time I became aware of what I now call 'the voices'. That second dialogue that plays over and over in your head, constantly telling you not to eat and screaming at you if you do. I was so frightened by what I felt at that moment that I wanted it all to stop. But I had gone past the point of no return. I knew I had to keep going, to keep losing weight, to defy those around me who were slowly beginning to realise that the person they knew was changing.

I became hostile and highly emotional. I was spiralling out of control, afraid yet exhilarated. My life became about avoiding food, losing weight, and school. School was the only stability I felt I had in my world. My family life was falling apart and I was constantly arguing with my parents. Even when I saw my mother in tears, it wasn't enough to make me stop what I was doing, not only to myself, but to those who loved me.

I felt enormous guilt for all the pain I was causing and longed to run away, but I had nowhere to go. Sometimes I would sit on my bed, knees bent, arms around my legs, clinging to a pillow as though it would protect me from whatever unspeakable force was pushing me to the extreme. I would cry for hours, silent tears so that no one would hear me and ask me what was wrong or try to offer comfort. I felt that I didn't deserve to live, to eat, to be. I wanted to die. I hated myself, hated what I was doing to those close to me, hated the pain that was imminent every waking moment. But I knew I couldn't stop. I had to keep going at any cost. I just had to.

It was towards the end of that year I became a living shell. The tension in the family grew and when I looked at my mother's face I could see the pain etched in her expression, the sadness in her eyes. I couldn't bear knowing I was the cause of all her suffering. My own emotional pain was unspeakable. I tried desperately to immerse myself in studies for the end of year exams but found I couldn't focus. I broke down a week before the exams were due to start. The school counsellor held a meeting with my parents and it was decided that I would not sit for the end of year exams. I spent that week with my mother, who tried hard to distract me with shopping expeditions and long drives listening to my favourite music. She even tried to interest me in making use of her sewing machine, suggesting we buy dress patterns and material. But when the exams were over and I returned to school my depression escalated. I watched my friends excitedly discussing their marks and felt strangely misplaced. Sadly they weren't interested in what I was going through; some even laughed at me behind my back. It made me feel even more alone and misunderstood. Yet I couldn't reach out; I wouldn't let myself. I hid behind my hostile facade, pushing everyone away. It was a horrible, lonely existence and I was desperately lost in a world that I didn't understand.

At home, I felt an outcast. I convinced myself that my family did not love me and no longer wanted me around. I fell deeper into my illness: it was the only thing I had that gave me control and made me feel strong. And then I would fight battles within myself, the weaker part begging me to start eating and find myself again, and the stronger part driving me deeper into self-destruction. The more I listened to the voices, the more power I gave my illness, but I just couldn't stop, no matter how much I wanted to.

During the Christmas holidays, my parents rented a beach house up the coast. It was a great excuse for me to spend time on my own, running up and down the long stretch of beach, feeding my eating disorder and avoiding my family. I became even more withdrawn and distant, totally consumed by my illness. When school resumed, I did not return. I went back a week into first term because I wanted to say goodbye to my friends. I still remember turning to look at my three best friends before I walked out the school gates for the last time. They were watching me in silence, tears streaming down their faces, and I was crying too. I think this was the saddest day of my life.

I hadn't wanted to leave school but my parents decided that pulling me out might remove the pressure that was driving my eating disorder and therefore I would start to improve. But this only created a different kind of stress—the self-loathing of failure, of not being good enough, of sitting by and watching my friends' lives move forward feeling helpless, of knowing that my dream of doing my HSC and going to university was gone. My future stretched before me like a black hole. Empty, shrouded in uncertainty. My feelings of failure only fed my self-destructive behaviour and my weight plummeted to an all-time low.

Over the next year I went to various doctors, none of whom I could connect with. Some made me feel violated by the very nature of their questions. Others just had no idea how to relate to a teenager with an eating disorder. Eventually, I found one I liked. At this stage, I felt ready to try to put my life back together but I didn't know how. I had gone through two years of hell and I desperately wanted it to end. I was willing to try, and finding a therapist I actually liked was the first step, and a significant one in my recovery process.

There were times during the early stages when I would relapse because the voices terrified me. I was too afraid of what would happen to me if I did not obey them to even consider taking the risk. After a relapse I'd feel even more like a failure and chastise myself for not keeping with my recovery routine, and for disappointing those around me. Eventually, I learnt how to control the voices, and to truly believe my own positive reinforcement. It took a long time and was a very frustrating and difficult process. So many times, I wondered if recovery was actually possible. Could I really be happy again? Could I really eat without feeling guilty?

For a time, I constantly reverted to the anorexic mindset and I had to work hard to change my train of thought so that it did not become destructive. It's like learning to walk—you keep stumbling for a while, but eventually you work out how to stand on your own two feet and take a step forward. The initial process was a constant, conscious effort. I had to be aware of what I was thinking at all times so that as soon as a negative thought process would begin, I could pause it and then try to turn it around. Only I could do this. My family was very supportive over this period of time, however the strength and the will came from within me—recovery had to be *my* decision; no one could make it for me.

Slowly, I learnt to shift my focus to the future, to make plans, set goals, experience enjoyment. I learnt to put myself to the test and take risks.

The most significant risk was when I made the decision to leave home and move to another state. I had been 'in recovery' for almost two years, and felt that I was surrounded by too many reminders of the bad times in my life. Also, it was evident that the people whom I most needed to trust me still doubted me deep down because they were afraid that I would never get better. I knew that if I was to get my life back and find the person I had lost, I would have to make the ultimate break. It was one of the most frightening experiences of my life.

My parents were fearful that I would fall back into my old patterns and no one would be there to look out for me. They knew I'd be on my own, in the truest sense. But despite their objections, I packed up my belongings and boarded a train bound for Melbourne. My parents saw me off at the station, and as the train began to pull out, I smiled and waved to them, standing tall and trying to look as if I knew what I was doing. As soon as they were out of sight, I burst into tears and cried most of the way, wondering what would happen to me. By the time I arrived, I had done a lot of thinking. I knew I could either live or I could die. And I made the decision to live.

The first few days were the hardest, knowing it would be so easy to go backwards, and that no one would know if I did. This was the first time I became aware of another kind of guilt—the guilt of knowingly letting down the people who trust you. I had worked hard to earn the trust of my family again, and I knew I could never jeopardise that. It was my achievement. It was special to me; it meant everything because it had taken every ounce of courage and strength I'd had.

I made sure that I ate, and that I was healthy. I began looking for a job to support my new life. I had rent to pay now, and I had new responsibilities. This was a good feeling because it felt like I had ultimate control over my life, and whatever happened to me was totally my decision. This shift in control was critical to my recovery because for so long the eating disorder had the power: everything I did was driven by the voices. But once I started making decisions for myself, I slowly regained control and this empowered me. I went for a job in marketing, a field that had always interested me. It was for a large publishing company with some well-known and respected magazine titles, and I felt important when I was accepted for an interview. I tried hard not to pin all my hopes on this job because I didn't have many office skills. During the interview I was so nervous, but that afternoon I received a phone call informing me that the job was mine. How elated I felt! I knew I had done it all by myself, and felt immediately that this was a positive sign of things to come.

From there, my confidence grew. I worked hard at my job and this gave me a new focus in life other than my eating disorder. I was committed to my role, and my ambition got stronger as I became comfortable with what I was doing and with my colleagues and peers. I also made a friend who had a big impact on me in terms of who I wanted to be. She was five years older and seemed so together. I admired her and she took me under her wing. The two of us had so much fun and would often spend weekends at each other's place, talking and listening to music. She had so many dreams and aspirations, which really inspired me to think about what I wanted out of life. During my time in Melbourne, we became insepa-rable and people would often mistake us for sisters. We'd laugh and pretend we were twins. I hadn't felt so close to anybody in a long time, and I learnt how to be a good friend as well as realise that I was worthy of love myself.

I also formed a close bond with my boss, who became like a mother figure and, in a sense, looked out for me. I learnt how to fit in again, without feeling as though I was different from everyone else. Over time, my destructive thoughts became less as I renewed my focus on other things in my life. By the time Christmas came that year, I felt as though my life was really coming together. I was proud of who I was and what I had achieved since I'd been away from home.

The move was the best thing I have ever done. I learnt how to look after myself and how to form relationships with others. I made friends, found a place to live and landed an amazing job because I told myself I could do it. I began to like myself and, importantly, *believe* in myself.

The one rule that I never broke was to eat at least three main meals a day. As time went on, I began to experiment with different foods and different tastes and textures. It was a difficult hurdle, but one I was determined to jump. Slowly, I began to eat almost normally, and I learnt to control my thought processes during and after a meal. It took so much discipline but I became a very strong person—my strength is what helped me through this difficult and challenging period.

When I went back to Sydney to visit months later, I felt like a new person. I was looking forward to seeing my family and to showing them that this time, I was truly on the road to recovery. I don't remember what we talked about, I just remember feeling an incredible happiness and a renewed sense of belonging that I had almost forgotten.

I moved back to Sydney two years later because I felt,

in my heart, it was time to go home. I began to miss everything I had known before my eating disorder, especially my family and the environment I knew and loved.

I worked hard to put the pieces of my life back together again. I learnt how to love myself and love and trust others. I am now married to a wonderful, loving husband who understands me completely, and I enjoy a successful career that I have built up over the years. My personal mantra is 'at all times have fun, because if you're not having fun, something needs to change'.

Most importantly, I am happy in life and I have an inner peace that can never be taken away from me. That is all I could ever ask for.

Edited extract from How to Recover from Anorexia & Other Eating Disorders *(Hale & Iremonger, 2001).*

MELINDA HUTCHINGS is an author, media commentator and motivational speaker who inspires readers and audiences with her courageous story of turning her life around. Having battled anorexia as a teenager, Melinda is passionate about promoting positive body image and self-love, as well as empowering people to trust the voice that speaks from their heart in order to create a happy and fulfilling life. Melinda's books have helped thousands of people understand the dynamics of eating disorders from onset through to the recovery process. Her third book *Why Can't I Look the Way I Want?* was recently published by Allen & Unwin (2009) and her fourth book will be published in 2010.

Melinda was a Finalist in Cosmopolitan's 'Fun Fearless Female 2009' awards in the category 'Inspirational Role

Model'. An experienced public speaker, she has presented at numerous conferences and forums throughout Australia, including many of the annual Youth Forums at Sydney Town Hall which attract around 2000 high school students. As a freelance writer and media commentator, Melinda is often sought for comment about body image and eating issues as well as being profiled in mainstream media. She has appeared on *Sunrise*, *9am with David & Kim*, *Mornings with Kerri-Anne*, *Sky TV News*, *A Current Affair*, Lifestyle Channel, ABC Radio National, 2UE as well as being featured in *Who Magazine*, *Cosmopolitan*, *Woman's Day*, *New Idea*, *Marie Claire*, *Time magazine*, *Dolly*, *Girlfriend*, *Sun Herald*, *Sunday Telegraph* (Body & Soul), *Daily Telegraph*, *The Australian*, amongst others.

Melinda is currently working on her fifth book. Her website is www.bodycage.com.

'The Boxer'

Brigid Delaney

Summers until I was fifteen always seemed prolonged and drowsy, like a twilight that refused to set.

We spent them haunting the local caravan park, blowing our pocket money at the almost derelict seaside carnival, lingering at the doors of blue-light discos, browsing the stock at Sportsgirl and sitting in the plastic chairs of a cafe down the main street, eating fried food and drinking Coke.

We talked about bands and boys, although we had no lived experience with either—so our talk was wistful and indistinct. Nothing was tangible to us except the Christmas presents we received, the magazines we bought, a dress put on lay-by, a trip on the train to Melbourne, the sunburn on our backs and the pain of showering afterwards.

Back at school we struggled to muster any coherent narratives from these lovely, shapeless summers and time, and indeed life, drifted by in a pleasant haze.

All the books on adolescence that we used to steal from our parents' shelves talked about some physical awakening; the one in which our bodies would change, some spark of sexuality would ignite and flare and, for a while, we would look and act like muddled half people—a full beard on a boy with a squeaky voice, a blooming rump on a girl who refused to untie her jumper from her waist, a broad rower's build forming on the frame of a boy who liked nothing better than to spend his lunchtime alone in the library reading books.

And so while we steeled ourselves for the grim eventuality of this physical transformation, what the books, the parents and the teachers never mentioned to us was that *time* itself would change. It would cease to be fluid and formless. Things and events would happen to us. There would be stories to tell at school on Monday because stuff—real and exciting stuff—had occurred on the weekend.

Unlike other watershed moments, which stagger their visits to different people, time became transformed at the same moment for everyone. Year 11.

Year 11. Teachers referred to it sotto voce in the staff room as a 'difficult year', and there was the sense of a turning point about it.

The cards of this new game were cut the summer before school went back.

Girls who for years had seemed on the margin of things, their attendance in class sporadic, their names listed as 'absent' in school photos, fell away during the holidays. In February, as we filed back into school in scratchy, starched tunics, these girls would be missing. The Disappeared—no explanation, just a tacit understanding that finishing school was not for them.

Later they might be glimpsed in the winter across the supermarket car park, a child in a stroller (Theirs? A younger sibling? We never knew), shed of the uniform and all the innocence it bestowed on the body. By mid-year we had forgotten their names except for the most notorious of their number; girls of multiple pregnancies to multiple men, frequent court appearances breathlessly reported in the local paper, a hardening of their face and deadening of their eyes.

Our blurry state of girlhood was also turning into something brighter and harder. Any of us who still had a hand clutching at the toy box knew very soon we would have to let go.

In Year 10, troops on the front line, girls with overripe bodies and perms—the perpetual centres of the netball team—had reported back from their nights at football clubrooms, cousins' twenty-firsts, the sawdust-covered dancefloor of a provincial nightclub.

Their knowledge was hard-won through elaborate lies to parents, complicated alibis, falsified identification cards and uneasy collusions with bottle-shop attendants, and for a while it put planets between us.

For a while. But now the rest of us would catch up. Now we would all start to lie to our parents, and use the library photocopier to invent documents showing new birthdates, and trade the names of visually impaired bottle-shop attendants as if it was a secret code that would grant us admission into previously locked rooms.

Old cultures, old religions have their rituals for the young, marking their initiation into adult society—bar mitzvahs or compulsory military service or a spearing ceremony . . . In Hindu communities, a girl at puberty is initiated into womanhood via ceremonies lasting up to a week.

Where we lived was a ghetto of Irish Catholicism, where the person who sat next to you in Legal Studies had great-great-grandparents who'd planted potatoes alongside your great-great-grandparents in some rainy and grim part of Ireland. Where the laneways in the countryside around our town bore the names of our great-grandparents who'd come over after the Famine. Where our sense of self was inseparable from the song-lines of place and kin. We had our own ways, too.

Our ritual, our coming of age, was the Debutante Ball.

These were run by parishes and schools and came complete with a full set of rules and protocol. The girls asked the boys to partner them—and it was considered poor form to refuse.

We were required to attend dance lessons each weekend, where an aged instructor and his wife would take us through the moves of their era—the Pride of Erin, the charleston, the waltz.

Dresses were seldom off-the-rack numbers but instead made by one of the dressmakers who'd received positive word-of-mouth from parish mothers. They often worked from home and, during after-school appointments, would briskly wind tape measures around your bust and hips, you blushing while they noted your measurements in a neat hand in their exercise books.

Many girls wore dresses that had already been worn by debs of yore: older sisters, friends of the family, cousins. Mine, with its yellow stains under the arms, came to me via a family friend. The $50 paid for it was more a token than anything.

Girls who bought their dresses out of town or spent a lot of money on them were met with disapproval—overt glamour was suspect. No one wore anything that was remotely sexy and the talk was of chiffon and silk, ribbons and lace, not fake tan and tit tape and hair extensions.

In our deb photo (same photographer, same composition as our class photo—stiff, expectant), some of us look like overgrown flower girls who've taken the wrong turn to a wedding; others of us look shockingly matronly, as if some cruel trick of our clothes, the make-up and the light has morphed us into our mothers or great-aunts.

Few of us were graceful in our dancing, but all of us were proud. It was the dances and the dresses, the corsages and the corsets, the manner in which we were presented to the mayor and parish priest—with a curtsey and downcast eyes. We were admired as we slow-walked around the school hall, fulfilling some complicated and entrenched need.

It was about community—and by 'coming out' we, the children of the community, were becoming visible to it as adults. We had passed through some portal and this is where and how we emerged, on the other side, dressed in extravagant gowns, paraded past the elders of our tribe.

Ritual was already something very familiar to us. We had donned white dresses (smaller, though, and cotton, not silk or satin) in Third Class for our first Holy Communion, and studied with great solemnity for the sacrament of Confession. Three years later we'd pored over saints' names, which we would adopt when we underwent Confirmation. And now these same parish children were making their grown-up debut.

But for us, it was not the ritual that counted. All the weekends spent in the unheated church hall learning the shuffling, stiff steps, suffering the elderly man's papery hand on your back as he showed you how to dance, was really for only one purpose. The Deb Party.

Parish parties were nothing short of bacchanalian.

In junior school we had heard of legendary nights— barns set on fire, ambulances called to remote paddocks to sedate wailing girls, walls of houses destroyed, girls getting knocked up, on their backs in the dewy backyards or in the rumpus rooms, still scattered with dusty doll-houses and Action Man figurines.

If Arcadia was created in the hall with the dancing and the dresses, this was its opposite.

Accidents happened on those nights. Kids got into cars and drove off, unsteady and unlicensed. The sweat would still be drying on the boys' tuxedos when they'd be arrested, or punched up, or bloody from some fall down the stairs. Girls unused to drink would travel through a spectrum of emotions. 'You're my best friend,' they would whisper in your ear before crying stormily about some long-forgotten primary school rift, followed by more protestations of undying love and 'friends forever', then sudden accusations of betrayal.

Confessions would be made at the edge of the dance-floor about banal anxieties ('I really want to give up the clarinet but don't know how to tell my parents') or sweet crushes ('Primary school, I think it started then . . .'). On these nights the popular kids would be flawed and teetering towards some cataclysmic downfall while the kids previously invisible would emerge triumphant through some escapade—drinking a litre of gin, procuring marijuana or chasing away the ewes that came too close to the perimeter fence and party guests.

Unlikely couples would emerge—sitting next to a boy on a bale of hay who you once sat next to in Maths, you might find yourself in an urgent and messy embrace that would be over and forgotten by the time you opened another VB. Unrequited love was announced, and perhaps sated, but if not, it didn't matter—all declarations were forgotten by the morning.

Each year and each parish liked to think that their deb party was the most outrageous, the most anarchistic, the most chaotic. But ours really was. There have been too many parties since then, but never one that was this keenly awaited. And never one that in the days, weeks, months and even years to follow was dissected so thoroughly and with so much relish.

After we'd danced and posed for photos and discarded our dresses for party clothes, we went to the bush near the Tourist Information Centre where our alcohol was stashed. We then boarded a bus that took us to a farm where the party was being held.

My drink of choice was Midori. Without a mixer. Others also didn't muck around. Southern Comfort. Ouzo. Jim Beam. Sambucca. The milder girls drank cider but in such vast quantities, it ameliorated all their moderation.

The sky was gusty and huge, the air was cold, Nirvana had just released *Nevermind* and many of the boys had worn flannelette shirts in part because they were farm boys, but also because they wanted to look like Kurt Cobain. A mini-moshpit formed and some boys threw their shirts into a bonfire. Everyone slam-danced and no one took the bruising personally.

The party was great, as we knew it would be, but it was what came afterwards that made it memorable. Still vivid, all these years later, is the bus ride back to town. It may have taken half an hour, but in my mind it took a lot longer, and in my darker moments I am still on that infernal bus travelling down narrow, too-dark country roads. The driver's name was Barry and it is a mystery of memory that while I have forgotten so many names, it is Barry's that I recall with such precision.

There weren't enough seats on the bus so we crammed in, sitting on one another or sprawled in the aisles.

It wasn't long before the sickness began. There were rivers of it, with word moving up and down the bus as to who was the latest casualty.

Bernie was sick in a Just Jeans bag then passed it to Juliet, who was also sick in it and passed it to Peter, who was half sick in the bag and half sick on himself. I was sick on myself and two others—Kieran and Jo. I ruined Jo's shoes. Sally was sick out the bus window but a strong wind blew it back into her face and hair.

Anne was sick in the aisle and Patrick slipped in it— and he, too, was sick. The worst was Nigel. He was feeling really sick. He had to get the bus to pull over. He walked up the front, over the bodies of wretched debutantes lying in the aisles, over the puddles of sick, past the farm boys holding back the hair of the vomiting girls who, moments before, they'd been so desirous of kissing. When he got up to Barry and asked him to pull over, Nigel was sick in the bus driver's ear.

Friends who hosed down the bus the next day still discuss the carnage—like an understaffed hospital ward during a botulism epidemic. Barry is remembered with a wince as people shake their head and murmur 'poor man'. But it is testament to his skills that he got us to town safely. But not home. We were not going home yet. There was still the after-after-party to attend.

Kids who'd been sick on the bus decided it was merely a messy interlude and kept drinking. Others fell asleep in flowerbeds, clutching bemused garden gnomes. Some met anxiously waiting parents gathered in the chill under the solitary street lamp at the Tourist Information Centre.

We could only imagine what cruelties awaited them at home. Mum pushing them half dressed into a cold shower. The kettle boiling, dark circles of sleeplessness and disappointment under Dad's eyes. The stench of alcohol, cigarettes and vomit radiating off their child, like the most violent reproach to parenting.

But this was what Year 11 was about. Running wild, getting in trouble, doing things that we could talk about at school on Monday, *time* being transformed by events.

That night ended somewhere near dawn, in one of the stately old stone homes in town. A group of us, drinking port and smoking cigarettes (menthol probably nicked from somebody's mum's purse), sat around the piano singing 'The Boxer', an old Simon & Garfunkel tune that sounded good on the piano, with a tenor among our number carrying us along.

There were other parties that year. It was as if after that first one we discovered a thirst for them that continued at a furious pace.

We had tasted alcohol now and knew its strange power—the way it could contort reality, make us feel warm and brave and invincible, the way it heightened everything, from our connections with each other to our very selves and our lives—which, until then, had seemed contained and precise.

It wasn't long before marijuana started doing the rounds and that, too, made the most mundane moments seem profound: walking across a lit-up football oval at night, sitting on the hood of a car in a deserted beach car park, listening to The Cure in a friend's bedroom, discussing Keats's 'On First Looking into Chapman's Homer'.

There were parties everywhere that summer: in the old stone houses in town, furniture being torn apart to the beat of the Violent Femmes; or at the house of a boy whose parents were perpetually travelling, where the bathtub had been turned into a giant bong and crayons were handed out so we could write on the walls. Or a bash for a boy home from the army—everyone drunk and throwing pieces of KFC at each other; or at the Surf Life Saving Club, following a boy into the dunes, the night lit only by his cigarette end; or in a vacant shop listening to the Dead Kennedys, someone putting a hole in the wall, another lighting a small fire, kids sick in the street, everyone worried about the police. Or at the houses of boys who had only one name—Murph, Davo, Jacko. Teenagers who lived without their parents (an older sibling, a cousin, perhaps, and no one went to school), whose parties had the edge of kids with nothing to lose, no furniture that once broken would be mourned.

But they all ended the same way—a house somewhere with a piano, singing 'The Boxer'. It had become our coda for the night.

Of course, school finished—and some of us went away to university, others travelled, others stayed. The parties continued for a few years—usually on university break or at Christmas time. And although fun, they seemed diluted somehow. New places and people happened. There were new parties.

There have been a lot of parties since Year 11—maybe too many.

The beat goes on. But I can't help thinking that the best parties were those first ones. We didn't know what we were doing then and there was genuine surprise at the way nights would unfold—the way life was unfold-ing. It was only our song—'The Boxer'—our unchanged good night, that seemed certain. And as parties end now—shadows of disagreements never aired, half in love with some guests and hating the guts of the rest, old feuds and foes who must be avoided, revealing too much to people who aren't your friends, fighting with those who are—I think I would give anything to have some of that old certainty returned.

BRIGID DELANEY is a former lawyer turned journalist. She has been a staff writer and editor for *The Sydney Morning Herald* and her writing has appeared in *The Age*, *Martha's Vineyard Gazette*, *Griffith Review* and *The Guardian*. She now lives in London, where she works for the *Daily Telegraph*. Brigid is currently writing a non-fiction book about young people and consumer culture.

Nude Photo

Jo Dutton

I was seventeen. Perhaps. After years of freedom at an alternative school and some time travelling I was broke, at home and about to be brought into line. Tired of my lack of direction, my parents had decided that I should attend a 'proper' school and get my TER. My leaving. HSC. Whatever. That mark that meant you had the points to get on with a life. I was cynical and unimpressed by their ambition. Doubtful they could enforce my compliance; interested to see how they might manage it.

There were a few impediments. My reluctance, for a start, and the state schooling rules that meant only the high school fed by my old primary school was obliged to accept my enrolment, and I had no desire to go there. Fortunately, my younger sister was there and my parents wisely decided she wouldn't benefit from my attendance. The one state school I had a small and remote interest in attending refused me on the grounds of my previous schooling—or what they considered the lack thereof. My old alternative school had a reputation. Other kids had encountered this problem but had managed to run a case where they were accepted on exceptional grounds as creative types whose poor attitude to authority and lack of basic educational skills could be overlooked. Clearly, I was more damaged goods than a worthy case.

Showing much determination, my parents cast about for a solution. Finally, my clergyman father, to my horror, took a bold step in his parenting and had an idea about what should be done with me. No doubt much to the amusement of his religious rivals in the Catholic church, he set off, wearing dog collar and all from the Anglican rectory we resided in, and headed, with me reluctantly in tow, up to the local Catholic high school for an interview with the Headmistress. Despite the fact I wore only the barest of dresses and showed my contempt for the whole process with the most obvious of defiant teenage poses—crossed arms, hostile stare, feet on the chair—I found myself, after a brief chat (more an interrogation in which I only answered no, or no comment, as was my basic human right), waiting in the foyer of a truly awful piece of Catholic architecture while my father paid a deposit. He had no intention of allowing them to change their mind.

The summer uniform for the school turned up mysteriously in my cupboard. A pair of ugly blue sandals. Some pairs of white socks. A black plastic backpack, with a Latin logo embossed in gold. At the time I thought it was best not to even mention the strange objects to my parents in case it prompted them to talk to me about their hard-right parenting tack.

I did not allow those objects to impact on my life. I kept up my heavy schedule of acquiring a suntan and trying to get into the afternoon sessions at the beachside hotel on Sundays. Not easy when you look about twelve.

Perth in the '80s didn't have much to offer young people, but beer drinking in grassy yards, listening to great live music next to a perfectly blue ocean, was a pleasure.

I thought I fell in love. I thought again. Then I did fall in love. He assured me not to panic. So far, he said, your parents have not proved themselves to be monsters. He spoke too soon.

First term started and I was rudely woken by my mother offering the first of numerous cups of tea to get me going. Shocked, I actually got dressed in the grotesque clothes, which I only remember as blue and cumbersome. My mother dropped me off at the wicked black spiked gates. Interesting, I thought, how my father already seemed to have lost his stomach for the whole enterprise. I stood around, looking gormless. A bell rang. Every other blue-clad person deserted the quadrangle. I stood around a bit more. A teacher told me to get to class. I waited till he left and sat down on the steps. After a few days I got the hang of it. Go when the bell rings. Get out your books. Listen. Do not ask questions of teachers because a) they talk on and on; and b) it gives the mistaken impression you are interested.

Do, however, do what they tell you, no matter how nonsensical, otherwise you could be detained in ways that call to mind our current refugee policy. In essence, all advantage to the detainer and zilch to the detainee.

I was bored beyond belief. Truly, my routine made daytime TV look engaging.

I recognised no one in the school as an ally. I could not believe the other kids had been doing this for more than ten years. Some eleven. The seniors twelve.

Time was heavier than stone.

There was one teaching nun, and although it would be too much to expect a conversion, she was my saving grace. She was questioning and expected us to think critically. She was widely read. Highly literate. She was the only person who thought I had any talent as a writer, and praised my unorthodox approach to English, with a book of e e cummings' work and some wry comment on learning the rules before one breaks them. I was, I am certain, a disappointment to her, refusing to constrain my 'creativity' to the assessable norm.

There was one girl I was vaguely friends with. A few more I smoked with in the toilets. Another girl and I became mates in a mutual effort to evade the sports teacher. There were rumours of much improperness. The school priest, I was assured, was only interested in boys. The only other male teacher was having an affair with one of the other teachers. An affair so hush-hush only about 600 of us knew.

I went to school more often when the weather was bad. On sunny days it was almost impossible to stay, with the Indian Ocean just down the hill beckoning me.

If I went to the beach with my boyfriend we went where there was surf, but I preferred the beach where clothes were not compulsory and the surf was crap. I met old friends and walked the long hot sand up the coast until there was nothing but sandhills, beach grass and blue ocean. There were no houses. No coastal road. Only federal defence land, housing the SAS training base.

On the beach we lay happily for hours in sunbaking competitions, spread to roast with pure coconut oil. Our days were peaceful. There wasn't much to talk about. We had strange new lives and rarely saw each other off the beach. Sometimes we'd float, star-like. One friend told me if I held my hands behind my head I could float forever. I considered it. From the Indian Ocean it would be a long float until the shores of Africa. The only disturbance to our idyll was the army crew. They started to use the nude beach as a training ground. Helicopters would fly endlessly overhead in spying swoops. Then there were rappelling exercises down ropes. It was tedious. Nothing more than perving. Taxpayer-funded perving.

In the manner of the young, I wrote an outraged letter to the newspaper. The Defence Minister at the time had a name, Killen, which could neatly be changed to Kill'em. The letter complained about the waste of money and energy involved in this sanctioned voyeuristic exercise.

I was nearly seventeen. Attractive. The daughter of an Anglican minister. I didn't consider any of this when I sat down to write my witty piece satirising defence spending. The press went into a feeding frenzy. The attention rattled me. I might have written the letter like a smart-arse but my complaint was serious enough. That was of no interest to the press. The focus was entirely on the fact that my complaint was focused on activities at a nude beach. I remember how uncomfortable it all felt. My father was rather bemused. He'd thought the letter good. My mother fell into a simmering rage at what she believed was an elaborate plot to be expelled from a 'good' school.

I actually had not considered my letter to be any of the school's business and was amazed by how seriously they considered it was. Clearly, my mother had a better insight into their minds than I'd given her credit for.

My one good friend at school was banned from associating with me. The school P&C had an emergency meeting. They wanted me expelled for bringing the school into disrepute.

It came as a beautiful shock. A way out I had never even considered. There was nothing my parents could do if it came to pass. No wonder my mother was mad. I kept my fingers crossed but I was also outraged at school hypocrisy. Their holier-than-thou attitude towards a bit of nude sunbaking while continuously papering over allegations of sexual abuse in their own ranks stunk to high heaven.

No one, however, was more outraged than the old boys and girls of the school. An old girl took me to task while I put her groceries through the checkout at the local supermarket. She went on and on, almost frothing at the mouth, till the manager told her off for holding me up. An old boy called me a slut when he passed me in the car park as I made my way home from work.

My uncles complained from another state that they'd been forced to lie to my grandmother when they had intercepted her daily delivery of *The Australian*, so she could be spared the shame of seeing her granddaughter's picture splashed across the page. It would be fair to assume from my uncles' reaction that a) they were old boys of the school; and b) I had actually been photographed nude on the beach.

Neither was true. I was photographed fully dressed in a buttoned shirt in a lounge chair in my parents' house.

The Headmistress managed to hose down the P&C. You had to hand it to her—she really believed she could straighten me out given enough time. The holidays came and provided a cooling-down period. I was well and truly yesterday's news. My mother breathed a sigh of relief. My expulsion escape route was closed off. I tried to think of something else to piss them all off but it seemed far too easy to bother. As my boyfriend pointed out, almost everything I did, had they known the details, would have pissed them off.

That Christmas, with school finally behind me and the stupid all-important mark yet to emerge and dictate my entire future, I went east. Every thinking young person went east from the west. My boyfriend and I were off to Sydney. We stopped in to see my grandmother. She was a chain-smoking, cryptic crossword-addicted darling. She had more vices than her entire family, and more charm.

Sometimes over the years she'd show me a letter, or an old photograph, and tell me something she thought I should know. This time was no different. She had something to fetch from her study she wanted to show me. She opened a scrapbook. In it were all the press pieces caused by my letter.

Maybe you'll be a lawyer, she said. *This is a good letter.*

I laughed and she did, too, in that too-many-smokes rattle of hers.

And this—it was the picture from *The Australian*. *You look quite the young Mia Farrow*. I had no idea who she was talking about but I recognised a compliment.

I thought . . .

I didn't know?

Yeah.

I'm old, she said, *not an imbecile.*

I smiled.

You don't always have to do what other people expect, but don't always go the other way just to show them how independent you are. You could end up cutting off your nose to spite your face.

Her directness took me by surprise, and I was a little unsure what to do with her insight. She patted my hand as if sensing I needed reassurance.

I could say I took her advice. It wouldn't be true. But back then we sat in her garden, surrounded by all her beautiful work. I ate strawberries straight from the plant while she smoked. The photo drama and my mangled education was behind me. I had an old Holden, a boyfriend and enough money to last till we hit Sydney. Life was sweet.

JO DUTTON lives with her family in Alice Springs. She is the author of two novels, *On the Edge of Red* and *Out of Place*. Her short stories and poetry have been published in various journals and anthologies, and widely broadcast on ABC Radio.

Straight As to Double Ds

Kathryn Eisman

I'm not a 'walk around nude' kind of girl. I see some women stretched out on Bondi Beach, all silky-bronze-skinned Brazilian bikinied and utterly topless, and I am shocked into admiration. Their breasts float on their chest as they walk towards the water with the same poise as if dressed in a couture gown. Nature has ensured that I would be arrested if I ever went topless at the beach. If not, I think I might have to perform my own citizen's arrest.

I didn't grow up in a 'naked' home. In fact, to this day my mother and sister (and, thankfully, brother and father) have never seen me topless. For an extroverted natural-born performer, I'm actually quite shy. So what greater torture than to decide, at the age of seventeen, when my breasts had seen the light about as often as Paris Hilton's natural hair colour, I decided to become a model. And not just any model—a swimsuit and lingerie model, of course.

I first walked into one of Sydney's premier modelling agencies a few days after finishing my HSC. All I had was a photograph some pervy Club Med photographer had taken unbeknown to me while I was doing water aerobics in Noumea on a holiday with my family. A photo I'd bought from the noticeboard in reception more out of shame than pride after I realised people had started to stare at me during our communal dinners. In it I was wearing a white string bikini and a rather unsophisticated flower hairclip that I thought was the epitome of beach chic. *Vogue* it was not.

This unusual profession had first been suggested to me when I reached fifteen and the lanky 'stick legs', which inspired my family to insist on me regularly performing the 'stork dance' (don't ask, you don't want to know) for friends and relatives, were suddenly considered more elegant than awkward. While it had often been suggested that I model, those suggestions tended to come from sleazy guys at parties, guys you wouldn't trust holding your Diet Coke let alone your career destiny. So I hadn't considered it seriously until the editor of one of Australia's top fashion magazines happened to move in next door to my parents' house one fateful day and told me I was 'wasting' my seventeen-year-old body if I didn't start modelling. Immediately.

I didn't want to waste my seventeen-year-old body. And to be perfectly honest I needed a break after an HSC year that felt more like an episode of *Survivor* than final year at private school. First, I'd contracted a case of glandular fever so severe I was bed-ridden for months and hospitalised twice, only to then be diagnosed with epiglottitis (a rare throat infection), which was discovered just hours before I needed an emergency tracheotomy. Not only did I have to sit most of my exams in isolation (due to missing the actual exam dates), I sat them in class-rooms conveniently placed adjacent to the playground, where I could hear all my friends laughing and having water-balloon fights. What's more, during my 3 Unit Ancient History exam I had to try to focus on Julius Caesar instead of the fact that my dad was having sextuple (yes, that's six) bypass heart surgery. At the exact same time. I had crammed and somehow managed to get the marks needed for the UTS Communications degree (around 95 per cent) that I had set my sights on. After a year of barely surviving, I couldn't wait to be a little superficial.

So there I was, walking down the steps of the model-ling agency's Elizabeth Bay terrace, perspiring with fear. Clinging on to this one photo and a scrap of hope. The agents took a good look at me as if inspecting a new car, concurred that I had 'potential' and agreed that, like any new vehicle that comes into the dealership, I needed a 'test drive'.

This came in the form of a prestigious lingerie casting that same afternoon in a suburb of Sydney I had never even heard of. I caught two trains and walked the remain-ing two and a half kilometres to the 'studio'. When I arrived all hot and sweaty a very cool-looking woman asked to see my 'book' (which, I later discovered, was a collection of photographs). Feigning my best expression of professional regret I pretended that it was at the agency (of course I didn't have a 'book'), and showed her my holiday snap. She looked puzzled and asked me to try on five pairs of bras and underpants and told me she'd take a few polaroids of each look. I was terrified; I could actually feel my eye starting to twitch in its socket. I came out of the change room in my first pick, a lacy flesh-coloured lingerie set—the type I could imagine my grandmother wearing—mute for the first time in my life. She asked me to turn around. I turned around, about four times, before she finally said, 'Okay, you can stop turning now.' Two changes in and she was ready to send me on my way. 'Thank you, that's all I need to see.' Since she had seen more than virtually anyone I had ever known, I tended to agree.

Later that afternoon I got a call from my would-be agent. I had the job. It was their mature ladies collection. Strange for a scrawny seventeen-year-old who was a size 8 at best, but considering that my bra size was akin to that of a breastfeeding mother I suppose it made sense. Even if I was modelling the mature ladies collection, I was still modelling. They were thrilled; I was thrilled. Then came the details.

'So it's David Jones's Elizabeth Street store, seventh floor. Own hair and make-up. Okay, Kathryn?'

The phone clunked before I could reply.

Not only had I been seen in my underwear by fewer than four people (including the lady at the casting), I was not exactly adept at professional make-up application.

When I arrived the following week for the job I was surrounded by models up to ten years my senior. They were the 'lingerie set'—the glossy-haired, pouty-lipped girls you see smiling at you from the swing-tags of bras; the girls who get the plum TV commercials for breakfast cereals because they look like they've actually eaten breakfast at some point.

On a very long rack behind the catwalk hung a few lonely pieces of underwear. Beside it on a large white card read 'KATHRYN—six changes' and a few pictures that looked more paranoid than polaroid.

All the other girls seemed to know each other, as if they had all attended Hot Model High while I was the new girl from Can't Believe I'm Here College. I tried to act as if I knew what I was doing but realised how ridiculous that was when it came time to change in front of everybody. There were all these naked girls carelessly swapping their clothing, laughing, talking about what they had done that weekend. I was so nervous I didn't even know what day it was. I didn't want to look like a prude so I, too, slipped off my bra and put on the huge black brassiere hanging next to my name. Then it was time to put on the underpants. This was when I realised I was the only one not wearing a nude G-string (standard model equipment) underneath my underpants. I felt more naked than on the day I was born, like an exhibitionist, ironically, for the first time in my life. And then the music started.

I could hear that the floor outside had filled up with people. A rather abrupt woman dressed in black and sporting a Madonna-esque headset told us what order to walk in by pointing and shouting, 'You, you, you, you.' And then it was show time.

I had no idea how to walk down the runway. I had spent most of my school days on the track and field team and had only just recently learnt that a lady crosses her legs when seated. So I approached the other girls: 'So sorry to bother you. I've never really done this before. I was just wondering, how do you walk?'

'You just walk,' one of them told me in a less than helpful tone of voice, her eyes never looking up from the mirror where she was artfully placing a stray hair behind her ear.

'Just do it, don't even think about it,' said another star tutor.

Rather than concentrating on walking, I was concentrating on not running to the bathroom to throw up. I decided that while the girls from Hot Model High might make sexy students, helpful teachers they were not. I was going to have to cram for this test, too.

Fortunately, I wasn't the first cab off the rank, so I tried desperately to peek from behind the curtain so I could watch the other girls do their thing. They seemed to sashay effortlessly down the catwalk with that smug semi-smile on their faces. I noticed some rested their hand lightly on one hip. Some did that back-and-forth thing at the end of the catwalk, shifting their weight from one leg to the other, a move that makes no sense in real life but looks perfectly natural when done in heels and suspenders in front of a crowd. I wasn't trying to choreograph my signature walk. I was just working out how not to look like a baboon with the grace of a front-row forward dressed in grandma panties.

And then it was my turn. I had never been more exposed in my life; suddenly I wished I had grown up in a 'naked house', or Nimbin. But as soon as I stepped out on the catwalk, those fears disappeared. There I was, in my favourite department store in my least favourite outfit, living my dream.

KATHRYN EISMAN is a best-selling author, TV presenter, producer, columnist and previously a reluctantly scantily clad model. Her first book, *How to Tell a Man by His Shoes* (Pan Macmillan), which she both wrote and illustrated, was an international bestseller published in eleven countries. At nineteen, Kathryn was the youngest Australian writer ever to receive a coveted three-book deal. Her second book, *How to Tell a Woman by Her Handbag*, was released in Australia and the US in 2007. Kathryn has recently returned to Australia after a four-year stint in New York as the lifestyle presenter for NBC's *Today* show. Kathryn is now the presenter and producer of *Xclusive*, Arena TV's flagship entertainment show.

Choosing Life

Gabrielle Lord

The way I understand things now, problems in adolescence start in the earliest days of childhood.

Before that, as the embryo grows in the womb, maternal support is total—unaffected, for the most, by the mother's ideas about embryology. The growing life is provided for, the mother's systems maintaining steady support—until the first step towards independence: birth.

From then on, the baby, toddler, child and adolescent find that maternal—and paternal—support is conditional rather than the given that it was *in utero*. This support (or lack of it) can range from complete neglect right up to complete care, just as parents can range from schizophrenic smackheads to conscious, loving and emotionally mature people. My parents—like most of us—fell somewhere in between.

My father was an emotionally distant and detached medical practitioner, struggling to meet the needs of establishing a practice while at the same time supporting a growing number of children (there were finally six of us—nine pregnancies—thanks to Catholic ideology) and also trying to pacify (and sedate) an increasingly anxious, inadequate, depressed wife.

In my family, children were not allowed to say 'no' and as any early childhood student knows, it's very important for youngsters around eighteen months or so to start realising that not only are they 'separate' and 'different' from Mama, but also that they sometimes don't want the same things as she does—and not at the same time. Wise mothers learn to deal with the 'no!' of the two-year-old by other means than head-on confrontation. Not mine. The battle of wills between my mother and myself must have gone on long enough to exhaust her capacities, because by the age of six, I was sent to a convent boarding school to help her cope better with a four-year-old and a new baby. Expelling me from the family home and separating me from my parents and beloved younger brother had a devastating effect, seriously damaging my capacity to love and trust. Learning to care for myself at such a tender age imposed a burden that no six-year-old child is able to carry. My father went along with this, as he went along with almost everything my mother proposed.

The problems that this too-early separation from my home caused me were never acknowledged, let alone addressed. A six-year-old needs the care of a mother, not a flock of sanctimonious, celibate and emotionally cold women draped in black. What does a six-year-old do with a life-threatening asthma attack in a dormitory at 2 am? No use calling for Mama.

In these convents, the physical and verbal abuse meted out by our so-called caretakers understandably made me more wary, uncommunicative and distrustful, if not contemptuous, of the adults surrounding me.

As a consequence, once I became an adolescent, not only did all the issues of puberty arise, but also those unresolved separation and autonomy issues from early childhood. No wonder my teenage years—up to and including a youthful marriage at eighteen—were conflicted, bewildering and painful for me.

Life is a continual growing *away* from earlier stages of development and *towards* autonomy and self-direction; from total dependence to mature self-sufficiency. Ideally, this is supported by emotionally mature adults. But too many of us, myself included, fail to find this support and become 'stuck' somewhere, in childish, irresponsible and rebellious behaviour. (This is one way to 'break away' from parental authority, but it is an unsupported break, and therefore the inexperienced young person flounders, trying to find a sense of self. Without the mirror of a mature and loving adult, a young human being cannot learn emotional intelligence. And emotional wiring has an effect on intellectual development, as researchers are now starting to discover. Faulty wiring in early childhood, further compounded by faulty wiring in adolescence, seems to lay the foundations for later mental, intellectual and emotional disorders.)

In the 'poisonous pedagogy' of the nineteenth century, examined at length by writers such as Dr Alice Miller, the clearly stated adult aim was to 'break the spirit' of young children, displaying the same cruelty used in 'breaking' animals—that is, sufficient brutality to terrorise them into submission. Generally, this was attached to moral teachings regarding parental authority as well as prescriptions to sexual 'purity'. Multitudes of generations of human beings have been raised ('razed') in this manner and, in too many cultures, this is still the case. Fortunately, more enlightened attitudes now prevail in Western countries as to both human and animal welfare.

Sadly, by the time I'd been pushed out of the nest, I'd missed out on certain important *humanising* experiences due to a mother who was not able to tolerate 'difference' of any sort. For her, 'harmony' between parent and child could only be achieved by a young person's perfect compliance and agreement. This non-negotiable sub-mission was also demanded in the convent boarding schools that I went to—or, as they would have termed it, 'obedience' to the 'representatives of Christ'. (No wonder I grew up hating Jesus.)

By the time I was eleven, and after years of brutalis-ing experiences at the hands of the Dominican nuns (the same order who brought us the Inquisition) and an inci-dent involving Frank Carmody, the paedophile gardener employed at the convent, I was sent to a different order.

By the age of thirteen, I'd been told hundreds of times that I was 'selfish', 'lazy', 'a bad example to the younger ones', that I had no 'backbone'—that I was a 'spineless jellyfish'.

I took no interest in school work, preferring to read smuggled books under the desk. I was always in strife, never able to be 'good' in their terms. Although by then outwardly tough and bold, I was in that saddest of places for any young creature—emotionally and psychologically isolated, without one human being in the world to whom I could turn—no one who could be trusted.

Every adult around me had an agenda for me. The nuns' was to turn me into an ideologically correct and nicely comported Catholic 'lady' (what a word!) who would marry a similarly subdued grazier or lawyer and start growing a large Catholic family. Possibly earning a degree *first*. My mother's agenda, while embracing much of the nuns', also included wanting me to follow her tastes concerning what shoes and clothes to buy and how to have my hair done, while at all times heeding her advice on how to conduct my life. Very simple, really. 'Why can't you just do what you're told?' was the battle cry. All I had to do was conform to her desires. Unfortunately for both of us, I had a few desires of my own. My father seemed not to notice me (or anything much at all, come to think of it).

By the time I was sixteen, the year of the old Leaving Certificate, we boarders would sit in the Senior Study Room, darning our school stockings, listening to one of the nuns reading *Pimpernel in Prague*, a story about a priest in communist Czechoslovakia, or other improving texts, while all around the sandstone fortress the '60s (and the parties) were raging. I remember sitting over my darning one such Saturday night, listening to the music from a party not too far away, and making a vow to myself: in just a few short months, *I'd* be out there and I was determined to do everything! Experience everything! Be as wild and bad as I could be! Although at that stage I'd never heard the phrase 'sex and drugs and rock'n'roll', I know I'd have adopted it immediately as my mission statement.

Such were the results of eleven years experience of extremely expensive convent institutions.

I was not provided with any living skills, nor was there any wisdom or even ordinary practical teaching about how to be a woman. How could there be? The women who 'taught' me lived in a self-limiting world of religious subservience to a God who expressed himself through a hierarchy of old men wearing peculiar clothes. They, too, lived a similarly sexless life—cut off from any first-hand experiences of living with women and fathering children. We were taught theological gobbledegook about the 'mystical body' and nothing about the human, female body that we all actually had. Apart from (presumably) passing on the required state curriculum, they added little except religious 'colour'.

In Year 11, a friend and I spent an illegal hour or so in the library, carefully liberating (with a wet sponge) the glued-together pages in the art books, including the 'centrefold' in a large book of Renaissance art works—Botticelli's *Birth of Venus*. We also tried to erase the hand-drawn black ink drapes added by some nun to the pictures of marble statues from Classical and later eras. (In Dubai a few weeks ago, I saw the same thing on the pages of glossy magazines—where women's décolletages, deemed unIslamic by prudish censors, had been scribbled over with angry black pen strokes.) My school friend and I got into serious trouble for 'vandalising' the art books. Even then, I recall thinking, 'Who are the vandals here?'

But rebellion is no way to get ahead (ask Lucifer), and thus I had no idea of what I wanted to 'be' once I'd left school. Without any wise guidance (and even if there had been such a person, I doubt at that stage that I'd have paid any attention), I drifted into an Arts degree for a few months but didn't attend any lectures or tutorials and was deemed to have failed by Easter. Then came a few jobs, another failing stint at teachers' college and then marriage to a nineteen-year-old teacher—another lost child. Somebody *wanted* me and I had never experienced this before.

One great benefit bestowed—although quite unwittingly—by those who supervised my adolescence was the experience of living under a totalitarian model and the ability to recognise it thereafter. We were called to wait for hours in a corridor, outside the Mistress of Discipline's (sic) room, while everyone else went down for dinner, not knowing what 'charge' had been brought against us this time. Nor were we permitted to speak in our own defence—this was termed 'answering back'. (Well, yes. The right to speak in one's own defence is enshrined in the law, but not in those places.) We had to obey orders unquestioningly and authority had to be respected simply because it *was* authority, not because it deserved respect. (Happily, although the nuns could—and did—beat us savagely, they couldn't shoot us when we 'sinned', although my father did threaten to have me committed at one stage—'And don't think I can't; all I need is another doctor's signature'—when I disobeyed him.) These experiences have given me a good nose for sniffing out fascism, no matter how it might disguise itself as religion.

This is the sad tale of a very particular adolescence and one that no doubt reads strangely to young people now. But a troubled adolescence very often can be traced to the loss of a loving relationship between the child and the parents. A person doesn't have to be incarcerated in a convent for this to be the case. It can happen in families where there is a religious or other agenda—wherever parents use a child to gratify their own needs rather than support the child in his or her efforts to grow and embrace life. This sort of abuse can range from the grossest forms of sexual abuse right through to the subtlest manipulations. Fostering good relationships with young people means treating them with the same good manners and respect as you would anyone else. Once young people reach the age where they can no longer be physically restrained (as they can when they're smaller and weaker), the only bonds parents have to keep their children onside are the bonds of love. If those bonds are not there, kids simply leave home. At best, they'll visit once a year or so, at worst they can start showing up in refuges, on police running sheets, as social workers' cases. By then, it's often too late.

I could have ended up like that, but early motherhood put a brake on me, as did country living, where the usual options for women—having babies, cooking and tennis—failed to tempt me. I enrolled again as an undergraduate and realised that I wasn't 'lazy'—that once I'd found academic subjects that engaged me, that *I* wanted to do, I was up there with the best of them. Studying Anglo-Saxon (as Old English was then termed) as an external undergraduate fired my imagination and I wrote poems about Beowulf and the wife of the king he served.

I'd always written. I shocked my mother with a draft crime radio play when I was about nine, enjoyed writing 'compositions' as they were termed at school, and also the odd poem. Unfortunately, one of these was found and ridiculed by a teacher. Another, a docile piece about a religious topic (I could fool them when I wanted to) won a competition.

My vocation started in earnest when I read a sentence by Gertrude Stein who'd written, 'I decided when I was thirty I'd write'. I put the book down and thought, yes, that's what I'll do. And I did, getting up at 4 am and putting a couple of good hours in every morning before getting my daughter off to school and me off to work. After dinner, I'd do another hour or so before falling into bed. I wrote two novels that ended up in the bin, but learnt a lot by doing so. The third one, *Fortress*, was an international bestseller. At that stage, I hadn't noticed that I was starting to make a living writing about *fear*.

But the early emotional deprivation played out and I didn't make wise choices about how to live life or with whom to live it—actually, I didn't *know* there were such things as choices. I was driven headlong by my anxieties and obsessions. I drank and smoked and did a lot of 'recreational' sex. I thought I was having a great time. And some of the time, I was. At least, in the earlier years . . .

The turning point wasn't one thing—I wonder if in any life it ever is only one thing—but a series of events. These culminated in the decision to quit drinking, in which I was enormously helped by the AA program, and to seek professional help—in my case, somatic psychotherapy—which contributed to developing my stunted soul. In addition to these great changes, I must mention certain pivotal books, of a psychological and spiritual nature, especially *A Course in Miracles*, which turned many of my hostile attitudes around. Together with 12-step invitations to develop self-awareness and self-reflection, personal practices developed that allowed ongoing emotional and psychological growth. A wise psychologist many years ago said to me, 'the potential of a person is unlimited' and, somewhere, I knew that was true. At any time, anyone can make a decision to change, to have a future different from the past. But it takes commitment and perseverance and a certain doggedness. There was no fairy godmother, although many people have shown me great kindness over the years, nor was there any prince on a white charger, although once again, I'm indebted to several 'princes' for the life skills they helped me develop.

There was, however—and this is available to everyone and at any time, if only they can get out of their own way—the unfolding goodness of life itself, something that, most of the time, I have finally learnt to trust.

I sought change at depth because the level of suffering had become unbearable; it was a case of change or die. These days, I wake every morning to the gift of a new day in which I can live and love and work and play. Often I can say together with my (very) distant relative W.B. Yeats:

when such as I cast out remorse
Everything I look upon is blessed.

GABRIELLE LORD's first novel, *Fortress*, was an international bestseller. Since then she's written sixteen more novels, including series novels featuring PI Gemma Lincoln, *Baby Did a Bad Bad Thing*, *Spiking the Girl*, and the soon to be published *Shattered*, and those featuring Dr Jack McCain, forensic scientist with the Australian Federal Police, *Death Delights*, *Lethal Factor* and the recent *Dirty Weekend*. Gabrielle's novels have been translated into French, German, Dutch and several other languages, including Serbian. Two novels have made it to the screen, *Fortress* and

Whipping Boy. Several are currently under options. Her first young adult novel, *Monkey Undercover,* was published in May this year and she is currently working on another, larger young adult project. Gabrielle's interests are mainly concerned with living life as widely and deeply as possible.

My Glorious Teens

Kelly Foulkes

I used to be the editor of my school newspaper—until I wrote this story, was suspended and given a leave of absence to 'think very carefully' about what I'd done.

MACABRE SCIENCE PROJECT GOES HORRIBLY WRONG—FAREWELL FLUFF

Today, the last of the chickens from Ms Silvers' Year 12 Biology class died, one of only two to survive more than two weeks after hatching.

The ill-conceived project was devised by the aforementioned teacher earlier this term as an experiment to show students how the birds could be nurtured from eggs to life.

It all started innocently enough—at the beginning of the term, twenty-eight students received an egg each and were instructed on how to look after them, by keeping them warm and turning them occasionally. Some wrapped theirs in cotton wool or kept them in jacket pockets. Others held theirs constantly, eyes never leaving the speckled shells.

After a day, some of the more careless students had already said goodbye to their eggs by leaving them in backpacks, to be cracked by heavy textbooks. Three days after that, four were declared dead when examination showed them to be cold from neglect. More followed, becoming the innocent casualties of schoolyard fights and, one suspects, somebody's lunch. Michael Matthews certainly seemed to be tucking into egg mayonnaise sandwiches a lot that week.

A pitiful total of eight chickens actually managed to emerge from their shells, a low success rate but amazing, considering the odds stacked against them. Night one saw the offing of another two, creatively named Chickie and Ron, when their parents failed to seal their shoeboxes properly overnight, and the unwary chicks managed to be 1. suffocated by the blow heater placed too closely and 2. eaten by the family cat.

Over the following weeks, four more died in unreported circumstances. There were tears, but the students responsible seemed largely unrepentant. Lindsay Craig was heard to remark, 'I just got so bloody sick of the cheeping.'

Minnie and Fluff were the only two left, when Minnie finally succumbed to a strange illness that had been causing her eyes to roll for the previous few days. And then it seemed time was up for Fluff. Poor Fluff, the last of a sickly batch, didn't have a chance. His owner, a certain Melissa Santi, was proudly extolling Fluff's hardiness and her superior parenting skills when Fluff wandered off the end of her desk, fell to the floor and lay twitching before finally ceasing to move at all— a fitting end to a doomed project.

Investigations into the deaths continue, but one suspects this will be the last Year 12 Biology experiment involving living creatures for some time. No doubt questions will be raised as to the suitability of it as a study at all, and this reporter for one hopes there will be a formal review of the curriculum. As Derryn Hinch would say: shame, Year 12, shame!

I spent my suspension playing pool in the back room of the local pub, slightly mystified as to where I'd gone wrong, and had even more time to think about it after getting busted by one of the teachers and having my leave extended by another three days.

I wasn't part of the Biology class—perhaps that's why I didn't fully grasp how traumatised everyone was after the experiment cruelly ended, and how sensitive some were about the whole dead baby chicken thing. And I was shocked when I found out Ms Silvers had burst into tears after reading my article. Most of the people I'd spoken to hadn't seemed too fussed—they'd appeared to just shrug it off. Some told me all that feeding with eye-droppers was driving them crazy.

I certainly didn't expect my boyfriend's older brother to be so upset he wouldn't be in the same house, and definitely not in the same room, as me. My relationship didn't last long after that but, looking back, the article was probably one of my lesser crimes.

'You think you're so bloody clever,' I was told. But I really hadn't thought that at all. I thought I was being funny. I just wanted to make people laugh. But alas I made them want to brain me instead.

And I only wanted to make them laugh in Mr O'Donnell's Maths class back in Year 8. While he had his back turned, I started clowning around with some scissors and my tongue, pretending I was going to chop it off, so I wouldn't have to answer one of his deadly on-the-spot quiz questions about Pythagoras's theorem. Instead, he thought I really was trying to chop my tongue off—the school had its fair share of self-harmers—and ordered me to the counsellor, who recommended a rigorous schedule of extra-curricular pursuits to my parents.

That resulted in two years of netball training and performing arts such as acting, singing and debating. This was unfortunate for my parents and two younger brothers, who had to hear some of the key songs from *Les Miserables* several times a night for three months. I suspect *they* needed counselling by the end of it, as my Cosette sounded like a cross between a bagpipe, a banshee and Kate Bush. Also unfortunate was my netball team—my lax attempts at being a Goal Attack always seemed to let the opposite team score after I missed and they powered away on the rebound. Thankfully, I wasn't so bad at the debating.

My teachers called me disruptive, unfocused and thoughtless. Report cards always seemed to say: *Kelly has so much potential—if only she would try harder, she might be able to achieve it.* And that was from the teachers who liked me.

I studied French for the entirety of my high-school years, but have the unfortunate ability to delete all but the most irrelevant trivia from my memory. I still know every single word to Vanilla Ice's 'Ice Ice Baby' (*Stop! Collaborate and listen . . .*) but cannot for the life of me manage more than *voulez-vous coucher avec moi, ce soir* in French—and they didn't teach that in class. Maybe the key is to sing it.

I guess you could say I was undisciplined. But I did have a mother whose answer to HSC-related stress was to go to the flotation centre for a spell, or to get a shiatsu massage. I developed a habit of meditating whenever I was strung-out about not getting enough study done, using my thumbs to dig into pressure points on my head, which was meant to relieve stress. Spending all this time meditating led to further anxiety and the need for more frantic meditating. It was a vicious cycle. I don't understand how I got good enough grades to make it into university at all.

It's hard to accept that you don't fit in. I always used to look at the popular kids and think the ability to act cool was something their parents must have taught them. How did people know that Nike Air Maxes were a must, yet Dunlop Volleys were for losers? Or that you should let your fringe swing nonchalantly in front of your (heavily kohled) eyes, not gelled into a solid wall above your forehead?

The most important skill you could have at my last school was to give the appearance of aggressive ennui. You were never meant to smile or appear as if you were actually enjoying yourself. Far better to opt for an aloof, bored pose, designed to scare off any adults or people not brave enough to attempt conversation.

My problem was that I had too much natural enthusiasm to keep up the studious apathy adopted by many
of my peers. This was something I tried to hide, but it
always revealed itself, like a kind of Tourette's for dags. I
went to the gym a few times a week (circuit training with
my mum at the local aquatic centre) but was ashamed
to admit it, because it was simply too uncool. You had to
appear as if your dress sense or your figure just came out
of nowhere. I had this friend who used to secretly go on
these crazy diets all the time—one where she was only
allowed to eat apples for an entire day, then bananas the
next, then cabbage. I'd always crack by mid-afternoon and
had to scoff anything at hand, but she could keep it up
for weeks.

It pained me to have two younger brothers, and I blamed
them for not being able to pass on all those handy hints
and tips that older brothers and sisters knew to make you
cool. All we seemed to do was argue. I always wished my
parents had had three girls—or just the one child, me. I
used to lie awake at night fantasising about my mum
driving off with me in the passenger seat, leaving my
brothers behind at the supermarket. After which, she
and I would take a road trip across the country, having
adventures like Thelma and Louise, minus Brad Pitt . . .
and the cliff.

But it seemed there was no escaping my brothers who,
instead of helping *me* look cool, came to me for help—
well, for music advice anyway. My weekend job at a local
florist, scouring the soupy buckets out with bleach, meant

I had a disposable income of forty dollars a week to spend on CDs and the occasional under-age gig.

There would be a gentle rapping on my bedroom door, and Ross would poke his head around and ask, nervously edging closer to my CD tower as if it were a shrine, could he borrow the new Regurgitator album? I could tell the deference to me was killing him. I would make him buy me lollies and promise fervently not to scratch it, or I would shake my head as if the decision was hurting me more than him and say, sadly, *no*.

I had a penchant for anything angry, played loud. Looking back, it was all pretty tame but I thought I was totally hard at the time, listening to N.W.A. and Public Enemy, Henry Rollins, Metallica, Soundgarden and Nirvana. I had friends who were into bands like Megadeth and Slayer. Unfortunately, I was very into the whole grunge thing. And by the time I was sixteen, I had all the (unflattering) accessories to match: Blundstone boots, flannelette shirts, a red bandanna and greasy hair parted in the middle. It was probably the first time I was ever in fashion.

The first two CDs I bought were *Run-D.M.C.* and (to my endless shame) the *Beaches* soundtrack. The first because it was a favourite of my friend's older brother, whom I quite fancied, and the second because I'd seen the movie four times and knew the words to all the songs, including Bette Midler's seminal classic, 'Wind Beneath My Wings'. Aside from that aberration my music taste was, largely, influenced by the boys I liked.

Having been to all-girl Catholic schools in my early years of high school, I only discovered that boys existed when I was fourteen. (I don't count brothers as boys.) We moved around a lot, and I went to a few different schools, mainly because my parents couldn't decide where to settle down—Perth, where my mum had grown up, or Sydney, where my dad had nice local pubs on every corner; *Cheers*-style establishments where everyone knew his name.

Nikki and Belinda, my friends at the time, were horrified when they found out I'd never kissed a boy on the mouth. They took pity on me and insisted I learn the ropes from Maurice, a guy they could always rely on for a good kiss. I was led to understand he was a rite of passage for every self-respecting young woman.

Maurice lived in East Balmain in a sandstone single-storey house. I'd never met him before. It didn't matter, said Nikki and Belinda, who decided to turn up on his doorstep one afternoon, with me in tow.

I remember him answering the door. He had the cutest long fringe with a short back and sides, and looked languidly disinterested when they floated the idea of him kissing me while they timed us to see how long we could last. I could hear a Daddo on the TV, which was blaring in the background. My heart was racing, and we didn't even make eye contact. He shrugged his consent, and before I knew it we were lip-locked and swapping saliva for the next 120 seconds, out the front on his parents' wraparound porch. I could taste that he'd been eating peppermint cream-filled Cadbury chocolate.

Who knows what his recollection of the experience is, or if he even remembers it. Even then I was wondering, 'Does he do this all the time? How many other girls has he kissed before? What will he think of me when we're finished?' I didn't want to stop when I heard Nikki's digital Casio watch beeping to say two minutes had passed, but could sense he was winding up and pulled away.

As if the pressure of kissing boys wasn't bad enough, there were always the demands of fashion to contend with, and Fridays at our school, when you didn't have to wear your uniform, were a nightmare. I really wasn't the snazziest dresser in my early teens. Used to wearing school uniforms or random tees and shorts on the weekend, I was filled with dread at the idea of mufti days, and would spend a week going through everything in my mother's closet, having rejected my own clothes immediately. Apart from my school uniform and sports kit, I only seemed to own desperately daggy old jumpers hand-knitted by various elderly relatives or 'My Parents Went to Bali and All I Got Was This Lousy T-shirt'-style tops.

One Casual Friday horror included my favourite pair of high-waisted, acid-wash denim jeans (slim-fitting at the ankle and ballooning, in MC Hammer-fashion, around the thighs) with my mum's treasured brilliant white and bubblegum-pink LA Gear sneakers. Leaving the house in a 'Mind the Gap' tee from my aunt's recent visit to London, I shrewdly swapped it for Mum's electric-blue rayon blouse in the bus depot restrooms. It had puffed sleeves with ruching all the way down from its thick shoulder pads, which made me look scarily similar to a valance. To top it off, I scrunched my hair dry and used a banana clip to secure it in place atop my head. The most disturbing thing: it wasn't even the '80s anymore. My contemporaries were wearing halter-necks and Bermuda shorts from Esprit, paired with stylish white Reeboks, subtly scuffed.

I would like to think I am well beyond committing such fashion faux-pas nowadays, but just last summer I had a very similar look going on. At least now, harking back to the era style forgot is fashion-forward. Sometimes it only takes time for fashion to catch up and for a faux-pas to become a statement. But I'm not sure what my look was saying back then. It prompted some older, rougher boys on the bus to affix me to the handrails with their school ties, leaving me shouting for help at the back of the double-length bus as we passed my stop, unheeded by the driver until we reached the depot. So maybe the statement was 'tie me up'.

All teenagers have the most ridiculous sayings. And the longest running and most versatile of ours was *mad*. Everything was mad, which was pronounced *maard*, and accompanied by an ironic shake of the head that could mean something totally cool or totally sad. It was hard to work out which of the two it actually was, and I'd find myself nodding in agreement with someone who had meant the exact opposite. See? Not cool.

Man was another. Everyone was man (*maaan*), including my mum, who would say, 'I'm not your man, I'm your mother.' She thought we were insane, and was also not overly fond of the Niggaz With Attitude blaring from my bedroom.

My body matured—ahead of my brain—seemingly overnight, but in actuality over Year 11 spring break. I went from being teased mercilessly for my flat chest to being teased mercilessly for my double-D cups, which were so prominent they made an appearance in the departing Year 12's muck-up day revue, as balloons which finally burst in the rugby shirt of the boy who wore them. I sat in the front row, teeth gritted in a smile, willing myself to laugh along with the 500 other kids in the school gym. Ho, ho, those balloons sure are funny!

I felt scarred for a while after school, haunted by memories of the ski trip where I got banned from the last day of skiing after being nabbed imbibing a nightcap at the local bar by the Phys Ed teacher, Mr Roberts, and of being part of the school band's appalling rendition— with me as back-up singer, holding my ear à la Bono in Band Aid's 'Do They Know It's Christmas?'—of 'Making Whoopee' in assembly. (Why, oh why, did we choose that tune? Why weren't we stopped?)

But the best thing about sucking so badly at school was feeling compelled to leave Sydney for some time, travelling overseas and then coming back to find I didn't really care anymore who remembered my turn as Kelly Bundy out of *Married . . . With Children* in my final week for Year 12 Slave Day. It's quite liberating to be totally anonymous for the better part of a decade, then find yourself back and living about 500 metres from where you spent most of your formative years.

I still make terrible fashion mistakes, and am happy to listen to anything from the Kings of Leon to Dolly Parton, although perhaps not the Divine Miss M. Now Ross lends me CDs, and is gracious enough not to make me promise not to scratch them.

So I've moved on, and I hope there's no hard feelings all round—from my brothers, from Maurice, from my poor teachers. Unfortunately, I don't think anything will ever redeem me in Ms Silvers' eyes.

KELLY FOULKES is the editor of and a contributor to *Sensory* (2000), an anthology of young Australian writing. She has worked as a freelance journalist for various publications including the *South China Morning Post* and the now-defunct Hong Kong gossip rag *Entertainment on Style*. She has worked in publishing for over eight years in Sydney, Hong Kong and London, and lives with her husband in Sydney's inner-west.

The Power of Two

The three of us were in our best going-out clothes, our hair combed, our socks pulled up, our shoes polished, and feeling damn good about ourselves. The two women who stepped into the lift with us at our local department store obviously thought we had reason.

'What pretty little girls!' one of them cooed to the other. 'How lovely!' I felt a pleasant warmness creep up my face. She looked directly at me and smiled. 'And how nice it must be for you,' she said, 'to have such pretty friends.'

She bent down and rustled in her shopping bag, as my face burned a beetroot red. She emerged with two silver coins. 'Here,' she said, dropping one each into the upturned palms of my companions. 'Take that for brightening our day. God bless you.'

The lift doors opened and she and her friend trudged out into haberdashery. As the doors closed again on both the blessed and the unblessed, I laughed, a little too loudly. 'Ice cream on you two today,' I said, jauntily. I swivelled round just in time to catch them looking at their own reflections in the mirrored walls of the lift, exchanging secret little smiles.

The problem for me, entering those troubled, vulnerable, excruciatingly insecure teenage years, wasn't that I had bad friends, or even too few friends. It was that I had too many. One too many. For my best friends in the world were a pair of twins.

There have been numerous studies over the years on twins, on triplets, even on the difficulties for quadruplets of establishing separate identities and going on to thrive in the world. But for their friends? Nothing at all. Yet while the products of multiple births bathe in the limelight simply for the good fortune of having shared a womb, revel in the admiration and curiosity of strangers for looking alike, and enjoy the company of close siblings, their friends live invariably on the cold, cold outer, in more ways than one.

When I first met Shelley and Karen, I was similarly beguiled. They had almost identical sky-blue eyes and long blonde hair, dressed the same, talked alike, and were almost inseparable. We lived in the same street and were the same age, so it was only natural that we soon became playmates. When we started at school, however, the dynamic subtly shifted.

It was my first taste of celebrity. They were the only twins in the neighbourhood and, at first, I enjoyed being the best friend of the schoolyard stars. I was happy to tag along behind them, warming myself in the reflected glow of their adulation, absorbing any worship they considered surfeit to requirements. All by ourselves, we were a tidy gang. We could play elastics, or skipping, without the need of anyone else to stand in the loops or hold the rope. We were three-fifths of a five-a-side netball team. Purely by dint of numbers, we were able to bully loners we didn't like.

Gradually, as we entered our adolescence and high school, and society became more complex, competitive and cutthroat, the power began to shift. Instead of all for one and one for all, it became two against one. And, regrettably, that one was almost always me.

The trouble was that Shelley and Karen were actually quite different people. One was brighter than the other. One was more athletic. One was more outgoing. One was more naturally popular. That was Shelley. Karen, as a consequence, was finding it tough to keep up. I found myself increasingly in the role of helping Karen cope, but working equally hard to make sure she—and I, for that matter—never eclipsed Shelley. That would have been more than both our fragile young lives were worth.

At lessons, I was best, so I was the one who always ended up helping Karen with her homework. On the quiet, Shelley often copied. The teacher put down the similarity of their work to comparable levels of ability. I was accused of replicating their homework, since the pages I handed in obviously weren't all that different.

At sport, Shelley and I were neck and neck at netball. But because everyone hung around and played in pairs, I missed out. When it came to choosing a team, the twins were an obvious package. With everyone else already paired up, I was too often the odd one out, sitting watching glumly, apparently friendless, from the bench.

As we grew older, relations became more fraught. At discos, we went as a threesome. Boys, however, habitually arrived in pairs. No guesses for who always ended up playing the gooseberry fool. On our birthdays, I had to save my pocket money for weeks in order to afford two good presents. On mine, I received a single gift of equal worth from them jointly.

But the politics between the girls was the worst. Shelley and Karen, like any good sisters, fought bitterly and each tried to recruit others to her cause. So often, Karen would make an extra effort to woo my friendship and, pathetically grateful for the attention, I'd take her side. Then Shelley would put in the hard yards and I'd find myself shamefacedly switching to hers.

As the week went on, each would amass a small army of supporters. As, supposedly, the best friend of both, I'd be sent scuttling between the two to try to re-establish cordial relations before the outbreak of school world war.

'But she started it,' Karen would protest. 'Yes, I know, I know,' I'd soothe, 'but she *is* bad-tempered, we both know that. And she can be a right bitch. But she's sorry she started all this now. She wants to be friends with you again.'

With Karen agreeing to a truce, I'd rush back to Shelley's side, a diligent and faithful first lieutenant. 'Karen's *sooo* sorry,' I'd whisper conciliatorily. 'She wants you to forgive her. She's premenstrual and crotchety, and knows it.' This was always a good card to play among fourteen-year-old girls. 'We both know what a cow she can be,' I'd add for good measure.

If it worked out, eventually the two sides would come together, peace would descend, and the sisterhood would be re-cemented with tears and hugs. The recriminations would come later, when they'd had a chance to discuss the week alone. Then they'd both confront me at my front door.

'You called Shelley a bitch,' Karen would spit at me, holding her twin's arm tight. Shelley would look at me coldly. 'And you said Karen was a cow,' she'd bark.

'*You're* the bitch and the cow,' they'd then recite together, before swinging haughtily around and setting off for school, my whole world crumbling in their wake.

By the time I'd arrive, the word would be out: I'd tried to separate the twins and cause a rift in their unbreakable birth bond for some unknown, malevolent motive of my own. Now, no one was speaking to me. And no one would—until the twins would finally decide I'd been punished enough.

Shelley and Karen left school as soon as they could in order to earn money as insurance clerks in the city, to marry young, have kids and divorce. I stayed on, and their absence felt like a weight had dissolved from my shoulders.

I didn't realise it then, but the twins had given me the greatest of leg-ups in my quest for a meaningful career. By the time we parted ways in our older teenage years, they'd instilled in me a heart full of insecurity, a soul brimming over with sensitivity, and a psyche warped by wretchedly low self-esteem allied to years living as an outsider, an observer of personal politics red in tooth and matching toenail.

All the main requirements, in fact, for a life as a writer.

SUE WILLIAMS is an award-winning journalist and columnist who's written for all of Australia's leading newspapers and magazines, as well as having her own opinion segment on a TV show. Born in England, she has also worked in print and TV in the UK and New Zealand and spent many years travelling before settling in Sydney. She is the author of the biographies *Peter Ryan: The Inside Story*, *Mean Streets, Kind Heart: The Father Chris Riley Story*, *Death of a Doctor* and *World Beyond Tears*. She has written a travel book, *Getting There—Journeys of an Accidental Adventurer*, co-authored *Powering Up, Apartment Living: The Complete Guide to Buying, Renting, Surviving and Thriving in Apartments* and *The Spirit of Australia*, and contributed to a collection of short stories, *Love, Obsession, Secrets & Lies*. Sue's last book was the true crime *And Then The Darkness: The Disappearance of Peter Falconio and the Trials of Joanne Lees* (ABC Books, 2006), short-listed for the Gold Dagger Award in Britain for the international true crime book of the year.

My After-Formal Party

Lucy Lehmann

'My after-formal party was so cool. There were couples lying around all over the place just making love.'

As a waitress crossed the courtyard with our coffees, our conversation was suspended. A movement caught my eye and I glanced down at the bench on which I was sitting: next to my thigh appeared a bare, bony, hairy, brown foot. During the brief pause in his discourse, Jason had slipped off a sandal and comfortably stretched out one leg under the table. My own legs, a counterpoint to the microskirt I was wearing, were crossed so tightly that, when our coffees were finished, I virtually had to unknot them in order to stand up.

We had met at one of Paddington Town Hall's reggae nights. I had been unable to believe my luck when a handsome stranger with tasteful dreadlocks had grabbed my hand and pulled me onto the dancefloor. For months, I'd been searching for someone like him. Time was running out. The music paused, and I hastily invited him to my Year 10 formal; after four years at North Sydney Girls High, my social circle consisted solely of girls, and I was dreading the loss of pride that would occur if I were to turn up to the formal by myself, or with a dorky schoolboy who all the other girls knew from Debating, or with someone I didn't know at all, like the friend of the son of a friend's family friend. When it was time for the band to lug off their congas and roll up their leads, Jason, promising to accompany me to my formal in a fortnight, used my lipstick to write his phone number down my arm. I felt profoundly uplifted, as though I had just solved the very last problem of my life, and would be from then on free from all worries.

But, in the two weeks between the reggae night and the Year 10 formal, my ideal solution proceeded to multi-ply into a litter of unforeseen problems. I had wished only for a formal date—how was it that I had ended up with a full-blown first boyfriend? According to the contract into which I had unwittingly entered, Jason and I were obliged to phone each other daily, regardless of the fact that his workday was as barren as my schoolday of any profound or entertaining conversational material. It was also a requirement that I meet his coiffeured mother and try, with manners polite enough to charm the Queen, to counteract the impression created by my modified, skimpy, figure-hugging school uniform. I had to wear the ring he had given me, its small, dark stone reminding me involuntarily of a blackhead that required squeezing. I had to ensure that my friends, when we were all out together, didn't forget that I had put my age up a year, to sixteen. I had to sit on his knee and hold his hand and greet and farewell him with a kiss on the lips. And

I simply didn't know what I was supposed to do with the feelings that his presence—or, rather, his existence—provoked in me. So I just suppressed them—feelings of being fatally trapped, painfully embarrassed and, most inconvenient of all, one particular feeling that I could only describe as the complete opposite of horny. Far out of my realm of experience—I'd never even properly kissed a boy!—and with Jason's naked foot and his enthusiasm for after-formal parties bumping around persistently in my mind, the problems were left unchecked as I threw myself instead into the task of sewing my dress.

It was grey velvet, in an Empire-line style, which I thought was sympathetic to my late-developing breasts, and had a decorative hem, which I would come to regret, of black glass beads and tiny jingling bells. Jason, when he arrived to pick me up, was in full formal regalia. His dreadlocks, and the fact that he was cute, no longer at school and drove his own car, were effectively cancelled out by his matching polyester paisley bow tie, cummerbund and breast-pocket handkerchief. As I sat beside him in the passenger seat, where he presented me with a single red rose amid baby's-breath, I felt a parabolic increase in the pressure of those problems that had been building up inside me; since our coffee last weekend, Jason's references to his own after-formal party had become more and more frequent, like a person whose conversation, towards dinnertime, turns repeatedly to food. With the same casual confidence exhibited by the bare foot that had nuzzled into my thigh as I'd sipped at my coffee, he was anticipating nothing but total fulfilment. My jumble of incomprehensible feelings, which had so far led to no action except prolonged, inconclusive discussions with friends, would not withstand the force of such confidence: in approximately four hours, my formal date and I would be at the after-party, making love all over the place.

By the time I got out of his car, I was in such a state that when he touched my back to guide me into the Sydney Uni Refectory, only with an enormous effort of self-restraint did I manage not to spin around screaming and swatting his hand off me. Another effort was required when we sat at our table and he put his hand on my thigh, which went rigid every time he squeezed it. Finally, after failing to evade the compulsory photo session, where I was forced to smile for the camera while his arm was dropped like a red-hot chain across my shoulders, my self-restraint was utterly depleted. I cast a 'Help me!' look at my friends and dashed to the toilets, the bells on my dress tinkling all the way.

'What can I do?' I cried to two friends who had surreptitiously followed me. 'If he touches me once more I'm going to kill him!'

'Could you tell him that you just want to be friends?'

I shook my head vigorously. The utterance of a dishonest statement—obviously, I didn't want to be his friend at all and, in fact, wished at that moment that he had never been born, and even that his parents had never been born—didn't bother me, but the prospect of further physical, visual and aural contact with him was unbearable. 'Where is he now?'

Clare stepped out and soon returned, reporting, 'He's back at our table talking to Sal and Annie.'

Our table was scarcely metres away from the exit door.

It might have been possible to take a route that would keep me out of his line of vision, but as soon as I made a break for the door, my hem would start jingling, alerting him instantly to the sudden, unexplained departure of his new girlfriend. It would only be natural, even chivalrous, for him to pursue me into the night, where he would soon run me to ground in the dark, unpopulated shrubbery of Sydney University.

'You can't just be polite to him and get through the night?' asked Veronica.

'No!' I gripped her hands. 'He can't come to the after-party. He can't! He thinks we're going to have sex!'

There was only one course of action available. Clare and Veronica left the toilets, and I waited, my dress jingling as I shivered with tension.

After forty minutes, Veronica returned. 'He's gone.'

I was filled, from top to bottom, with a sense of relief, as I had been in an entirely different way exactly two weeks before. However, the feeling which, back then, I had interpreted to be the result of finally arriving at a glorious, long-imagined destination, I knew now to be only a temporary rest-stop on an interminable, wandering journey where I would be lost far more often than found; only for a moment could I believe that sending your friend off to tell your formal date to go home because you are having some kind of overwrought episode in the toilets was a satisfactory solution.

'How did he take it?'

'He was crushed.' Veronica was silent for a moment. 'Crushed! You should have seen him!' She obligingly distorted her face into an approximate replication of his as he had turned to tread with dragging feet across the

Arundel Street Footbridge. We both burst out laughing, then slapped our hands over our mouths.

'Poor boy,' said Veronica, gravely.

By the time I emerged from the toilets, taxis were arriving to take us to a house in a quiet street on the North Shore. There, I decided to get drunk on West Coast Cooler, hoping to exorcise a haunting feeling of guilt, but was stopped by the fear of vomiting, and only ended up depressed. I sat on a sofa for the rest of the night, eating a bowl of peanuts. From there, I saw a small amount of kissing, several cases of partner-poaching, and heard an eyewitness report of a fingering incident, but I didn't see any couples making love at my after-formal party.

LUCY LEHMANN was born in Sydney. Her first novel, *The Showgirl and the Brumby* (Vintage/Random House, 2002) won the Kathleen Mitchell Award in 2004, for a novel by an Australian author under thirty. She is now writing her next novel.

Who's the
New Girl?

Rebecca Huntley

My all-time favourite teen movie is John Hughes's 1986 classic, *Pretty in Pink*, starring the ultimate '80s It girl, Molly Ringwald. She plays Andy, the smart, strong heroine from the wrong side of the tracks who lives with her dilapidated dad and raises herself, struggling with her outsider status at the well-positioned high school she attends. My favourite scene is when Andy is sent to the Principal's office after getting into a fight with rich bitch Betty. In the end, she's let off the hook, but the Principal can't help but dispense some 'sage' advice. 'Andy,' he says, 'if you put out signals that you don't want to belong, people are going to make sure that you don't.' Andy calmly responds to this with the words: 'That's a beautiful theory.'

Now, I am not for a second pretending that I'm anything like Andy, a willowy redhead from a disadvantaged background with, strangely enough, a very cool pink vintage VW and great taste in clothes. But I love this scene because it illustrates just how devastating it can be to be victimised at school and how often adults don't see the true nature of that victimisation.

These days, when I admit to people that as a teenager I was socially awkward and a target for bullies, they find it hard to believe. I suppose it's because I am the guest at the dinner party who will never shut up. No wallflower, me. But it wasn't always that way.

As a child, I was intensely shy. This shyness led to a general kind of social dysfunction throughout my childhood and early teens. It was made worse by the fact that I was the daggy, bookish daughter of intellectual types who valued classical music, art and travel over fashion, sport and fun. There's a photo of me as a twelve-year-old that encapsulates my early style. I am wearing brown cords, a button-down shirt and a jumper my grandma knitted me. I have huge tortoiseshell glasses and a short, boyish haircut, dictated by convenience rather than fashion. I am smiling broadly as I pose for a picture in front of the Trevi Fountain. I had spent the morning in the Vatican Museums, thrilled at the artefacts and paintings I saw there. Move over, Mary-Kate and Ashley.

These days, of course, it's somewhat cool to claim a nerdy past. I have read countless interviews with stars who claim to have been 'drama geeks' or 'book nerds' at school, unable to land a date with the opposite sex or ostracised for being too tall and skinny. (As a hardcore, genuine nerd, I am always a tad sceptical about such claims.)

Looking back on my early teens, my overriding memory is of having to navigate my way around my own unpopularity. I always felt out of place. This was made worse by the fact that until I was fifteen, my family kept moving cities all the time, which meant I had to constantly change schools. We moved approximately every two years, mainly from Adelaide to Sydney and back. Whenever he could, my dad would also shift us to England for a few months of sabbatical, after which we would travel around the Continent in a beaten-up old car. It all sounds terribly glamorous and exciting. Certainly, there were amazing aspects of this vagabond existence. Like learning about Rome by actually visiting Rome. Or spending a whole English summer out of school, teaching myself American history and reading all of Jane Austen's novels. But this adventurous lifestyle meant I was rarely at one school long enough to make friends before I was packing my bags to head off somewhere new.

The cycle was always a predictable one. I would arrive, the nervous new girl. A group of girls, sometimes on the prompting of a benevolent teacher, would adopt me, much like a stray kitten is taken on by an animal-loving family. But because I was a dag with odd tastes and no real mastery of playground politics, I would eventually become unpopular with the cool kids. This stage would often last between six and twelve months, during which I dreaded going to school. I felt tense as I walked the corridors, in case I bumped into those who had decided to hate me for reasons best known to themselves.

My worst memories? At thirteen, I used to wait by a large palm tree in the car park for my mum to pick me up after school. Every afternoon a group of girls who had taken a particular dislike to me would gather nearby so they could all walk home together. They would pass me in silence as I stood stock-still in an attempt to blend into the bark. Without fail, one of them would make a barely whispered comment about me and all would respond with laughter. Weirdly enough, I never asked my mum if I could be picked up in another place. Perhaps I considered the teasing inevitable.

At two of the high schools I attended—one a posh private school, the other a selective public school—I went through a few painful months of having no one to sit with during break times. I would try to while away the long minutes of recess and lunch in the library or walking around the school perimeter. Then there was the time in Year 9 Maths class when a note passed around between a group of girls 'accidentally' got passed to me. The note was all about me, how annoying and ugly I was. I read it in shock and passed it on.

Writing, thinking about it now, it all seems so trivial, and the hurt I still feel about that time, even after all these years, seems somewhat melodramatic and self-indulgent. Thankfully, my mum didn't think so at the time. Every day after school, I would come home and we would sit in her room so I could recount the most recent humiliation or spiteful comment. She always listened without judgement, offering support and unconditional love. She never said any of the things parents say in these situations like 'just ignore them' or 'they'll get over it'. She never once implied I had done anything to deserve the rough treatment. As a high-school teacher, she had seen this scenario countless times and understood what rampant and unchecked bitchiness among girls can be like. She took my concerns seriously and knew that, even though my stories sounded silly, the treatment being dished out at school was the most important issue in my life and thus important, full stop.

Of course, as my father used to say, 'This too shall pass.' And it did. After a hazing period at the new school, things usually calmed down and I eased into being accepted. And I was happy. I felt like I knew who my friends were, where to go at lunch, and that school was a safe place not a blackboard jungle. I was like John Travolta—popular then desperately unpopular then popular again.

Of course, this was always the very moment it was time to pack our bags and move again.

When I turned sixteen, things got better. My dad finally had a job he felt he could stay in for more than a couple of years. I had been at my high school for three years at this stage and had settled in. The worst of the bullying was over for me. At this time, I became friends with a girl in my Ancient History class; let's call her Clare. Clare was fabulous. She was skinny with a mop of curly brown hair, big blue eyes and the most infectious laugh. The thing I best recall about her is how much she laughed and what a happy person she was. She was also a fantastic artist, with groovy handwriting that looped and swirled across the pages of her school notebooks.

I would visit Clare at her house and she would play me her favourite Jimi Hendrix and Led Zeppelin songs on her sister's hand-me-down stereo. She would insist I lie on the floor of her bedroom, a speaker at each ear, so I could appreciate the true texture and depth of 'Are You Experienced' and 'Stairway to Heaven'. Chaperoned by her sister and her boyfriend, Clare and I went to see U2 live, one of the best music experiences of my life. I watched as Bono pulled a girl from the audience and danced with her to 'All I Want is You'. 'Why couldn't that be me?' Clare and I exclaimed to each other.

A few months into our friendship, other girls at school started making comments to me about Clare. 'Why are you friends with Clare? You know she's a leso,' one girl in Home Economics said to me. 'A leso?' Too smart by now to admit I only had a weak understanding of what 'being a leso' involved, I did know it was short for lesbian and being a lesbian was bad. 'How do you know she's a leso?' I enquired. ''Cos she's always all over people, hugging them and smiling and stuff' was the response. This tactile behaviour was part of Clare's charm, as far as I was concerned, but now I was being told it wasn't okay, that it was even suspect. I kept hanging out with Clare, although I stopped returning the hugs quite so much. The comments kept mounting. 'Clare's such a lesbian. It's *so* obvious.'

Thus far in my life, I had never been on the other side of the bitchy barrier. It was me people whispered about. It was me people lobbied against. It was me who attracted the unattractive names. All these comments about Clare were upsetting but also intriguing, a totally new experience. I finally felt accepted. I was in a position to be the one spurning rather than the one spurned.

I'd like to say that I resisted these attempts to get me to de-friend Clare. I'd like to say that all my years of being bullied had taught me a lesson—treat others as you would like to be treated.

I'd like to say that happened.

It all came to a head during a PE class. Something shifted in me that morning. I woke up and I didn't want to see Clare. In fact, I was deliberately late to school in order to avoid her at rollcall. We shared PE and she was thrilled to see me, while I acted stand-offish. Clare kept asking what was wrong. Why was I avoiding her? Why didn't I want to stand next to her? Others, those who were leaders in the Anti-Clare caucus, were watching as all this played out on the sunbaked tennis courts. I turned suddenly and, to my own surprise, said in quite a loud voice, 'I don't want to stand next to you because you're a lesbian.'

What happened next I will never forget. Clare just looked at me in shock. Her face fell, then crumpled into a full-blown sob.

'I'm not a lesbian! That's not true. Why would you say that?'

She stared at me and cried as her question remained unanswered. How could I answer it—'I said you're a lesbian because other people say you are and I am too stupid and weak to think for myself'? Instead, I was totally lost for words and utterly ashamed of myself. I had hurt this person profoundly, in front of her tormentors; someone who had only ever been lovely to me, introduced me to real rock'n'roll and organised for me to see Bono in the flesh.

The PE teacher barked at us to stop misbehaving and keep playing whatever dumb game we were playing at the time. Clare quietly sobbed in line while I stood there, ashen-faced.

I have a vague memory of apologising to Clare later in the day. She took the apology with a quiet dignity, but we both knew she hadn't forgiven me, and the friendship that had been so much fun was now over.

We continued in school together, even sharing classes

until Year 12. We were 'say hi in the corridor' friends but never close again. I know there was a time when she hated me, deservedly.

At our ten-year school reunion, after one too many red wines, I found Clare in the crowd of all-too-familiar women, pulled her by the arm into a corner and apologised profusely, saying that what I had done to her still made me cringe. She laughed it off. Maybe it was just a blip in her recollections of high school. Or maybe, even after a decade, she still couldn't admit to me how much I had hurt her.

Looking back on my teen years, the bullying I encountered has had largely positive effects on my life. Always being the new girl transformed me from a shy type into a not-so-shy type. I can certainly walk into a room of strangers and feel comfortable, start a conversation with anyone, tell a joke and make others feel at ease. I know how to stand up for myself, knowing that if I can't, no one else will. And I value the friends I have in life, knowing that life without friends isn't much fun.

But I do think about Clare and wish I had the courage and strength of character at the time to ignore the 'leso' comments and stand by our friendship. I didn't please anyone by giving in to that pressure to reject her. I wasn't more accepted by others as a result, just less acceptable to myself.

REBECCA HUNTLEY is a Sydney-based writer and social researcher, with experience in publishing, academia and politics. She holds degrees in law and film studies from the University of New South Wales and a PhD in gender studies from the University of Sydney. She is the author of *The World According to Y: Inside the New Adult Generation* (Allen & Unwin, 2006). She writes regularly for *Vogue*. Rebecca is the author of the *Ipsos Mackay Report*.

The Imaginary
Life of Lucy

Patti Miller

With apologies to D. H. Lawrence,
Doris Lessing, Virginia Woolf,
Patrick White and Anaïs Nin.

No one at my new school knew I was really a mysterious, pale, dark-haired girl. I stood in the heat of the bitumen quadrangle, red-haired, red-faced, straight-bodied and, watching the other girls mill about in tight groups, lost my childhood confidence in a moment. Fresh from the farm and a one-room country school, I was immature, years behind, but quick at imitating, and within a few months I laughed and talked as they did. Thoughts and acts lost their innocence and were accompanied by a witness who registered everything, a shadowy observer. None of the writers I read all day did anything to dispel that shadowy self; how could they have dispelled themselves?

It was easier to live an imaginary life. Imaginary life had stronger colours, deeper shadows, more insistent rhythms—and I could be anyone I wanted to be. I selected the name Lucy after discovering it was my mother's first choice for me. I thought it poetic, and wondered discontentedly why she'd changed her mind. Lucy led the life of art.

It was the first year of high school and life outside the classroom was awkward. I blushed, my eyes sliding sideways, if any boy spoke to me. My uniform was too big because it was a hand-me-down from a cousin, my school stockings wrinkled around my knees, my hair was badly cut. But, unseen, I was the D. H. Lawrence heroine who lay in the sun on a hillside one afternoon, wrapped in a blue cardigan.

The sun penetrated Lucy's skin, into her bones, into her mind, dissolving the cold clots of thoughts. Turning over, she let the sun warm her right through; she let her shoulders, her thighs, soften in its heat. The stiff sinews of her emotions loosened and became fluid as the rays kneaded through her. It was the autumn sun and because it had little time, it was urgent, not slow and careful. It melted fiercely, golden fire aiming down through the blue sky, focused alone on her. It poured honey on her legs and she pushed the blue wrap from her body and lay surrounded by the prickle of autumn-yellow grass. She let the honey flow between her thighs on the warm silence of the hillside.

In the night, Lucy was the space between the stars. She could hear the sound of flowers folding in the evening and the crystal note of stars moving in their spheres. The darkness pulsed; she felt the beat of its heart, steady like the breath of a sleeping creature. She was made of dark space. The moon was silver and alone above her. She asked the moon to enter the dark cave inside her so that she could carry her hidden across the day. The moon entered her quietly; she lay cool and round inside her, waiting for the sun.

The people she knew away from the hillside were neither sun nor moon. Earthworms, she thought. They didn't look up from the business of eating dirt. They were cold and soft and could not face the sun or moon. They attended to dates and times as if their lives depended on it.

A soft rippling of the fingers of the wind played down her body and sent shivers over the sun-honey on her skin. The hillside was quiet except for a late cicada shrilling in the almond tree behind her. The world was far away and she was scornful of its clothed paleness. She spread her arms and legs in the grass and felt the prickles massage her shoulders and the backs of her legs. The sun poured between her thighs and entered into the cave of the moon and she disdained the world.

Another day, in late high school, I was the Doris Lessing girl sitting resentfully in church in my little town, stifled by the forms of religion I had to enact, critical of the narrow lives around me. No one suspected that the freckle-faced girl with the mantilla veil and look of condescension was not praying but in fact planning her escape, ready to leave for the city as soon as her matriculation results arrived.

'This town on the veldt,' thought Lucy, and wished she could say 'veldt' because it sounded wider and more isolated than 'plains'. She sat in church studying the lined but well made-up face of Mrs de Burgh, who always sat in the same pew. She was a blonde, tired, altogether disappointed woman in a pale blue suit that had been smart five years ago. She was tall and would have been pretty before she married Mr de Burgh, who was short and round and solicitous of her. She had borne him three tall, good-looking sons as a kind of reproach, as if she were saying *I can do this all on my own, they have nothing of you in them*.

Lucy wondered why Mrs de Burgh had married him. She knew the rumour; her first son was the illegitimate child of a rich lawyer from Sydney and Mr de Burgh had offered to marry her because he had always longed for her tall, blonde unattainability. Lucy didn't care. She believed she was finding a kindred soul in the first son, Sebastian. Her mother scoffed gently at the fancy name. He was already at university, studying politics and sociology. They had stood outside the church discussing ideas and didn't go inside until the service was half over.

'This is just a Sunday morning social club.' Sebastian tossed a kurrajong pod up and down as he leant against the railings. He looked disinterested but she knew he was watching everyone.

'Yes,' she said. 'They're here to show off their new hats. They don't even know or care there are kids out at Nanima Mission who don't have enough to eat.'

'You sound like a revolutionary, comrade.' He was laughing but she felt complimented.

'Of course. I want to turn things over. The Aborigines at Nanima don't stand a chance. Do you see any at the Catholic school? They are all kept out at Nanima in primary school and when they do have to come into town for high school, they all drop out because they are intimidated by the white kids and their whole history as victims.'

'So, what are you going to do about it? Do you think political action is going to make a difference in a small town?' He was serious but there was something in his tone that was undermining. He had not wanted her to have an analysis. He had only wanted to impress her with his knowledge and his distance from this tedious place.

'I don't know yet,' she said. 'But I will do something.' She felt superior, even to Sebastian. She would show all these tired people that she would not ever permit life to trap her. She would never marry a Mr de Burgh of any kind and end up with a neatly pressed suit and a look of terrible disappointment. Soon she would leave and find people who lived intensely and broke out of limitations. She smiled and walked away from the heat of the morning into the cool church. She didn't listen to any of the prayers or the sermon but planned where she would live when she moved to Sydney.

On another day, perhaps twelve months later, I had left school and lived on the bottom floor of a Darlinghurst terrace with Ruth and Naomi, who both had rich parents in Edgecliff. Upstairs, Naomi made love to her Chilean boyfriend who had been tortured in Santiago and who borrowed money from me for acid trips. The world of the farm where I'd grown up, which had stretched to the horizon, was shrinking. It could not have contained so many characters drifting in and out of the flow of days. I was the Virginia Woolf girl who moved through the day as if in an invisible stream.

❖

Lucy stepped away from the bus stop and into Victoria Park. The morning was bright, as if issued fresh to a child running out into it. She had started out early and there were still dew-drops on the undersides of leaves of grass, splitting the light, spilling the light; exquisite diamonds spilt carelessly by the darkness. They shot out fiery sparks, glittered dangerously, messengers of the fire and beauty hidden in the easy, ordinary light of every day. Brighter than stars and more piercing than diamonds; she had to blink, shade her eyes, hurry away from the miniature explosions.

She was frightened. The world was more secret and strange than she thought. This striving for knowledge was nothing when light was split by the tiniest drop of dew. *I am powerless, empty*, she thought, *and I am fooling myself by trying to fill the emptiness with knowledge.*

Nonsense, nonsense! She deliberately stepped off the narrow dirt path she had been following across the park. The goat path, it was called, worn into the grass by thousands of students taking a short cut to the gate in the iron fence of Sydney University. Lucy walked to one side of the path and watched a woman with black hair and brown skin who was standing at the gate.

The woman was also dressed in black and brown, a woodland creature waiting for her lover who would not come. She was dressed so that everyone who saw her that day would remember her for the rest of their lives, yet her lover would not arrive.

Lucy looked away from the woman. She wouldn't take her pain, but only her black and brown delicacy, a faun waiting by the iron gate and sharp fence. She looked back down the slope to the blue rectangle of the swimming pool. It was empty, a flat blue sheet surrounded by high fences, dreaming quiet cool dreams before the onslaught of summer children ruffled and tore its smooth blueness. The children would be oblivious, sunk in the fabric of time. To them a splash of water was an exquisite joy.

In the sky, city swallows were swooping, curving, flinging, always with perfect control as if held by elastic; buzzing flies were returning and returning; the sun was spilling in soft gold, pure good temper at first but, later in the summer, ill tempered and harsh.

She stepped high up through the gate into the university grounds and the faun-woman did not forget the young girl who passed by her with a hungry glance the morning her life took the first of its tangents. It only took a moment. Tangents were everywhere. The woman already knew he would not be arriving. One of them, she couldn't tell if it was he or she, had stepped onto an invisible tangent like a crevice which would lead them onto another circle.

I wasn't going to the university to study. I worked as a waitress at the Professors' Club, not yet ready to save the world. I changed into my waitress uniform, which was pink and three sizes too big for me, and tried to collect trays in a manner that demonstrated I was the professors' intellectual equal. I didn't study at Sydney University for another decade, after I'd had two children. Then, as I walked across Victoria Park, I cried for the girl who had dreamt along the path years before me.

Months later, still a teenager, I lived in New Zealand. I found another dreamer living in a yellow and red and blue room in a wooden house under a mountain. We made love by a river on the Coromandel Peninsula and I gave birth to a golden boy. But I wanted to return home to Australia. I became the Patrick White woman who longed to head out into the void of the inland. The dreamer wanted to stay behind in fertile places.

'I will show you the beauty of dryness,' Lucy said to her young husband.

He had taken her to a valley in his country in a last effort to keep her there. They climbed up to the highest point above the valley, slipping on the muddy path through ferns and rewarewa and rimu, dark green dampness all around. Up and up they went until they scrambled over a final jutting outcrop. Before her was the valley, smooth and pleasant. The hillside opposite seemed to wear a green mink coat decorated with peaceful miniature cows. A stream flowed through the cleared land and the hills beyond were cloaked with dark dripping bush.

'Stay here, where it is fertile and welcoming,' he said. He feared the dryness she spoke of. Dry places were to journey through, not to live in.

'You would grow roses around the door.' Lucy was full of contempt. She could see him imagining a white-walled cottage, red blooms.

He felt her scorn and was hurt but wanted to know her strange spirit, which wouldn't accept comfort. 'We can go to your dry country if that's what you need.'

'I can't live in your country.' Lucy pleaded now, knowing she had what she wanted. 'It's too moist and green. I am not myself here. I'd rot if I stayed. I don't want to settle. I would decay. I need hot wind and dry earth.'

Because he was a writer himself, he couldn't resist the onslaught of words. In a few weeks they had packed their bags, gathered up their child and set off. He watched her joyful dismissal of his grassy country as they left it behind. He feared she would stride out into a place of dust and sticks and forget that a child needs moistness.

'I have a delusion,' Lucy confessed as they headed towards her country. She liked to say all that could be said, write all that could be written. She was angry and impa-tient with the unsayable. 'I found the name of it in a book. It's called an oyster delusion. It means that I rock to and fro like an ordinary brown oyster in the tide of events, occasionally bumping into a rock or two—and then, one day, I produce a pearl of great beauty. You see, I need to go back to my dry inland sea so I can produce my pearl.'

She wanted lizards in the dust, cicadas drumming shrilly after years of silence, hot red winds, the dreaming land beneath and around her. She was a crypto-eagle who aspired to soar, and did in fact in thoughtscape and dream, but her nature could not exist without the warm return to her husband and so neither of them was truly at risk. She remembered the unresentful silence she felt in the dry seabed of her childhood, the crest of trees bent over in obeisance, the dust flirting in the light, the cows milling, threatening with their placid eyes. She smiled, thinking how she would puzzle her husband with the strange things that comforted her.

I want to claim this is entirely true. Of all these writers from my teenage years, Patrick White is the only one I still read—I live in his worlds for long ages. But inhabiting a fictional world, how can I know if I am truthful or not? I did live in the damp fertility of New Zealand in my late adolescence and have a child; my partner and child did come back to Australia with me.

In Australia I became immersed in the stories of knowledge. I began studying and writing at the university that began its life in an old department store. In daily life there were essays to write, a child to take care of, rent and telephone bills to pay. I became the Anaïs Nin woman who recorded her life in her journal almost as soon as she lived it, absorbed in her own being and the creation of her own reality.

Lucy waited at the railway station to change trains. She was returning to the city after a week with her childhood family, which was starting to crumble. It wasn't just that each of them was leaving one by one, but also that the circle of belief that her parents had been able to maintain for so long was fragmenting. Now she feared that even their faith was beginning to seem illusory and their whole world was shimmering like a mirage.

Along the platform, Lucy saw a beautiful girl, nearly a woman, the same age as she was. She had pale skin, dark hair, a European face, but she looked familiar. She wanted to speak to her, but she felt shy, held in by the enclosed world of her childhood.

She looked at her sideways to drink in her mysterious beauty, the beauty she had always wanted; impenetrable eyes, a sensuous, playful mouth, qualities of contradiction and hidden possibilities. How Lucy disliked her own country-girl face. It was a lie. She was not a cheery girl with her feet firmly on the ground.

Lucy found her seat when the train arrived and the beautiful woman sat next to her. She felt a leaping joy, as if she were her lover. She felt selected by the one she wanted to select.

'I've met you before,' the woman said.

'Then I *do* know your face.'

'You read to our writing class. You were a friend of the tutor and you read a piece about making love to a lover who had been away for months.'

The train jolted into movement. It was an old train and they were in a compartment with wooden panelling and leather seats. They were in their own moving world, out of time and place. The conversation was, from the first instant, intense and formal. It was as if they had met for a mythic purpose.

'I have always felt so boyish,' Lucy said. 'I am small-breasted and straight like a boy.'

'How can you say so? When I saw you read I thought you were the most feminine woman I had ever seen. No, not feminine, womanly.'

'But I'm not curvaceous and womanly in my body. I'm not contained mystery like you are.'

The train sped across the plains and up into the mountains. Lucy was far from her childhood, which was crumbling behind her, and not yet immersed in the life of the mind in the city. It was becoming dark and the woman's face glowed in the dimness. The air around them was warm and fecund as they created worlds of intenseness and purity. Outside there was velvety darkness; passengers disappeared, the train disappeared. They moved through the warm night of themselves as they rushed towards their separate futures.

But even in the city no one knew I was really a mysterious, pale, dark-haired woman. I stood in the heat of the busy streets and lost all confidence in a moment. Thoughts and acts had lost their innocence a long time ago and were still accompanied by a witness who registered everything, a shadowy observer. None of the words I wrote all day did anything to dispel that shadowy self; how could I have dispelled myself? It was easier to live an imaginary life.

Edited extract from The Last One Who Remembers *(Allen & Unwin, 1997).*

PATTI MILLER is the author of five books: *Writing Your Life*, *The Last One Who Remembers*, *Child*, *Whatever the Gods Do* and *The Memoir Book* (Allen & Unwin, 2007). She writes articles for newspapers and magazines, works on manuscript development for other writers, and teaches memoir workshops in Australia and overseas. After nearly twenty-five years in the Blue Mountains bringing up two sons, she lives with her partner in Kings Cross—or Potts Point (depending whom she is talking to).

August the 27th

Tobsha Learner

It was a long London summer in the mid-'70s, in a decade of transition, that awkward moment after Vietnam, the Rolling Stones, Bowie and glam rock, Harold Wilson, unionism, Carnaby Street, miniskirts and the Pill. Looming just ahead was punk, Margaret Thatcher, the miners' strike and the blind nationalism of the Falklands. There was an optimism to the times, but then that might have been my youth. I was in the deciding decade myself, a time of life when every experience had that shimmering edge of excitement—the apprehension of the new.

In retrospect, I wonder whether this wasn't the haze we all functioned in back then as a result of the drugs we consumed—marijuana, speed, psychedelics, all of which coloured the drab mock-Tudor suburbs of north-west London like a garish hand-tinted black and white postcard. In those days rebellion hadn't been swallowed up, regurgitated and branded by the advertising world—we were teenagers who strove to be individual, to stand out, not to disappear in a generic sea of denim. I made my own clothes—skin-tight paisley maxidresses with elaborate necklines that pushed my breasts up into an innocent bondage; pill-box hats with net veils; shiny patent-leather platform shoes; striped crocheted woollen dresses (one of which my mother, appalled by its holey translucency, threatened to cut up with a pair of scissors). At thirteen I had suddenly grown breasts, my teeth had been straightened and I had gone from being an unprepossessing buck-toothed, skinny pubescent to a striking, voluptuous teenager.

Now, at sixteen, I was fierce, uncompromising, opinionated and bursting with a newly discovered sexuality that must have been intimidating as well as daunting to my youngish mother and my stepmother—both virile women themselves.

My father, a mathematician who drove a motorcycle, sported a beard and wore John Lennon glasses, was a youthful forty-year-old. When he picked me up from school on the bike the girls used to ask me who my boyfriend was. Like I said, it was London in the '70s—pre-AIDS—and parenting was not the intensive grooming it can be now. My generation wasn't brought up—we were thrown up, let loose, left to forge our own mistakes, and some of us survived and many of us didn't.

My parents were left-wing Australians, part of the wave that had fled the repressive Australia of the 1950s—Prime Minister Menzies' Australia, then a post-war, bleak anti-intellectual wasteland. My father had taken his doctorate at Cambridge, where I was born, followed shortly by my brother, then my sister later in London. We moved temporarily to America where my father spent a two-year sabbatical at the Berkeley campus in California in the early '60s. My mother used to tell a story of taking me to a folk music concert as a tiny child during which Joan Baez introduced a young singer called Bob Dylan— one of those family anecdotes when the personal brushes up against the mythical but it gives you a sense of my parents: liberal, intellectual, playing out the intensity of student life in that era. They were young—twenty-four when they had me—optimistic, culturally curious and lucky enough to find themselves in the right places at the right historical times: California in the early Kennedy years, London in the swinging '60s.

After the sabbatical my family returned to England. When I was eight my parents went through a sad, and perhaps inevitable, divorce. My father's leaving was traumatic for me; I have very strong memories of wrapping myself up in an old coat he had left behind—still imbued with his scent, it transported me right back into his arms. At the time I recall being enraptured by that B-grade film *The Parent Trap* (the original), convinced that if I applied the same strategies the twin sisters used to bring their estranged parents together, then I, too, might be able to magically reconstruct the family—only it wouldn't be my dysfunctional, tense and unusual family but a Disney one with calm, undramatic parents who adored each other and with no shouting behind locked doors. All the wishing and spell-making changed nothing but my parents remained friends and my mother got custody.

My father remarried and became a weekend dad (Sunday lunches at the local Wimpy Bar), while my mother had her own relationships. Unknown to me, this separation from my father was to foreshadow the tragedy that was to come—the illogical physics of emotional history: sometimes the timeline folds back on itself to give you a faint sense of future events. I have now lived long enough to observe this phenomenon—but what can one do with such information?

But let me return to that hazy hot London August. Earlier that year my mother had gone back to Australia to work for Gough Whitlam for twelve months and had decided my father should take custody for that period of time. She sold the house to my father and stepmother, who had moved in three months before. At last now there was the semblance of a nuclear family, although unconventional, and my father and his wife adapted to the chaotic challenges of dealing with three teenagers (my brother was fifteen, my sister thirteen), the two oldest of whom were already fiercely independent.

There was a severe drought in London that summer. The government had posters up encouraging people to share bathwater and there was already a hose-pipe ban, which was awkward for me because I was growing a quantity of marijuana in the back garden and my bed of pot was swiftly becoming a green island surrounded by patchy dry lawn. This wasn't behind my father's back— he smoked occasionally himself—but these were innocent times, tolerant times. I suspect that future generations will view us with the same puritan eye the Victorians must have reserved for their liberal grand-parents, who still remembered the ribald hedonism of the eighteenth century.

I had spent most of that August holidaying in Provence, France, with my father's cousin Saku. Saku came from the Protestant side of the family (as opposed to my mother's Jewish side) and was half Indian and half English. Exotic and striking, she had been a beatnik in the early '60s and had dropped out of the drama course at the Guildhall School to marry a Swiss sculptor in a small border village near Geneva. They lived in a commune originally set up by an American couple fleeing the repressiveness of President McCarthy's America.

I adored Saku and her husband and had spent several previous summers escaping into their artistic, hippy lifestyle; skinny-dipping in the rivers of Provence, trekking through the Cévennes mountains, sleeping in their basic cottages—unrenovated stone huts with no running water. Paradise for a completely urbanised teenager—I suspect some of these experiences have shaped me into the pantheist I am today.

This is where I was on the night of the 26th, sleeping in Saku's remote shepherd's hut in the Cévennes. That night I had a dream my mother had died. It was so realistic I woke up weeping, absolutely convinced it was true—perhaps it was a secret anxiety about her being so far away in Australia, perhaps it was a premonition, either way I never acted upon it. In those days, phoning internationally was a big event and besides I was nowhere near a telephone. I dismissed the dream as nonsense and went back to London the next day as planned to my father and stepmother.

At the time I had a Danish boyfriend—a classical guitarist moonlighting as a barman at the Marquee Club in Soho. He was twenty-four years old and now, when I think of the eight-year age difference between us and despite my precociousness at the time, I find myself doubting his integrity. Nevertheless, reunited after a month apart, it was with him I was making love that summer afternoon on the floor of my bedroom. And now, in the motion of standing naked, lifting myself away and up from the carpet, I noticed in the blur of post-coital consciousness two odd events taking place outside my bedroom window. Firstly, the neighbour, who had a long-standing feud with my mother, was walking down our front garden path for the first time in ten years; and secondly, she was flanked by two policemen. My initial thought was that the police might be arriving to raid the illicit crop in my back garden, and I had just pointed this out to my boyfriend when there was a heavy knocking on my bedroom door. 'Don't come in!' I yelled out because we were both still nude, but my stepmother walked in regardless, followed by my sister.

I think I first knew something was dramatically wrong when I saw my sister's face. It was white, completely white—blank, in deep shock.

In a monotone, my stepmother told me that my father had been killed. Also in shock, she appeared scarily collected.

There was a pause, a tiny silence. Then I let out one single scream—a primal howl that seemed to shoot down into one's most primal fear to haul up grief that had been unimaginable until that moment. Even now I find it hard to describe that moment, that animal shout of outrage and horror in the face of sudden and irreversible loss. Those of you who have experienced it will know that howl, that bellowing instinct.

After that I became very calm. Wrapping my dressing

gown around me, I went downstairs with my stepmother and confronted the policemen.

It must be an unspeakably terrible job to be the uniformed messenger of death, but here they were, ridiculously English and ridiculously ill prepared. In those nightmarish situations you hang on to impossible notions—mistaken identity, the absurd hope that he might not be dead but injured. But my father, a meticulous man, kept all of his personal details in his wallet, including blood type, age, name and address. Such evidence was indisputable, even to an impassioned sixteen-year-old who wanted more than anything in the world for the facts to be wrong.

He'd skidded into a lamppost on his motorcycle for no apparent reason and had died instantly. One of those freak accidents where the possibility of being killed outright as opposed to being brain damaged or merely ending up with a broken arm was incalculable—even for a mathematician.

I remember cross-questioning the policemen; how ridiculously young they appeared close up, unnerved by the emotional maelstrom they now found themselves in. It must have seemed bizarre—the teenage girl naked under her dressing gown, the young stepmother mute, the older foreign boyfriend standing around helpless, the little sister weeping.

Somewhere in the house the phone rang. It was the local doctor offering Valium to the recently bereaved: this was the level of bereavement counselling in the mid-'70s. In England in those days any display of extreme emotion was considered embarrassing and something to be done in the privacy of one's home (a notion of which my dramatic Jewish mother always seemed wonderfully oblivious). I think I told the doctor to fuck off.

At the time my brother was out with a friend, so somebody rang his friend's father, who arranged for my brother to be driven back to the house. It was left to me to tell him as my traumatised stepmother was in no state to be authoritative.

For decades I carried the memory of this as one of my most painful; the experience of having to tell my fifteen-year-old brother that his father had just died. To my surprise, only a few years ago, my brother told me he had already guessed by the time he'd arrived back at the house. But the agony of that memory has not dissipated: my brother, so streetwise and skinny in his long-collared shirt, his platform boots, his tight flared trousers, so cocksure, felled by this moment. It was in our entrance hall, the loss of a future innocence falling away from those ridiculously slender adolescent shoulders as he covered his face with his hands, his elbows resting on the mantelpiece.

With my stepmother in deep shock, my siblings both grieving, the household was now minus a competent adult; I found myself walking around to the house of the woman I had regarded as my second mother, the mother of my best friend. This was momentous as I had been banned from the house following my recent teenage rebellion but instinct carried me around the corner nevertheless and into the second household of my childhood.

I think they must have known the moment they opened the front door. Any transgression I might or might not have committed was instantly forgiven. My best friend's mother walked back to the house with me, where she put the kettle on and comforted my step-mother. Grief has blurred the memory, but I remember that at one point we were all sitting around the kitchen table, drinking tea, when somebody asked the time, and we all looked up at the electric kitchen clock only to discover that the hands were running backwards and now stood at the time of my father's death a few hours earlier. There was most probably a prosaic explanation but in those minutes of great unfurling tragedy you look for meaning in the most mundane places—like the mystery of his cat, who went missing.

There had been two cats in the house—one belonged to my stepmother, the other was my father's. This one disappeared that afternoon, never to be seen again, as if the animal had somehow sensed the finality of my father's departure that morning, an apparently ordinary depar-ture barely noticed by anyone else.

And if I had known the cataclysmic effect his death would have on both myself and my family, then I might have taken more notice, might have been more acutely present in the moment; but I was sixteen, extraordinar-ily wilful and independent and defiant in that frightening way sixteen-year-olds can be, believing as they do in their own invincibility and, poignantly, immortality.

My father's death changed my life—of this I have no doubt. He was the linchpin to so many things—an understated patriarch who might have provided a con-tinuity of domesticity, the likes of which my siblings and I had not experienced since my parents' divorce. Within six months our family house was sold by my stepmother, and I was squatting in Harlesden with five men as my flatmates. My sister was taken to Canberra (it was argued by my paternal grandfather that the youngest should be with her mother), followed a year later by my brother, and two years after that I also migrated to Melbourne. It is possible that if my father hadn't been killed our family might have stayed living together in London. More importantly, the experience of his death gave me an entirely different perspective on the fragility of life; on determinism and free will. The seemingly arbitrary circumstances of his accident had a profound effect on my belief system.

Later that summer, on a train trip—the back views of English gardens flying past, the idiosyncratic microcosms of other people's lives that always seem to force you to reflect on your own—I vowed always to live life for each moment and to live it to the fullest. It's the kind of philosophy you'd expect a sixteen-year-old to adopt, but mine was underpinned by the visceral understanding that it could be snatched away so suddenly, in a death that might have no meaning except the one projected upon it by others. I don't know whether I have succeeded.

TOBSHA LEARNER's plays include *Wolf*, *The Glass Mermaid*, *Fidelity*, *Witchplay* and *Miracles*. Her books include *Quiver*, *The Witch of Cologne*, *Tremble* and, more recently, the novel *Soul* (HarperCollins, 2006). She has sold more than 200,000 books internationally and divides her time between Australia, the UK and the USA. Tobsha's website is www.tobshalearner.com.

'Dear Jacinta'

Jacinta Tynan

I wrote a letter to myself the day I turned thirteen. It was written on Anne of Green Gables stationery and wasn't to be opened until the same day ten years later, when I would be twenty-three. When I would be a woman. '*I got my first bra today. I bet you have several now,*' was one of the first things I wrote.

I didn't actually get the bra *that* day. That was poetic licence. I thought it would sound better when I opened the letter at twenty-three and looked back on myself, remembering fondly how new it had all seemed and how daunting, remembering the frightening time when my breasts had started to form and I would have done anything to stunt their growth, to hide my puberty from the world.

Anyway, whatever day it was (in fact, I think I was twelve), it was big. Mum took me to Barter's at Miranda Fair, distinct for its whispered silence and shiny cream lino floors that squeaked when women (always and only women) moved through. There were rows and rows of bras big enough to fit my fist—both my fists—and some even accommodated my palms spread wide. I know because I attempted it in complete fascination and awe.

I preferred the haberdashery section, with its endless wheels of ribbons in every colour. We had to stick with navy blue ones for primary school followed by white for high school, but I always chose the satin ones, thick and tied in a long bow at the end of my plaits, which I kept until I was fourteen when Rachael Miller pointed out, 'Don't you know plaits are for primary school?' Then I asked Mum to pull the front back in a bow, leaving the rest long like in *Little House on the Prairie*, until Tara Boyd got a mohawk and, not that I wanted one of those (she was suspended for it), but it inspired me to shave the back of my head and flop the rest of my hair over it like the other girls were doing.

But that wasn't until Year 9. When everyone was wearing bras. In Year 7 (actually, it was Year 6, but I wasn't admitting that to anyone), there was only me.

I hadn't asked Mum to get me a bra. I would much rather have gone without. But she must have noticed I was wearing singlets (yes, plural) under my school uniform and keeping my blazer done up in summer and my arms crossed at all times. She picked me up from Miranda station after school and said, 'We'll just pop into Barter's', and the first I knew of it was when she told the nice old lady with the purple hair who smelt of Johnson's Baby Powder that 'we need a bra for my daughter', her hand resting encouragingly on the nape of my neck. 'It's her first one.'

'Oh,' the purple-haired lady cooed. 'You'll want a trainer then. How lovely.' And I was ushered into a curtained change room with a faded blue velvet chair, where she measured my chest with a swift hand and a tape measure, nipped out for a few minutes and came back with two tiny things—one in skin colour and one in pale pink (I loved the pink one instantly). She taught me how to fasten them at the front. Double A. Easy. No one had ever seen me naked before, not since I'd needed a bra, but the Barter's lady seemed indifferent, fluffing around me as if she'd seen it all before. All I cared about was that no one would spot it through my uniform. That would be my worst nightmare.

I got away with it for a good year and then I must have become complacent and let my guard down because I was sitting cross-legged in the playground one lunchtime when Gwen Adams and Fiona McCarron crept up behind me, yanked down my summer uniform zipper and flicked my offending bra strap. 'She's got a bra! I knew it. Jacinta's wearing a braa-aa!' I wanted to run and lock myself in a toilet cubicle and never come out. Instead, I decided to be mature and reached down, coolly sliding the zipper back up and informing the sniggering group I was sitting in, 'Well, you'll have one, too, one day. It's natural', rolling my eyes. But I wasn't proud. I was mortified. Having boobs was the worst thing you could wish on a girl. It meant social exclusion. At least until Year 9.

I didn't tell anyone I had my periods either. Not for at least five years. I didn't write about them in my letter, even though I well and truly had them at thirteen, because I was still in denial. Mum was well prepared. I was her second daughter (and two younger sisters were yet to reach puberty) so she was armed. She bought me a special pencil case (a pink and green striped one) and stocked it with Modess Sanitary Pads, instructing me to use them when I first saw blood and come to her when I ran out. I had no idea what she was talking about. I was eleven. But my mum was wise and I had already cottoned on to the fact that there were some things women had to bear in silence and so I must just go with it. I had heard the Girl Guides talking about it when I was a Brownie. They called it 'your monthly' and shared stories of its horror and inconvenience. I just wondered how I was going to do ballet with those things shoved between my legs.

When they came, The Monthlies, I never did ask Mum for a refill because I was too humiliated. I just pilfered the stock that was in the bathroom cupboard and hid them up my jumper at school or in my Art History textbook when it was time for a change. Some of the girls were onto me, though. Leanne O'Leary and her faithful pre-pubescent entourage bailed me up in the locker room and cut to the chase. 'There's a rumour going around you've got your rags.' ('Rags' was the other word for it, although we called it 'George' and some girls' mothers also called it 'The Curse'.)

'I do *not*!' I burst out laughing at the mere absurd suggestion, my hands sweating as I gripped tighter to the pocket that concealed my Modess stash. *Please don't see it. Please don't see it.*

'You can tell,' Leanne went on. 'You walk like a woooman.' And she did some silly teasing twirl and I said, 'What would *you* know, anyway?' and bolted to the bathroom where I successfully completed my pad-change manoeuvre and then burst into tears. Forget about tampons, which would have helped keep the whole thing a secret. I hadn't even heard of them. Not until

Year 12, when Elizabeth Bell-Ross gave everyone lessons. By then, periods were all the rage.

I also asked myself in my letter about love. '*Have you been in love yet?*' I wrote.

Unlike my breasts and my periods, love was still in front of me. I fell head over heels in love at fifteen.

Simon was fifteen as well and loved me, too. Thank God. In fact, he loved me first and told me so in a friend's back garden, where we'd all gone for a party after our Year 10 formal was cancelled as punishment for two girls who got caught sniffing deodorant on our history excursion to Canberra. We'd gone to see New Parliament House under construction and check out the War Memorial but we were bussed home early after the girls got high by spraying their pillows and inhaling. I think that's how it worked. So after a meeting with our parents—all of them, not just those of the deodorant offenders—the formal was called off and we went to Imogen Wilkinson's house instead, where Simon (someone else's formal partner) told me he loved me.

'You can't possibly love me, you don't even know me. And anyway, you can't be in love at fifteen!' I reprimanded him. But he was and so was I, and he took me on a date to the Old Spaghetti Factory and kissed me at the Opera House where, at ten, I'd decided I would have my first kiss, and he walked beside me on the gutter side of the road. He was wise, my first love. At sixteen he insisted I look at myself in the mirror every day and tell myself 'I am beautiful'. 'Yeah, right!' I'd scoffed. But he was totally serious. He was a rugby halfback and got pissed with his mates but he loved me like there was no tomorrow and wanted me to see why.

Maybe he knew he wouldn't be around forever to tell me himself because he wasn't. By nineteen, Simon was gone, hit by an oncoming car and killed instantly. The only boy I'd ever loved—the only person outside of my family whom I'd *chosen* to love and who'd chosen me— left me without warning. I knew it at the time, woke up with a start at the precise moment, it turned out, crying for him, pining for him. When they broke it to me the next morning, Mum and some of his friends, Dad misheard and thought they were telling me he'd met someone else, that that was why I was doubled over, wailing, 'No, No, No', so he rubbed my back and told me there were plenty more fish in the sea.

Simon didn't mean beautiful as in pretty when he told me to look in the mirror, although he thought that was the case, too—he meant beautiful on the inside. He knew me better than anyone and so he knew that I gave myself a hard time, the hardest of all. It didn't help that I was white. It was tough growing up white. Especially in The Shire.

Being white was a darn sight better than being a wog, that's for sure. It would've been hell being a Greek or Italian kid in the southern suburbs of Sydney in the '70s. Their parents ran the greengrocers, the fish and chip shop and the corner store, and their mothers met them at the school gate wearing headscarves and speaking another language. They stuck together in the playground away from the Anglo bullies, eating salami and sticky cakes. If you didn't have blonde hair and blue eyes in Caringbah, you had no chance. But to be white as in having skin so fair it was almost luminescent, skin that would never change colour no matter how hard I tried (and I tried), was the next worst thing. Red was easy and slightly less conspicuous than white because at least it looked like I was giving it a go, but red was painful and only ever met a sorry end in rows of blisters and great flakes of skin peeling off me like scales before it returned to the wan hue that got me into trouble in the first place.

Once, when I was sixteen, I went brown. After an entire summer of careful concentration, precision-timing my exposure like a Christmas pig, my skin started to look a little golden, and I had never been happier. I couldn't wait to get back to school where I could start Year 11 with a bang, tanned and fitting in. But when I stretched out my legs next to the other girls against the science lab wall, I felt like a fraud. Their brownness was long-lasting—tans that came naturally and went beyond the first layer of skin. It was in their blood. And they weren't even from Yowie Bay. Mine was hard-won and feeble and motivated by self-loathing. It was all over by the first weekend of term anyway, my glowing moment as transient as the summer. Or not even that.

To have luminous white skin in a land of crochet bikinis was torture. This was the birthplace of *Puberty Blues* and I was letting the side down. I was never going to be a surfie girl, didn't want to be, but it would have been nice to at least be able to blend in. Instead, I was ridiculed.

At swimming training, where I looked sickly in my royal-blue crossback Speedo one-piece, I overheard a boy protest (it wasn't that hard to overhear—he created a scene right in front of me) at being on the starting block next to the 'ghost'. I cut an article out of *The Sydney Morning Herald* about parents forcing their children to do sport and stuck it on the fridge, and I was let off the hook.

I couldn't wait to get out of The Shire. Somewhere, I was sure, there was a land where brown skin didn't equate with kudos and birthday party invitations. I concentrated on ballet, where I could wear—had no choice but to wear—those thick pink opaque tights that homogenised all of us in a land where posture was king and one could stand out with an arabesque. Acting classes were non-pigment-sensitive, too. At fourteen, I took myself off on the train to the Australian Theatre for Young People (where that Nicole Kidman from *BMX Bandits* had gone), wearing KingGee overalls dyed pink with multiple ribbons in my hair and earrings made from plastic farm animals like Molly from *A Country Practice*, and forgot that I had no tan.

I had freckles, too, lots of them. I tried blotting them out with Mum's Revlon foundation but then it dawned on me that maybe freckles could work to my advantage if I could just get enough of them because they could all join together for an all-over glow. Nicole Kidman had freckles and she was on the cover of *Dolly*.

One of the arty types from school asked me to pose for her photography assignment so she could enter it in the *Dolly* covergirl competition and I shot back, 'Are ya right?' and bolted up the corridor laughing. It's not that I didn't want to. It's just I didn't want them all saying I was up myself. Sarah Nursey was a *Dolly* covergirl, for God's sake. I saw her in the flesh once with the Ascham girls at Edgecliff station and I was mesmerised. Curly blonde hair, piercing blue eyes, caramel skin. She had made it and she was only sixteen.

'*Hope you're pretty because you're certainly not now*', I'd written in my letter at thirteen. '*Forever trying: sunbaked in a bikini today, growing your hair but addicted to chocolate so have bad skin and cellulite.*'

Mum tried to teach us about beauty, me and my three sisters. We were each given Clinique facial soap on our twelfth birthday, plus toner and moisturiser. 'Pull your shoulders back,' Mum reminded us constantly. 'And stop talking through your nose.' We had elocution lessons to be sure of that. But as much as Simon told me I was beautiful, I was never going to believe it.

I didn't think I was fat, though. But suspicion was cast that I was on a diet when I almost fainted in Ancient History and Sister McKay ordered me to the infirmary classroom for a good lie-down. It was actually period pain but I couldn't own up to that because I was fifteen and still the only one who knew I had my periods. So they sent the school counsellor to my bedside, the same one who'd consoled me when Nanna died after being too selfless to tell anyone she had a lump in her breast.

'What did you have for breakfast?' Mrs Connolly asked me, concern etched on her face.

'Weet-bix?' I responded with a question mark because I wasn't sure if that's what she wanted to hear. It wasn't. She gasped. 'That's simply not enough for a growing girl like you!' and what followed was a lecture on loving

myself just the way I am and how to be any thinner
would be just plain unhealthy, not to mention unbecom-
ing, and from now on I must have two pieces of vegemite
toast as well. I told her it was *two* Weet-bix with sugar on
top, but she hushed me and insisted I come and see her
if I ever experienced feelings of self-doubt. About me or
my body.

Anorexia was the word Mrs Connolly had not been
game to utter. We called it 'Anna'. I knew what it was but
I was never in danger of getting it. Not like one school
friend, who ended up in a special Anna hospital where
they watched you eat and weighed you day and night like
cattle. I went to visit her, all the way over on the North
Shore, and was horrified to see her looking worse than
when she went in. Vacant eyes, sallow, and on a drip. She
sat on the end of the bed and kicked her legs because,
she reckoned, if they were going to force-feed her, at
least she could exercise to keep the weight off. She was
so much prettier when she had a body, and so much more
lively. Couldn't she see that?

I didn't write about sex in my letter because I didn't
know what it was.

Simon and I never slept in the same bed. He came on
my family's caravan holidays where he slept on a collaps-
ible bed in the annexe with my brothers, just as when he
came to stay at home he slept in Dad's study or in one
of my brothers' rooms.

I learnt about sex in the caravan park. Well, I learnt
that something like it existed.

It was the Panel Van Convention at Valla Park near Nambucca Heads that first got me thinking. There were rows of them, in colours I'd never seen on our family cars. Our Valiant station wagon had been brown, the VW Kombi was blue. These panel vans were orange and purple, black, lemon—there was even a rainbow-coloured one with bubble windows. They were parked with boots open like giant jaws so you could see inside— a privilege usually only bestowed on anyone lucky enough to be invited in, like the girls hanging ten nearby with Farrah Fawcett hair and terry-towelling short shorts. I could appreciate this was a once in a lifetime opportunity and I couldn't get enough. I stared at the carpet on the walls, the built-in beds with their purple satin sheets, which matched the curtains, the ghetto-blasters, playing Marvin Gaye, embedded in padded white vinyl like in the Joyce Mayne catalogue. One van had a decoupage of girls with no tops glued to the roof.

'Feel free to get in,' one panel vanner said to me as he polished his bumper bar, which shone enough that I could see my own reflection. He had long hair and a KISS T-shirt. I hated KISS. I found the whole extended tongue idea off-putting and preferred singers whose faces I could see, like Cat Stevens, Neil Diamond and Billy Joel. I loved Carole King, too, and could sing every word of the *Evita* soundtrack, and *Cats*. Dad bought me a cord-less microphone for my fourteenth birthday so I could hook it up to the stereo and sing along as if I was starring in the musical, which was almost as good as the real thing. But not KISS. KISS was for offbeat people. Like panel vanners, and that girl in my year who wore the oversized crucifix necklace with no Jesus. KISS was for people who had sex. So I declined.

One girl lost her virginity in Year 12 and no one would speak to her. It was pretty off. Not even the Day Girls were doing that. At my Catholic boarding school, I was a weekly boarder who went home on Friday nights, so I floated somewhere in between the very distinct worlds of Day Girl and Boarder, and belonged in neither camp.

The Day Girls were a different breed. They went to nightclubs and wore eyeliner to school. They didn't do their homework and they sunbaked with their uniforms unzipped and baby oil lathered across their shoulders. They smoked with the Scots boys, their uniforms hoisted up, behind Edgecliff station. They pashed them but they didn't have sex with them. So they said. When they invited me out one Saturday night in Year 10 I didn't want to go, but I had to. Who else was I going to hang out with?

Mum dropped me off at the nightclub in Paddington. She thought it was better that way—at least she would know where I was. I wore my pink bubble shorts from Sportsgirl, blue and white striped tights with black flat winklepickers and I can't remember what on top, but I know it wasn't a bra, which is what the Day Girls were wearing. When my eyes adjusted to the darkness inside Paddo's, there was Chantelle Duponte in a pointy black bra like two ice-cream cones, a black vinyl miniskirt and fingerless gloves, dancing like Madonna in a cage. I thought she was part of the floor show, that this was how she paid the school fees, but then I noticed the other Day Girls were in bras as well, their fringes matted in knots, their lips painted black, and I wanted to die.

I bought a vodka and orange with the $10 Mum gave me, and skulked to the bathroom where I waited for time to pass. Waited until 10.30 pm, when Mum would be out the front in the Kombi to whisk me back home to Yowie Bay and Carole King.

After that I went out with the Boarders. I fitted in no better there at the Royal Oak, where the girls all wore fob chains, Liberty-print blouses and family signet rings, but at least I was safe. And at least I had Simon. For a bit.

The thing is, I wasn't sure what you were supposed to do at pubs. There didn't seem much to talk about when we were at school all week together anyway, and the country boys we hung out with, in their moleskins, striped shirts and jumpers around their waists, only seemed to want to drink. Lots. It was better when we went to the Midnight Oil concert. At least there I could dance and sing along, even though I couldn't make out Peter Garrett. He was way off in the distance, a gyrating stick figure. One of Simon's tall farmer friends hoisted me onto his shoulders so I could see. 'US forces give the no-o-od . . . na na na na na na na na na na na na na na . . .' But then a security guard yanked me off and we were all sent outside. Hanging outside the Horden Pavilion with nothing to do except smoke. And I didn't smoke. I couldn't wait for the night to end.

I couldn't wait for my teenage years to end, either, so I could get on with this business of life. So far it all seemed like a waiting game to me. That's why I wrote the letter, I guess. To take me forward to a time when I could decide what's what instead of having to spend my Saturday nights at the Gresham, counting down the minutes in the toilets on my fake Gucci watch from Bali until it was time to go home to my Jane Austen novel, so at least I could say I'd been out. To a time when I could be a journalist for a women's magazine, or host my own TV show, or act in feature films. When I could be who I wanted instead of always having to hang on. '*Are you on TV yet?*' I had asked of myself at twenty-three.

When I started at uni, I got a rude shock. There were girls called Women's Officers who told us we had to stand up for our gender—it had never occurred to me we'd been missing out. There were drawers of condoms we were encouraged to use but I still wasn't sure what for. A lesbian tried to chat me up and I ran from the uni bar in tears. There were B&S balls with people throwing up on the dancefloor and girls squatting next to the blokes pissing against a barbed-wire fence, their drop-waisted skirts hoisted up. My parents got divorced after my dad moved in with someone else. And in that first year, when I was still a teenager, I experienced death. There was no mention of any of that in my letter at thirteen. That I would know love then have it snatched away. And I soon came to realise it was what was *not* in that letter that said the most. Beyond my first bra, beyond falling in love and being on TV, I could not have predicted any of it.

JACINTA TYNAN is a journalist, author and columnist. Her first book, *Good Man Hunting* (Random House, 2005), has been published in three languages. She is a news presenter with *Sky News Australia* and writes a weekly column for Sydney's *Sunday Telegraph* newspaper, before which she was a national news presenter/reporter at ABC TV. Jacinta's journalism career has also included presenting ABC TV News in Darwin, being the weather girl for WIN TV Canberra and the Thredbo Snow Reporter. She was inspired to write by her great-uncle, John O'Grady (Nino Culotta), author of the 1960s bestseller, *They're a Weird Mob*. She is also a keen actor, having written and starred in two short films and acted on stage in productions including *The Vagina Monologues* at Sydney's Ensemble Theatre. Jacinta is also a patron of the SISTER2sister Program, which mentors disadvantaged teenage girls. Jacinta's website is www jacintatynan.com.

Humiliation
and Lust

Leigh Redhead

The indignity started when I was ten. I woke up one morning with tits.

By tits I'm not talking proper breasts, more like puffy protuberances, not big enough for a training bra but sufficient for me to wonder what the hell they were doing there. I was horrified.

'No one will notice,' said Mum. Yeah, right. I already stood out. I was the new girl at Stanwell Park, a coastal town south of Sydney, and the kids already thought I was weird. Our house was a ramshackle rental decorated with batik wall-hangings and seagrass matting, and Mum and her much younger boyfriend listened to jazz and grew dope plants down the side. All the other girls lived in two-storey brick homes and their bedrooms were chock-full of pink ruffles, Barbie townhouses and horse posters. They had actual fathers, ate white bread and were all called Amanda. My friendship with the Amandas was provisional. They'd deign to play with me as long as

I took the part of the wicked witch to their fairy
princesses. I didn't really mind—as far as I was concerned
the witch had a greater dramatic range.

It was sports day, so I had to wear the school T-shirt
that always cracked Mum and her boyfriend up when
they were stoned: 'Stanwell Park—All the Way Straight'.
The top was bad news, and not just because of the motto.
My new breasts made the soft fabric pinch into a line
that ran from nipple to nipple. I tried to ignore it and
repeated what my mother had told me as I lined up for
morning assembly. No one will notice. No one will
notice. It'll be okay.

And it was. Until the head Amanda, a psycho bitch
who'd informed me on my first day of school that the
elasticised front panel of my sundress made me look like
a 'pregnant goat', pointed and screamed.

'Boobies!'

I kept my face straight. Maybe she wasn't talking
about—no, wait, she was. As the whole school watched,
she crouched down in front of me, tugged at my T-shirt,
pursed her lips and made a wet, slurping sound.

'Mummy! Let me suck your titties, give baby some
milk!'

Waves of laughter swelled, broke and washed through
the crowd, from Sixth Class to Kinder. Even the teachers sniggered and I could've sworn the Headmaster put
his hand over his mouth and pretended to cough. Embarrassed wasn't the word. Hot blood flooded my cheeks and
I looked to the sky. I had become obsessed with UFOs
and hoped this would be the moment space aliens finally
swooped down to claim me.

It wasn't.

My mum eventually got spooked by the proximity of the Lucas Heights nuclear reactor, so we moved to Elands, a small mountain town on the mid-north coast of New South Wales with a large alternative community. I'd never lived in the country and imagined it would be just like an Enid Blyton book with quaint stone cottages, rolling green fields and an abundance of bluebells, buttercups and hollyhocks, whatever the hell those were. I'd have loads of friends who'd be just like the kids out of the Famous Five, and in between catching smugglers and international jewel thieves, we'd have wonderful picnics on chequered tablecloths with sandwiches and cake.

I was wrong. The roads cut out of the mountain were steep and dusty, the bush dense and tangled, and instead of a historic cottage we lived in a converted bus. There was a complete absence of any kind of cake, but if you were lucky you might happen upon the occasional slab of black bread smeared with tahini and gritty white honey.

And the other kids . . .

On my first day of school I realised there were two factions. The hippies, progeny of the alternative types who were rapidly taking over the town, and the straights, sons and daughters of farmers and the folks who had worked at the timber mill before it shut down. I knew I belonged with the former. I lived in a bus, for God's sake, with a canvas bag for a shower and a toilet that was little more than a hole in the ground. My mum was even doing rebirthing with their mums, but it didn't matter— they couldn't see past the clothes.

The hippy kids wore sarongs, faded and laddered Velvet Underground T-shirts, ripped jeans, ultra-short denim skirts and Hawaiian shirts knotted at the waist. They went barefoot, had wild manes that smelt of sassafras (the herbal cure for head lice that never actually worked), multiple earrings and scraps of leather around their wrists and ankles. After a year of trying to fit in with the Amandas I wore my mouse-brown hair centre-parted and tucked neatly behind my ears and my wardrobe consisted of pink, frilly outfits from Best & Less that made me look like a girly little swot. The cool kids immediately pegged me as a straight.

So did the straights. Farmer's daughters Bethy and Kim let me play with them, but it was the Amandas all over again.

'Me and Kim are the prettiest princesses,' Bethy told me. 'We have the best jewels and the biggest castle. The king that's your dad is a poor king. You live in a shack.'

Whatever. I was over playing princesses and secretly tracked the hippy kids out of the corner of my eye. They always roamed around in a gang, stealing off into the scrub at the back of the school, hiding under demountable classrooms, whispering secrets, exchanging knowing looks. I just knew they were up to no good and, goddamn it, I wanted a piece of the action, which was weird. Despite my unconventional upbringing I'd always been such a nice girl, polite and eager to please. My favourite activity had been reading quietly and I would have done anything for a gold star, smiley stamp or plain old pat on the head.

But the hormones were beginning to bubble up, bringing with them an intense yet nebulous desire for naughtiness. I wasn't sure what form this bad behaviour would eventually take, but I'd already started sneaking sips of my mum's Green Ginger Wine and had noticed that whenever I gazed upon Dr Who's pouty teenage assistant Adric, watched the Hot Gossip dancers prance around on the *Kenny Everett Video Show* in their suspenders and stockings, or saw Joan Jett's 'I Love Rock 'n' Roll' on *Countdown* (we could only pick up the ABC), something stirred.

The leader of the hippy kids was a girl named Una. A year older than the others, she had waist-length black hair and underneath her tight, tie-dyed singlet her boobs were bigger than mine. Kim saw me looking and her face curdled.

'Una's a slut, she's done it.' She made a circle with her fingers and thumb and poked another finger through so I'd get the drift. If she'd meant to turn me off it hadn't worked—I was even more intrigued. I belonged with the hippy kids, but how to make them accept me?

I decided I needed a bike. Although their folks were officially 'alternative' they all had bikes, brand-new BMXs bought with the proceeds of parents' dope plantations, and every Saturday at the local market they'd gather then take off down some dusty road, too far for me to follow on foot. My mum was on the pension and didn't have a crop, so I pestered my dad in Sydney, and when he unveiled the bike at Christmas my heart sank. It was a dragster. Wide handlebars, elongated seat, daisy basket on the front. Impossibly cool and retro now, but social death in the early '80s. Still, it was better than nothing. I thought.

One Saturday I found them down a rutted laneway bordered by two scrubby paddocks, building a ramp.

I peddled closer, affecting nonchalance, completely unaware that my long floral dress was draped unflatteringly over the dragster's long seat. Stafford, a skinny dude with a rat's tail at the back of his head, saw me and pointed.

'Hey, look everyone, Leigh's got an erection!'

I wasn't exactly sure what an erection was, but had a feeling it was something rude to do with dicks. The embarrassment was so acute, tears pricked my eyes. I skidded, did a 180 and tore off back down the lane, legs pumping.

Not long after that I got my period for the first time. Some girls looked forward to it, apparently. Not me. Word on the street was no one else had theirs, which would make me even more of a freak, and I could just imagine all the fresh opportunities for humiliation that awaited me. These started on the first day. As if the dark brown blood and the pain like a knife stabbing my guts weren't bad enough, there was Mum's reaction. When she caught me rinsing out my knickers she was happy.

'Wow,' she hugged me and rubbed my back in the way of hippies since time immemorial, 'this is wonderful. Some amazing things have happened since we moved to this place!'

Then she handed me a sanitary pad the size and density of a house brick, and drove me thirty k's to the nearest town so we could use the public phone to call my dad and deliver the joyous news.

'Some amazing things have happened since we moved to this place!' she told him before handing me the receiver. I remained silent until she nudged me and nodded encouragingly.

'Uh, I got my periods,' I said.

'Gee,' my dad sounded as mortified as I felt. 'Congratulations.'

The next day Mum went to the library and borrowed every single book of the human reproduction and 'now you're a woman' variety for me. I thought the twenty or so volumes were unnecessary. I may not have known what an erection was, exactly, but I knew about sex. We'd lived in one-room apartments for years and my mother had never been the quiet type. Also, every time we were unfortunate enough to come across a couple of animals mating at the zoo, or see two dogs stuck together in the street, she'd treat it as an impromptu Sex Ed class and say loudly, so everyone around could hear, 'You know what they're doing, don't you, Leigh? They're *fucking*!'

The books were certainly graphic and didn't hold with the old 'when a mummy and a daddy love each other very much' business. I saw terrifying pictures of erect penises (finally, I knew what Stafford had been talking about) and read cheery descriptions of what happened when you lost your virginity. Hymens stretched to breaking point until they were rent asunder, agonising pain, rivers of blood. I must have gone pale because Mum walked over, glancing at the book.

'Well, you'll have to be careful. You can get pregnant now you're menstruating.'

I gave her an 'as if' look. I mean, I hadn't even kissed a boy.

She crossed her arms. 'Don't roll your eyes. I wouldn't be surprised if the other kids are sexually active. Especially Una.'

A few weeks later there was a movie night at the community hall. *Apocalypse Now*, playing on a 16 mm projector. I sat in one of the hard wooden chairs, next to Mum, staring at the screen but not seeing anything. I was still obsessed with the hippy kids. The gang wandered in and out from time to time and kept disappearing under the building. Desperate to know what they were up to, I formulated a crude plan. I waited till Una headed for the toilets, finally alone, then sprang from my seat and caught up to her just before she entered the cubicle, breathlessly blurting out the line I'd been rehearsing in my head.

'I don't know what you're doing under there, but whatever it is, can I join in?' I couldn't believe I'd said it and resisted the urge to gasp and clamp my hand over my mouth. I had to be cool.

Una looked me up and down lazily, eyes like a cat, or perhaps a Mafia don. Her mouth curled up at the sides. 'You'd be too chicken.'

'No I wouldn't.'

She studied me for what felt like three years but was probably only half a second. 'I'll ask the others,' she finally said.

I sat back down, so excited my palms were buzzing. Man, I'd done it, and there was every chance I'd be going under the hall and I'd be part of the gang at last. Then I remembered Kim's finger actions and what my mum had said and I freaked. Holy shit. They were having sex down there. Had to be. How could I have been so stupid? What had I done? I remembered the books I'd read and I felt sweat pool under my arms and leak down my sides. I was too young to lose my virginity. I couldn't go through with it. I just couldn't. Maybe the others had said no and she wasn't coming back and—a tap on my shoulder, Una's breath hot in my ear. 'Come on. Come down.'

'I can't,' I whispered.

'Why not?'

I groped for an excuse and all I could come up with was, 'Because . . . I fell over just before and hit my head and I think I've got concussion.'

'Bullshit. They didn't want you at first but I told them you were cool. You don't come now, you don't get another chance.' She dragged me from my seat, out the double doors and down the path of flattened grass that ran down the side of the hall. My heart lodged in my throat and started to pound and swell. All I could think of was pain and blood, and I imagined my hymen as a wad of strawberry Hubba Bubba, blown too big until finally it burst. Jesus. As we ducked underneath the building I heard the faint thwack of helicopters and the orchestral swell of 'The Ride of the Valkyries' filter down from above.

The damp space smelt like concrete dust and rotting wood. A candle was wedged into a long-neck beer bottle and in the flickering light I saw the hippy kids sitting in a circle, looking up at me, some with raised eyebrows, others with crossed arms and sardonic grins. Another bottle lay on its side in the centre.

Stafford sighed, bored. 'Not Miss Prissy.'

A couple of them sniggered.

'Sit,' Una pushed me down next to him. 'Spin.'

I did as she commanded and the bottle skittered on the pebbly ground, finally pointing at Stafford. The others hooted and he groaned, got to his knees and shuffled towards me. I stopped breathing and my vision tunnelled and even though by that stage my belief in space aliens was pretty much hanging by a thread, I prayed for them to take me away, to no avail. What was their goddamned problem? Why would they only abduct fat Americans?

Stafford loomed in front of me. Terror-stricken, I squeezed my eyes shut and felt him squish his mouth against mine and move it around from side to side. After a few seconds he pulled away in disgust. 'You don't kiss with your teeth!'

Everyone laughed and I opened my eyes, confused. I'd read all the books. I knew there was a bit more to it than that, but Stafford had already moved away and was spinning the bottle again, brightening considerably when it pointed to Una.

That was it? Just kissing? I disguised my amazement by leaning back on my hands and acting like the whole thing was no big deal, while inside I felt like clapping and laughing out loud. This was the naughtiness I'd been waiting for my whole life, better than Adric, the Hot Gossip dancers and 'I Love Rock 'n' Roll' combined. Miss Prissy my arse. I couldn't *wait* for the bottle to point back at me so I could have another crack at it.

Only this time I'd watch out for the teeth.

LEIGH REDHEAD has worked on a prawn trawler and as an exotic dancer, masseuse, waitress and apprentice chef. She is the author of *Peepshow*, *Rubdown* and *Cherry Pie* (Allen & Unwin), a crime series featuring stripper and private investigator Simone Kirsch.

Starting Fresh

Maggie Hamilton

As I stood pressed against the ship's railing, staring down at the crush of people below, I knew my life was about to change forever. It was a surreal feeling—all around me people were laughing, shouting, crying, their voices filling the air. I looked up at my mother beside me. She was smiling through her tears, trying desperately to ignore the pain in her heart as we waited to depart. It was a bitterly cold May day in 1964. Around us endless snatches of conversations, frantic reminders and last-minute declarations of love were all lost on the wind. As the ship pulled away from the docks, the cascade of coloured streamers that had been thrown to family and friends began to snap and tear. The moment had finally come to leave England for the other side of the world.

When my parents announced that we were going to live in New Zealand, my sister and I thought they were joking because no one we knew had relocated so far away. The idea of leaving my friends was heartbreaking—it wasn't just the physical comfort of having them around that I'd miss, but the special moments and endless secrets we'd shared. The thought of not seeing them for some time, perhaps even years, was hard to take in.

But it's not just the loss of friendships you miss when you make a major move. The place you have inhabited from birth is as much a part of you as your own flesh— it imprints itself on your psyche. I loved the moors and mist-clad hills where I'd grown up, and the neat rows of houses that were nestled in our valley. Everywhere I looked held a fragment of my life. My most significant moments were imprinted on this place. It was impossible to imagine living anywhere else.

When it came to sorting through my things, I'd no idea what to keep and what to ditch. We were in the middle of one of the worst winters for years, which didn't help. There were blizzards, and almost overnight the roads around town had been transformed into gleaming tunnels of snow and ice. No one went outside unless they had to. I tried to imagine what it'd be like to have Christmas in summer, and for the weather to be warm enough to get a tan, but I couldn't get my head around how life would be.

I'd never been that adventurous as a child—probably because I'd been pretty sick. My bad chest had meant long spells of absence from school, and having to be wrapped up most of the year when I did go out. But as I packed up the world I knew, pausing now and then to leaf through the brochures on our new home, something shifted inside. Alongside my fear of moving on was a profound ache to embrace new people and places. Soon I couldn't wait for us to be on our way. I knew life would be different, but as we'd still be speaking the same language there wasn't too much to worry about.

The closer it came to the day of our departure, the quieter Mum became. Even though she was happy to take the plunge, and put on a brave face for us, she became acutely aware that she was about to lose every-thing that was familiar to her. It must have been impossibly hard to move away from the people and places she'd known for so long. It was here, in a cottage on the outskirts of town, that she'd birthed her two baby girls. It was here that she'd fallen in love and married. And it was here, as a teacher, that her life had become inextric-ably linked with many local kids and their families. Dad had left home when he was a teenager, so the whole process was easier for him. He tried to make Mum feel better about the move, but her aching sense of loss intensified as the weeks passed. As my excitement at leaving intensified, moving on was less of a big deal. I couldn't see why Mum saw the move as final, as we could always come home if it didn't work out.

Finally, the time came to leave, and it was impossible not to feel exhilarated at the thought of all the adven-tures before us. Instead of travelling by plane, we had six weeks ahead on a Dutch liner, during which time we would see Egypt, the Suez Canal, Sri Lanka, and other breathtaking places that were at present little more than names on the world map.

Once we'd set sail, all the conflicting emotions around our departure dissolved, and we were free to turn our attention to our temporary home—where to sleep, where to swim, where to play. There was so much to take in. I'd never had problems sailing, but once the ship got out into the open sea, I began to throw up. It was hideous, but there was little anyone could do. Apparently, it was a reaction to all the injections we'd had. I wanted to curl up and die, but I couldn't even lie down, because every time I did the room would spin. Suddenly, the whole idea of leaving everyone and everything behind seemed like the worst idea in the world. I spent my time engulfed in my own personal misery as I stared out at the steel-grey sea and sky.

Once I settled down a bit, Mum took me out on deck for some fresh air, which helped. I can still remember sitting out in an icy wind, torn between wanting to feel better and freezing to death. A day later, though, my seasickness was gone and I was fine. As one day disappeared into the next, the weather warmed. We packed away our heavy winter clothes, and enjoyed the luxury of sun on our skin. Within a couple of days I'd found a small clutch of girlfriends—some on holidays and some destined for new homes in the different countries on our itinerary. We were inseparable for much of each day.

We were also able to take our dog on board, which helped us feel even more at home, as we'd never been separated from him since he was a pup. Pip was in the kennels at the front of the ship. We weren't allowed to see him much, so as not to unsettle him, but that didn't matter. It was just good to know he wasn't far away. After a couple of weeks, the staff announced a fashion parade for guests. Suddenly, everyone was preoccupied with what to wear. A friend asked if Pip could join her in the parade, which seemed like a great idea. He loved every moment—until it was time to go back to his kennel.

Later that day, he escaped while being fed. We didn't hear about it immediately, because everyone was so busy trying to find him. By the time we started to look for him, he was long gone. It was as if he'd just vanished. In the end, the staff had the unenviable task of informing us that he'd probably fallen overboard as there weren't any railings at the front of the ship.

It was awful to think of Pip all alone in the sea, and no one even knowing he was missing until it was too late. The worst part was there was nothing we could do. Even if the ship turned back—which was never going to happen—there was no way you'd find a dog in the middle of the ocean. He could swim, but with nowhere to swim to, once he tired he would drown. As a few hours had elapsed since his escape, he was probably already dead. We were devastated. Then, just when we were about to give up, to our huge relief he was found in the laundry.

A few days later we were crossing the Indian Ocean when we learnt there was a major storm brewing. There's nowhere to shelter when you're way out to sea in bad weather. Once the wind got up, the waves formed massive troughs that tossed the ship about as if it were driftwood. The boat fought its way with agonising slowness up one steep wall of water after the next, only to come crashing down the other side. Even though it was the middle of the afternoon, the sky was so dark it was more like dusk.

When the storm was at its height, it was almost impossible to hear anything over the wind and the sickening thud of the waves as they hurled themselves against the sides of the ship. Everyone was left clinging to rails or whatever else they could hang on to. We were in one of the lounges, so we could see out. Chairs and plates and anything that wasn't bolted down went flying. We were all secretly terrified, but no one admitted it. There was no way you could go outside—it was too dangerous. Unlike Dad, who had been in the Navy during the war, most people hadn't spent any time out on the open sea, and few could swim. He kept on talking calmly to us throughout the whole episode, which was reassuring. But even that didn't prevent our periodic screams and nervous laughter. When the wind finally dropped an hour or so later, an eerie calm descended on us, as if nothing had happened. The experience left everyone shaken, but incredibly no one was hurt.

Then, a couple of days later, a man died. As no one had been told why, his death became a major topic of adult conversation. There were worries that this silence might mean the beginning of an epidemic—we were in the tropics now. As kids, we were more scared of supernatural repercussions. The mere thought of being in the middle of nowhere with someone who had died in mysterious circumstances was terrifying. Then the girls I hung out with began to talk about vampires, which only made things a thousand times worse. I can still recall the tight knot of fear in the pit of my stomach as I wondered if we'd be safe. This fear intensified at night, because *anything* could be lurking around in the darkness and you'd never see it coming—until it was too late. None of my friends admitted to how they were feeling, but secretly we were counting the days to the next port, where the body would be taken ashore.

The weeks fled, and all too soon we were nearing our destination. After the chaos of Singapore with its rickshaws, crowded alleys and night markets, came Fremantle with its black swans and Darrell Lea chocolates—and its eye-piercing light, which I love to this day. By comparison, Melbourne was icy cold, formal and a little foreboding. Then came Sydney. We sailed past the Opera House, which was still being built, and under the world-famous Harbour Bridge, which I'd only ever seen in books. It was such a special moment to experience the Bridge firsthand. Little did I know that this beautiful city would one day be home.

By this stage, Mum was becoming increasingly tense. The excitement of new places was now lost in her fears for the future. She told Dad that if she didn't like New Zealand, we were going back to England. That made us all anxious, because we hadn't reckoned on this. What if *we* didn't like New Zealand? Or what if we loved it and Mum hated it—would we really have to go back?

Luckily, our fears were temporarily allayed. The day we arrived in Wellington the harbour was picture-postcard perfect. And even though it was the middle of winter, the cool weather seemed relatively warm after an English winter. Our first few days were spent outdoors, enjoying the sunshine and fresh air. Everywhere we went were spectacular views of the harbour—there was so much space and beauty. Almost all the houses were built from wood. Many were on impossibly steep blocks of land. No one seemed worried by this, even though there was frequent talk of earthquakes. One of the greatest joys was trying out the new food—sweetcorn fritters, roast kumera, whitebait and pavlova—they were all delicious.

Within a couple of weeks, Mum and Dad had found us a great apartment in a quiet bay only a few minutes from the beach. It was perched on the hillside and surrounded by bush. You could lie in bed at night and hear the sound of the waves. It was brilliant. Shortly afterwards our tea chests arrived. It felt like Christmas as we opened them up and worked out where to put everything. Now, after the limbo of homelessness, it was time to immerse ourselves in our new life.

The first day at school was exhilarating and nerve-racking. I was eager to start my new life and make lots of friends. At first, it seemed easy—everyone was really welcoming, which was a relief. But within weeks the novelty wore off and the bullying began. I wanted to be like everyone else—but it was impossible. There was so much animosity towards newcomers that it didn't matter what I said or did—to most kids, I wasn't a person, just 'another Pom'. It's a soul-numbing experience to be face-less. Sooner or later you start to compromise precious parts of who you are—just so you can belong.

I'd spend hours thinking about how I could win the other kids over. I wanted them to see that I wasn't really that different, but every time I opened my mouth my accent betrayed me. I was younger and skinnier than most, so I was an easy target. The kids would pull me around by my clothes or grab my hair, or punch me when the teacher wasn't looking. Even casual conversations were fraught, because there was so much I didn't know about my new home. The only option I had was to take situations literally, which just inflamed the aggression. I'd mispronounce a place, or ask an obvious question, betraying the fact that I was an outsider. Now and again the girls would let up and I'd relax a bit, assuming that at last I was finally accepted—only to have awful things happen again and again.

Like most kids, I never said anything to my parents—I was too ashamed. You always assume it's your fault, and you're reluctant to give your parents more grief. I was also aware that Mum and Dad had enough on their plate starting a new life, and that they were both working incredibly hard. Even though I frequently felt sick in the stomach, I never cried. I was determined to be strong. Whenever it got too much I'd go down to the beach and stare out at the ocean, dreaming of ways to escape—only to realise there was no escape. I was who I was.

What made things worse was that Mum was really homesick. She'd break down and cry when she thought we weren't around. I just wanted to wrap her in my arms and keep her safe, but I knew that she'd be embarrassed for me to see her like that, so I pretended things were fine. Dad had his own sorrows, too. His mother, who'd seemed fine when we left, died, which was devastating. She'd been diagnosed with cancer just before we departed. Even though she knew she was terminal, she didn't say anything. This was yet another blow. Dad wasn't able to get to the funeral, which must have hurt. I guess that's one of the shocking things about growing up—you finally realise your parents don't have all the answers, and that they experience life's lacerations as well.

Occasionally I'd overhear Mum and Dad relating the cruel comments and jokes they'd had to endure at work. It made me feel angry and sad and utterly helpless. I'd lie awake at night, dreaming of how I could get enough money to take us back to England. But I was just a teenager—there was nothing I could do. When you move countries, you lose your points of reference. To survive you must take note of *every* nuance. This makes you exquisitely sensitive and vulnerable to whatever is going on around you.

In spite of this sadness there were many beautiful things about our new home. I loved the warmth, and the deep blue skies and the beach. Had the kids at school been more welcoming, it would have been perfect. I'd come home after school and go down to the sea with my little sister and Pip, and lose myself in the beauty of the ocean, and in the comforting green of the steep bush-clad hills. In quiet moments I loved to collect unusual stones and shells, or to climb the hill to my own special eyrie, where I'd look down on the jumble of houses that fringed the bay. But what really saved me in those early days in Wellington was the unfailing love of Mum and Dad.

After a while I made friends—good friends—and I came to feel part of my new world. Their kindness and generosity helped me flourish, and as our lives intertwined, new memories and precious rituals were formed. My years in New Zealand gave me so much, and for that I am deeply grateful. I've never forgotten the pain of rejection, though. It's not something you do forget. Although I wouldn't care to relive those experiences, I don't regret them, because they have made me far more aware of others—especially those who find it hard to fit in.

Once you've made the break from your first home, something inside you is forever changed. You belong everywhere and nowhere—the world becomes your home. And no matter how much you love where you live, there's always a part of you that aches for another adventure. And that's not such a bad thing, as there's an amazing world out there.

MAGGIE HAMILTON, an author and publisher, is passionate about life, books, films, people and travel to faraway places. She gives regular talks, lectures and workshops, writes for magazines, and is a keen observer of social trends. For the past two decades she has been based in Sydney, where she lives with her bookseller husband, Derek. Her adult books include *Coming Home, Love Your Work: Reclaim Your Life, Magic of the Moment* and *What Men Don't Talk About.*

Tenants

Heather Rose

At fifteen the only thing I knew of war was Mr Abetz. Mr Abetz had lost a leg in World War II and when he went swimming he took another leg—his 'swimming leg'—with him. I remember watching him on the path to the beach in the late afternoon, his good leg and his fake leg sticking out from beneath his black bathers and the white prosthetic swimming limb tucked under his arm. War could take your leg off, that's all I knew about it.

That year, the people next door upped and went to Singapore. Their house was to be rented.

'Rented!' said my mother. 'Oh Lord, I wonder who we'll get.'

I had never been inside the house next door, which was grey brick with a garage underneath and a small concrete verandah over the driveway. The family who owned it were the Porters. They had much younger children and Mrs Porter yelled at them. My mother often stopped to speak with Mrs Porter in the driveway, but we were not close to them in the same way we were to the people at the end of our cul-de-sac.

We'd been the first house on the subdivision so I had grown up with new arrivals. I knew everyone between our house and the paddocks up the hill, and all the families on the way down to the beach. My parents and some of the neighbours had regular dinners and barbecues. One house had a sauna in the backyard and on Saturday night everyone would get naked together. The women would gather at 7 pm and come home flushed and glowing, in time for the husbands to depart for their sauna two hours later. My mother had been known to meet people in the supermarket and say, 'Oh, hello! I didn't recognise you with your clothes on!'

The new tenants arrived on Harleys wearing black helmets without visors. Dan and Joe. They were followed by several women in a Kombi van painted green with yellow flowers.

'How many of them are there?' my mother asked. 'Quick, come away from the window.'

Only one woman became a permanent resident and she was called Gabe. She and Dan had a baby and when she carried the baby about on her hip I saw her stomach and I knew that in ways my mother and her friends would never be to me, Gabe was a real woman. She had long, wavy, ginger-gold hair and wore green velvet skirts and white Indian shirts that barely covered her breasts. I was so impressed by Gabe I decided to stuff my bra in the hope that my breasts would look like hers. Proud of the effect, I dropped by and Joe, the older brother, made me a coffee and then sat me down and said there was nothing more lovely than a woman who knew she was beautiful just being herself. He didn't look at my new 32C cup; he just looked into my eyes and smiled at me. A strong, clear, reassuring smile, and I wanted to shrink away and pull out the wadded tissues. It was the last time I ever worried about my triple A breasts.

I took to dropping over on weekends and after school before my mother got home from work. I was surprised my parents let me visit, but they did. Next door's was a house that played to a different music. The washing-up was rarely done. The frying pan was left on the sink with bits of bacon rind in it and the remains of baked beans. There was no schedule that said mealtime or bed-time. The milk was often sour and the bread was rarely fresh. The pantry had cat food, marmalade and Salada biscuits. People arrived and left at all hours of the day and night, cups of tea were made in brown mugs, con-versation drifted with the cigarette smoke, people slept and woke at strange hours. The curtains stayed closed all day and the grass grew long to the fence.

Joe chatted with me about books and writing, about music and school. He shared poetry with me and told me he was saving up to head off round Australia in the Kombi. Joe said the great writers were the Americans and the greatest of these was Kerouac. He lent me his copy of *On the Road*, which I loved, and Kesey's *Some-times a Great Notion*, which made me long to write a great novel.

Joe was painfully thin and energetic. He DJ'd at night and worked for a sound-equipment place by day. He had brown curly hair and a short beard. His nails were chewed right down and he had a way of walking that was slightly sidewards. I always wondered how he had the strength to ride the great Harley that waited for him on the driveway, its black metal ticking in the sunshine.

His younger brother, Dan, was tall and blond. The curly hair that hung down his back was tied with a strip of leather. He had washed-out blue eyes and his arms were tattooed with green dragons. He wore cowboy boots with metal wheels at the back that clicked as he walked. He smoked Drum, which he rolled slowly and gently in his grease-stained hands. Dan rarely spoke and didn't like the curtains open. He'd sit in the chair in the corner of the lounge saying nothing or nodding now and again to some remark, or a thought he was having. He'd be still for so long the ash from his cigarette would drop onto his jeans in little piles. Sometimes Gabe would go over and sit in Dan's lap and he'd rest his head on her breasts. The baby slept in his arms and it never seemed to cry. Some days Dan just stood at the kitchen bench the whole time I was there and stirred his tea. Other times I passed him on the driveway on my way inside the house. He liked to take his bike apart and put it back together, and all the pieces would be laid out neatly on a blanket on the concrete.

Their front door was always open and if I rang the bell someone always shouted down to come up so I stopped ringing the bell and just went up, calling out as I took the stairs two at a time. Often I found Gabe pottering about in the kitchen with the baby in a sling on her back. I thought that she and Dan were the most beautiful people I'd ever seen. They were both so tall and long-haired, so quiet and unimpressed with everything. Gabe's feet were usually bare and her legs were covered in golden hairs. When she dressed up to go off on the back of Dan's bike, she'd wear blue jeans, a black jacket and long leather boots. I waited for the day they'd ask me to go too. I longed to ride off with them but my father had banned that not long after they'd arrived.

'No daughter of mine will be getting on the back of one of those machines.'

If they'd asked me I would never have been able to obey my father. My hands longed to feel the weight of the helmet slipping over my head, the straddle of the machine. I always imagined I'd ride with Dan because Joe seemed too fragile to hold on to.

Joe had been married, he told me one day. But now he was divorced.

'Why?' I asked.

'I couldn't do it after I came back,' he said.

'Back?'

'Vietnam,' he said. 'I thought you knew. Dan and me. That's how I lost my lung and all this,' he said, patting his excruciatingly thin chest. I saw then that while Joe's rib cage filled out on one side, it had collapsed on the other, and this was what gave him the peculiar skewed leanness I had never understood before.

'She lives on the other side of the river, the ex,' he said. 'My boy, too. He was born just after I was called up.'

'Don't you want to live with them?'

'I can't. I'm not good with any of that anymore.' His hands shook as he rolled another cigarette. 'She still calls.

'It's nice being with people who don't know,' he continued. 'It feels kind of safe. We've been in bad places, Dan and me. That's not good to be around too much. Dan was a prisoner over there. They kept him in water. Now he can't sleep more than two hours at a time.'

He smiled a little at me. 'Like Frost said—"I took the road less travelled by, and that has made all the difference . . ."'

I knew nothing about Vietnam. No one had taught me about it at school, no one seemed to mention it. It was 1979, less than six years since they'd come home, and their war was as far away to me as Mr Abetz's.

'Joe and Dan were in Vietnam,' I told my mother.

'I know, dear.'

'Joe lost his lung and stuff.'

'Did he? I expect he's on a benefit. It was a mistake, that war. They shouldn't have gone.'

'But they were conscripted.'

'Yes,' she nodded. 'They all were. To help the Americans.'

'Didn't we win?'

'No. No one won.'

Winter came and went, and I lingered in their lounge room drinking International Roast. Their friends dropped in. There was always music playing—Bob Dylan, Joni Mitchell, Led Zeppelin, The Doors. One day I found a stack of *Forum* magazines on the coffee table and spent an hour or so discovering the various positions women arranged themselves in to be photographed naked.

I knew the house had a smell about it, but then all houses do. I knew there were conversations that went on that I didn't understand. Sometimes there was laughter about goings-on that I missed. But I didn't mind. I wanted to breathe it all in, I wanted to soak up their strange fabrics and food and dark house and make it mine. Sometimes I walked in the open front door and up the steps to be greeted by clouds of sweet-smelling smoke and all of them languid on the couch. But Joe'd get up and make me coffee and talk to me.

That burgeoning subdivision on the river had been

built for public servants, bureaucrats, nurses and teachers who worked by day and cooked meals with two green vegetables and one orange vegetable at night. It was not for people with no fixed schedule, no suit or tie, no church and no marriage certificate.

One day I was home from school studying for exams and I heard cars pull up next door. I looked out my window to see two white panel vans and two police cars. Dogs leapt out from the back of one of the vans and began bounding about on their leads. From the other van, men were unloading boxes and carrying them into the house. It seemed very peculiar. I knew where Joe was working so I rang him.

'Joe, there are police at your house. They're unloading boxes.'

'I'll be right there,' he said.

Within fifteen minutes the noise of the two Harleys topped the rise along the beach and I could hear them rumbling all the way up the road to home. The police by this time were waiting in their cars. When Dan and Joe pulled up they got out and walked them inside the house.

Not long after, they took Dan and Joe away in one of the police cars. The next day Joe rang me and said it was best I didn't come over anymore. My parents were bound to have heard about the bust and he didn't want me involved.

'Bust?' I asked.

'Yeah,' he said. 'That stuff they were unloading. It was grass. Boxes of it. Crazy thing was, they hadn't even tried to make it look normal. There was so much under my mattress it would have been impossible to sleep on it. I mean, it was a joke.'

'But I saw them carry it in,' I said.

'Yeah, I know, babe, but you're not to tell anyone about that. I don't want you involved. Your parents will freak.'

'But it wasn't yours. They set you up.'

'They did, and I know that and you know that and that's all that really matters.'

They skipped through not long afterwards. One day they were there, the next they weren't. My mother said she'd heard from Mrs Porter that they hadn't paid the rent in months. She and I went over to clean the place up before the next tenants as a favour to the Porters, who were still in Singapore, although I think my mother just wanted to see inside. We took buckets and sponges, White Lilly and Ajax. The house wasn't so bad, although Mum said it was disgusting. It was empty except for the furniture that had come with the house. The cupboards in the kitchen were open and there were still crumbs on the bench. Down the hall I saw the bedrooms with their green and blue geometric wallpaper and round paper lightshades. I stared into the room that I figured had been Joe's and imagined the mattress on the bed perched on top of a vast quantity of marijuana.

In the lounge room the curtains were opened and for the first time I saw it in daylight with its mustard shag pile stained and flattened, the purple walls, the sofa with its brown check pattern, the orange lamp.

Joe rang one afternoon, weeks after they'd disappeared.

'Joe!' I said. 'What are you doing? Are you okay?'

'Sorry we had to dash,' he said. 'Got a little hot.'

He waited for me outside school the next day and

drove me in a white Corolla to a flat he'd rented. He was as thin as ever.

'Did you sell the bike?' I asked.

'No, I just thought you'd look a bit conspicuous in your uniform on the back, so I borrowed this from a friend.'

'I'm never going to ride on the back of a bike,' I said.

'Never's a long time, babe,' he smiled.

The flat was scrupulously clean with white walls and cream carpet and a tiny kitchen looking out onto a concrete backyard big enough for a clothes line.

'Dan and Gabe have gone north to get some warmer weather. I'm heading off soon to join them.'

'What happened—with the bust?' I asked.

'Dismissed,' he said.

Joe made me a coffee; seven teaspoons of instant, just the way I liked it.

'How did you get off?' I asked.

He laughed, his brown eyes bright against his pale face.

'Well, we actually had a smoke with the magistrate the night before the hearing. We were at a party and we shared a smoke with this dude. And then when we rock up to court the next morning . . . well, he could hardly say anything, could he?'

We laughed and chatted but something was missing. Perhaps it was the lack of clutter and strange smells. Or perhaps I had gotten older. I wondered what he wanted, this older man who had taken an interest in me.

'Don't tell your parents we saw each other today,' he said as I headed off down the street to catch the bus home. 'Your old man'll be after me.'

I nodded.

'I might not see you again,' he said.

'Yes you will,' I smiled.

'Just in case . . .' he said, handing me an envelope. Inside was a note.

Heather. Never forget to laugh. Try to read ten new books each year. Remember to be kind to all people, especially yourself. Never cut your hair. Joe.

I kept that note folded up in my wallet for a long time. I never saw Joe again. The house next door stayed empty for a year or more and then my parents divorced and our house was sold.

I drive by our old home every now and again. It has changed almost beyond recognition, but the house next door is still grey brick.

HEATHER ROSE is the author of two novels—*White Heart* and *The Butterfly Man*. *The Butterfly Man*, about the disappearance of Lord Lucan in 1974, won the 2006 Davitt Award for the Crime Fiction Novel of the Year and is long-listed for the 2007 IMPAC Literary Awards in Ireland. Heather is the 2006 recipient of the Eleanor Dark Fellowship for Fiction.

Poor Alice

Jill Morris

Under the House in post-war Queensland was a mystic place that eavesdropped on many secrets.

High houses on tall stumps (the popular style of the period, designed for coolness and to escape floods) left a dirt-floor area underneath, often on a precarious, crumbling slope. The 'ceiling' was festooned with cobwebs and the area always harboured a cloying, musty smell. Children, discovering the flattest place, perched on discarded tables and three-legged chairs to unearth secrets from one another while digging in the dirt for dinosaur-shaped arthropods.

Stump caps (the metal hats on top of stumps that protected the buildings from white ants) were cool repositories for fat green tree frogs with blue on their hips and beauty spots on their faces. We stroked but did not hold. 'Slimy' was not the word—a cold flatness, like a threat from the centre of the earth.

At night, those stump caps were a link to another, more necessary, activity. On a trip to the lavatory out the back before bed ('lavatory' being a new, nicer word to replace the 'dunny' of the previous generation), you had to reach above one stump cap to flip a light switch (but hopefully not a frog), making the precarious bulb hanging from a wire swing into life.

It gave just enough light for a child in pyjamas to head for the little timber hut out the back, complete with its thunderbox and pile of tissue papers that had arrived wrapped around apples, or newspaper cut into squares and hanging on a string to the right of the occupant— the position taken today by an ornate chrome dispenser and toilet paper painted with fish and flowers.

Life in those old Queenslanders so revered today involved nightly trips down the back stairs in the dark; a little hand creeping under the side of the house halfway down for the light switch; possible contact with an indignant frog; then a terrifying few minutes perched on the wooden seat, listening to the wriggles of unknown nocturnal reptiles in the suburban bush.

Our outhouse was hidden behind a timber trellis covered in thick vine, which was home to many noisy slitherers, so I was always keen to bang the cover down and race back to the warm light of the house.

Home for my sister, my mother and myself was a high house on stumps at Sandgate, a seaside suburb of Brisbane. Holidays meant trips by train and service car to the tiny dairying and citrus settlement of Montville (in the hinterland of the Sunshine Coast), now a popular tourist village, where we stayed with an ex-Sandgate neighbour we called Auntie Frizz.

I now live twenty kilometres from Montville, this final residence probably chosen because of childhood memories. My house, an imaginative hexagon perched on a green hill outside Maleny, is not built on stumps;

but walking outside at night onto the concrete slab 'verandah' can bring contact with a frog or a snake, while hunting owls and grunting possums produce an orchestra of night calls. Our toilets, of course, are inside.

In 1949, the year I turned thirteen, Under the House in one of the dwellings in the main street of Montville (the *only* street at that time) was menacingly low; only just high enough off the ground to fit us as early teenagers while we were still short. Any girl stretching into puberty, pushed along by a sub-tropical summer, was pleased to bend her neck to fit. We all wanted to grow *up*; but no one wanted to admit to growing *big*.

The mountain cool of Montville was a welcome escape from boiling Brisbane. My sister and I, with other girls of similar age whom we picked up along the street (sometimes two, sometimes more), trawled the safe, quiet little village in skimpy handed-down cotton dresses and bare feet. When hunger drove us inside, we gobbled scones from Auntie Frizz's wood-fired oven. A generous woman with tight spiral curls and large working hands, Frizz didn't seem to mind us descending like locusts, and taking off afterwards for another house to see what else we could get.

Now, I wonder whether that kind woman and her family, with their curly hair and olive skin, were descendants of the Kanakas, South Sea islanders abducted from their homes and brought to slave on Queensland's early sugar plantations. Perhaps those large brown eyes hid a sad family background—but at that time it was not our concern. We cared only about our own comfort—and the scones.

One sun-filled morning, while Frizz and my mother

were having a cup of tea in Frizz's kitchen, our gang headed for our favourite hiding-place, under another house on the main street. It was a tumbledown, 'rented' place, the home of a girl I shall call Alice, and the best thing about it was that there was just enough room underneath to fit us—and our secrets.

Our secrets in 1949 were cheap—like those of all teenagers at that time around the world. We had no money, and no real jobs. Our 'jobs' (wiping up, emptying chamber pots, feeding chooks) earned us pocket money and free encouragement from mentoring adults. Perhaps they mentioned our names when we needed a push-along for a career; or wrote a letter of support when we needed to get into a school or an apprenticeship. We were not politically powerful like today's teenagers. Unlike them, we were not a 'market', because we had no buying power. The word 'teenager' had barely been invented— so we were desperate to grow up. There was childhood and adulthood and nothing in between; we were children, desperate to become adults.

As we squeezed under Alice's house that day in December, we did not discuss why my father had died in the war; why the Japanese had almost been given all of Queensland north of the Brisbane Line; or why women were being asked to give up the jobs they had taken over in wartime, when they were needed. Fiercely independent, hard-earning widows like my mother seemed rare—a single parent against her will, with two growing girls always wanting new dresses (which she made for us on her trusty Singer sewing machine). At least we rarely needed shoes, slipping through dust and sand happily in our Queensland-toughened bare feet.

We discussed which boys had looked at us and which had not. And why. We talked about the adventures ahead, the mysteries to be explored. We longed to glimpse again the treasure of Montville: a butterfly collection stored in dark timber cases in a spooky room of the schoolhouse across the road—100 multi-coloured beauties under glass, with wings stretched to the limit and anchored by bright silver pins.

We discussed daring invasions that might distract the owner of the three-storey shop (the only shop in Montville), allowing us to explore, unnoticed, all the way to the roof. (That shop is now a classy restaurant and I still have not been game to ask permission to climb to the top.) We speculated on the mystic activities that might be taking place up the narrow stairs.

But the greatest mystery of all was shocking us at that moment under Alice's house.

In 1949 Montville, we visitors from the outer space of Brisbane were mesmerised by the ice-blue eyes of Alice, who squatted with us under the house while her baby stepbrother wailed at us through the floor. As the sound blasted through the worn gaps between the broken boards to the whisperers hiding underneath, Alice looked guilty—and terrified.

She was rarely allowed to join us. Her cotton shifts were even more threadbare than ours, and always too small—although Alice was so thin you couldn't imagine anything being too small for her. She was like a little old lady at twelve, curly blonde hair puffing around those iceberg eyes and falling onto a pasty neck. A wartime childhood diet was probably showing on all of us, but Alice's skin was almost transparent.

Above us, hiding somewhere in a house strangely devoid of furniture, Alice had a stepmother she resented but whom we all frankly admired, a glamorous beauty with Rita Hayworth hair and a smile for every visiting child, who wore her baby son like an adornment whenever she decided to pick him up. But the baby was clearly Alice's responsibility and she wore his body like a hump as she raided their kitchen for food to shut him up. Poor Alice. We felt sorry for her, but on that day I particularly remember, she was free—we had sneaked her away to play and share secrets under her own house.

I can still hear her wispy, croaky voice: 'He beats me, you know.' Stated simply, but with terror in her eyes, silently pleading: 'Do something about it! Help me!'

Who could be beating her? we wondered. In answer, she rolled her eyes skyward to the floor where her father's heavy tread was vibrating the timber boards. He did walk heavily through that house.

Should we believe her? we asked ourselves. We had seen Alice lie, when she stole a handful of lollies from the shop and turned her blue eyes like innocent lights on the shop lady, denying the accusation. So when she complained to us, we perched on our moral molehill and silently, unanimously declared her dishonest.

I remember Alice's sentence, so I must have heard it. But I was not ready for a secret I didn't understand. And I was afraid, too, of that man upstairs.

With all the security of our safe family backgrounds, we other girls, a conspiracy of ignorance, changed the subject—to butterflies, or boys, or lunch. Or the mandarin farm we hoped to visit that afternoon. More free food.

Was Alice just an unhappy stepdaughter, trying to get attention anywhere she could? Had her father come back from the war (I don't recall him having a job) and taken out his frustration on his resentful twelve-year-old daughter from an earlier marriage? Did Alice really have to look after that baby as much as she said she did? Was she just a whinger? Or was she an abused child who later moved on to a marriage of abuse, after a miserable childhood?

I remember thinking rather meanly that Alice was lucky to have a father at all. Mine had just died, and I, like all teenagers, was the centre of the world. So everyone, including Alice, should be sorry for me. Now I appreciate how much my mother did for me, as a young widow trying to be two parents, feeding and clothing us, getting us to good schools, taking us on any holidays at all. I'm sure Alice never went on a holiday. She remained trapped within her secrets—or lies. And the larger mystery we were all tussling with—why people went to war and killed one another—has still not been solved.

I can't find that house now—it lies buried somewhere under a string of galleries and high-flying restaurants. It whispers at me as I drive past on my adult rush from Maleny through Montville to Mapleton and Nambour. No matter what architecture, timber and concrete we use to disguise history, a piece of land holds the spirits of those who have lived there before—a tiny piece of the planet used for different purposes by a succession of generations.

Alice's eyes still burn in my memory today when I wonder whether to speak out in a political dispute; whether to make an effort to prevent a sacrilege by destroyers of the natural environment; or to support a fund-raising cause that is easy to ignore.

In that little gang of girls in 1949, we lost an important moment when we could have helped another human being. How many more opportunities did I lose in those self-centred teenage years? Or since?

Poor Alice.

JILL MORRIS is the author of more than 100 children's books and the director of independent children's publishing house Greater Glider Productions, which is based at the Book Farm in Maleny, Queensland. Her latest book is *Argonauta, Octopus Navigator* (Greater Glider, 2006). Jill was a columnist for *The Age* for twelve years and has served on the Australia Council Literature Board and the Australian Society of Authors' Committee of Management. She has also worked in radio, television, film and theatre. In 2005, Jill was honoured with the Dame Annabelle Rankin Award 'for distinguished services to children's literature in Queensland'. Her website is www.greaterglider.com.au.

Fire and Ice

Lyn McPherson

'I hate you, I hate you, I HATE you!' Those three words resounded loudly through my head as I sat next to him in the back of his dad's inappropriately space-deprived vehicle. Engulfed in the stifling haze of silence, I struggled to contain my fury.

He seemed completely oblivious to my internal chaos, as his shoulder nudged mine at every greater-than-45-degree turn of the steering wheel. Was he purposely fuelling my anger? I could feel the rising temperature of my face accelerate every time he made contact. It was soaring quickly, to an almost uncontrollable level. 'Please, hurry up and get me home!' I chanted to myself in the hope that my thoughts would prevent the embarrassing scream of disgust inevitable at any given nudge now.

Thankfully, the car stopped seconds before the ensuing disaster. I promptly and politely thanked his dad for the lift, and flicked my hair 'accidentally on purpose' in his face as I flung myself out of the car in disdain. Avoiding even the slightest glance, I turned away and walked off proudly, ensuring he understood I didn't need him. Who did he think he was, anyway?

He probably had no idea what he'd done—or rather, not done! This insensitivity was part of his problem! Three opportunities he'd had—not one, not even two, but three—to ask me to couple skate and not one word! What was his problem? It was just super-sick! Who would want to touch his sweaty, stinky paws, anyway? What *was* I thinking?

No time to stop and greet the rest of the family. I ran to my room, slammed the door and fell on the bed, bursting into uncontrollable tears of humiliation. This lasted ages—well, about five minutes. My mind churned through visions of being stuck on that blue bucket seat while the ice rink turned into a magical, romantic movie set. He even had the audacity to sit in the same row as me—only five seats away! What a nog-head jerk! What was he trying to prove? Talk about rubbing salt into the wound!

Then, suddenly, the tears were replaced with anger and pride again. How could I let *him* get to me this much? I simply must move on! So I grabbed my trusted friend— my diary—and, with a sigh of relief, anticipating the release of my fury, I recorded the untainted truth: 'Duncan McPherson is such a jerk, suck, idiot, poor excuse for a boy! I just HATE that guy SO much! How did I ever think he was cute? What planet was I on? John asked Sarah to skate, Mark asked Sally, even *Rob* asked Anne—can you believe that!? But Duncan just sat like a stuffed pig five seats away from me THREE times!!!!! What was he trying to prove? Who does he think he is?

I'll show that egomaniac! He had his chance. This is the end with Duncan McPherson! He's so hacked!'

Satisfied that I'd recounted the facts concisely and accurately, I decided to get on with my day. After all, he'd already ruined half of it; I certainly wasn't going to let him ruin another second. It was at that moment I heard Mum calling my name. Confirming in the mirror that there were no telltale signs of this pathetic emotional outburst as I walked out, I cooeed back, 'Yes, Mum?'

'Duncan's on the phone,' came her reply, to my absolute horror. It was absurd! What did this guy want? Feeling the blood rush back to my head, I knew that the emotionless perfection I'd just created had been destroyed instantly with those four words. What was I to do? Should I just tell him what an arrogant jerk he was? Should I refuse to speak to him? Was he calling to torment me further?

Realising his ego would only be further inflated if I revealed how upset I was, I decided to take the call: 'Hello?'

'Hi Lyn, it's Dunc, I was just wondering if you'd like to come to my school formal with me?'

'Okay, thanks,' I replied, staggered by my own response.

'Great, thanks, see you soon then,' came his reply. We both said goodbye and, as I hung up the phone, I simply could not contain my excitement. Jumping for joy up and down the passage, I made sure the entire family was blissfully aware of this incredible occurrence!

I must ring Sarah, Sally and Anne, I thought—they'll be *so* excited! This was the coolest thing. Skipping gleefully, like a five-year-old, to my room, I bounced all over my bed as I made the necessary announcement to each. Screaming with delight, I discovered that Sally and Sarah were going too! They got invited at the ice rink. Life was the best!

I had to get this down: Diary, where are you? 'Dunc is such a spunk!' I wrote. 'He is the best guy in the universe! I'm going to the school formal with him—yay! yay! YAY! And guess what??? Sarah and Sal are coming too!!!!! This is the best day, oh my GOSH! Life is so cool and Dunc is SO hot!!!'

I wrote in my diary almost every day as a teenager, for about six years. It really kept me sane, as it was a safe place for me to express and release my feelings. I always felt like I had finalised something or made sense of it once I'd written it down.

I also wrote poetry, and later songs, to express just about every emotion imaginable. My diary was my best friend. I could confide in it any time. It accepted all my moods; it never judged me, and it allowed me to always be completely truthful. I expressed anger, pride, joy, frustration, disappointment, sadness, and every other possible emotion in my words.

Whenever I felt rejected or at a loss, somehow offloading my feelings in this way allowed me to feel a little lighter and more able to cope. I still remember, when I argued with Mum, for instance, how writing about my hurt allowed me to disengage from my feelings, clear my head and figure out a more productive way to manage the situation. It was a bit like downloading a big file; once it was out of me I felt like I no longer had to worry about it as much. My thoughts were there in black and white, accessible if I chose to go back to them, but they no longer consumed me to the same extent.

I also discovered clarity and meaning. I derived conclusions and strategies, which I'd write down. This was a great way to learn about life because I was able to look back at my emotions and the resulting tactics or conclusions in order to figure out whether they'd been effective and accurate or not. I remember linking over-reactive emotions to non-sensical strategies, resulting in a conclusive strategy to be less over-reactive emotionally (not always easy as a teenager).

One funny example of this was when I received my first (rather unexpected) French kiss. I was in a dark corner at a blue-light disco, with a distorted version of 'Tainted Love' obliterating any hope of verbal communication. Suddenly I believed I was going to choke to death; it felt like there was a giant snake stuck in my throat and it was terrifying—I couldn't even speak and tell it to get out! My head was held firmly in the grip of an over-enthusiastic hand, adamant that I would share the passion. I was completely horrified and absolutely amazed that anyone could find this enjoyable. I developed a strategy: to keep my mouth tightly shut at all times while kissing. This was a somewhat ambitious plan and it failed—that particular boy had a rather determined tongue! There was much discussion in my diary about how to resolve this problem because I really liked the guy. The conclusion was a decision to beat him at his own game—get in first! I had to be less emotional though and find the courage to confront my fear! This was a brilliant strategy. It really worked, because there wasn't enough room for two determined tongues at once!

I remember vividly how heartbroken I was when the relationship with my first real love ended. I had moved on to writing songs at that point, with the occasional diary entry. It's absolutely fascinating to play those songs now. You would never believe they were all about the same person: titles included 'Don't confuse me', 'Together forever' and 'I don't want to want you anymore'.

When we are teenagers, we're often on an emotional roller-coaster. The things that are important to us create such intense feelings. We are hormonal souls, but not yet used to our hormones, and I know that mine were really crazy back then.

Our teenage years can also provide an exciting journey of discovery. We are creating the woman we will soon become. We are learning how to be a woman, even though we are not one yet. Life is blossoming and so are we.

Interpretations and conclusions of life, derived from my teenage years, defined and created me—just like they do all of us. It is obvious to me now when I look back, that my words created the 'me' of today. Fortunately I have a true perspective on this because as soon as I could write, I wrote. I wrote about the way I saw the world around me. My poems reflected often latent questions regarding race, spirituality, human interaction and animals from the youngest age. Later my detailed diaries recorded emotions and interpretations of life, rather than actual events.

After I matriculated I started a degree in psychology, which I felt restricted my thinking and prevented my mind exploring the things it needed to. I wrote about this too, not in a diary, but on bits of paper that I keep finding even today!

Then I started nursing, where I did much deep analysis of life through poems and prose on night shift. While the lights were down and the patients slept peacefully, I wrote. I wrote some of the most discerning material I've ever written. I've often wondered if the energy and the stories, the dreams and the losses, from all those dormant souls somehow entered my consciousness. I wrote about the homeless, the abused, the power of the mind, destructive emotions, life, war, peace, analogies for living, life philosophies, love, global issues, humanity, relationships, feelings, fantasy, spirituality, aging and even death. Night shift nursing became a catalyst for empathy and understanding beyond myself, which was unrestricted and revealing. I learnt a lot about suffering and the human spirit at this time and lost much of my naivety. I became incredibly attached to my patients as a nurse and found it impossible to leave my emotions at work, but it was through nursing that I learnt how exceptionally diverse and empowering writing can be.

❧

Today, I am the happily married mother of two little girls: Jasmine is seven and Angelique is five. You will never guess who I married: Duncan McPherson! We have now learnt how to communicate properly, and we find it hilarious when we look back at how different our individual understanding of shared teenage experiences was.

At fourteen, I lived across the road from Duncan, in Adelaide. We were really good friends (most of the time)—we had a somewhat love/hate relationship. We used to go ice-skating, roller-skating, bike-riding or just hang out together and with friends.

When we finished school, we lost touch for a few years. Then, coincidentally, we ended up sharing a house together years later in Melbourne—completely platonically! In this time, Dunc became my best friend and confidant. He knew everything I felt and thought about. Nothing really seemed real until I told Dunc. He became my substitute diary.

We then lost touch again, only to rediscover one another, with our respective partners, in Sydney. I remember thinking what a gorgeous man Duncan had grown into, but quickly dismissed those thoughts as totally inappropriate.

The final twist of fate occurred when we just happened to end our relationships the same week! We hadn't spoken for months. We decided we both needed a flatmate, but this time it wasn't going to be platonic.

Two and a half years later, we were married. Dunc (the spunk!) is the most beautiful husband and soul mate to me, and the most wonderful father. I feel we were predestined to be with each other and I consider myself so blessed.

Most of my writing, throughout my life, has revolved around issues like equality, connection, justice, peace, freedom, environment, expression, passion and empathy. There is always a compassionate edge to it. I often have a particular focus on compassion and protection of those who are unable to express themselves—like children and animals. It's hardly surprising that when I became a mother, the aspects of society that did not support connection and compassion became quite distinct to me. My fairy-tale, idealistic dreams were met with the reality of an injurious birth as well as a number of other (mainly medical) challenges relating to my child and myself, which also opened my eyes.

I felt as though my life had gone into a spin cycle of confusion. Whenever I looked for answers (from friends, experts, other mothers, my own mother, books), I found myself going around in circles and getting nowhere. It was only when I stopped, briefly, let go of all the information, influence and panic, and let myself settle that the most profound resolutions came to me.

I saw that, in some ways, society has it all back to front and inside out when it comes to mothering. I felt I was supposed to face extreme challenges—to accentuate the reality of the world we live in. I realised mothers were given vital survival tools—instinct and intuition—for a reason, but often society discourages them from accessing, acknowledging and listening to this critical inner voice.

I had stopped keeping a diary, but I would often write a page or two when I felt passionately about something, or perhaps a letter I had no intention of sending. One day, out of the blue, I felt compelled to write a list of topics that, to me, felt inauthentic and destructive to modern mothers. I knew mothering would be a whole lot more natural, enjoyable and rewarding if we simply changed a few ways of being and doing.

Then, whenever I had a small block of time (which

was rare: Angie was a rather unwell six-month-old and Jassie was two), I would start writing. It's really difficult to explain, but I feel the most extraordinary answers and understanding came *to* me, and *through* me—rather than from me. Writing became a place where wisdom and clarity liberated me. It seemed to be a subconscious process, or perhaps even a gift from God, because it was only later that night—when I read what I'd written to Duncan—that we both actually 'got it'. We felt like we had just received deeply profound insights.

At the end of the process, my life was transformed. I was no longer influenced by the world around me, unless it felt right and authentic. I felt free. Solutions were coming to me without really even needing to search. Life became simple and incredibly beautiful. I felt an overwhelming need to share this gift with all mothers, and remarkably the publishing process flowed as fluidly as the writing itself. Before I knew it, *Intuitive Mothering* was born. It has its own life energy now, and is transforming the lives of mothers and children all over the world. This ability to share and make a difference is to me the ultimate gift that writing can offer.

So, writing had made sense of life again. This time, however, the actual writing process provided the answers, instead of the answers coming through an exploration of conscious thoughts or feelings, and derived conclusions or strategies.

Writing is extremely cathartic. It is as diverse, flexible and multi-faceted as human beings. It is eternal and can be both introspective and altruistic, sometimes at the same time. It comes in different forms and can give us release, guidance, understanding, insight, acceptance and clarity.

If we just allow words to flow, we can receive wisdom and awareness beyond conscious thinking.

Some of the wisdom and awareness I've learnt through writing is illustrated in this story. In summary, I say: express yourself authentically because when you are true to yourself, you are true to others. There is penetrating beauty in truth. Our vitality and forming self is liberated through truth and authenticity. It's this sense of being real that is what makes each one of us shine. If we love who we are, completely and unconditionally, without judgement or expectation, we will be able to love others in the same way. We will also allow ourselves to transform and evolve, creating and fulfilling our dreams and living a life that we have chosen—a life authentic to each of us. It's in this place of being that the true miracles, and synchronicity of life, become our reality.

LYN McPHERSON grew up on a small acreage just outside of Johannesburg and moved to Australia when she was eleven. From the youngest age she wrote, keeping a detailed diary every day of her life. After spending her teenage years in Adelaide, she moved to Melbourne, backpacked around the world and landed in Sydney, where she fell in love with and married Duncan, her best friend of fourteen years. Lyn began a degree in psychology then switched to nursing, while continuing to write on the night shift. After she and Duncan had two children, Lyn wrote her first book, *Intuitive Mothering* (New Holland, 2006), which guides mothers to 'tune in' to their instinct and intuition, and 'tune out' the distractions that so often prevent truly joyful, connected, self-determined mothering. Her website is www.lynmcpherson.com.

The Waiting Room

Debra Oswald

Sitting in the doctor's waiting room with my mother, I shifted my bum on the squeaking vinyl chair and tried to control my shaky breathing. I wanted to look as normal as possible in front of the receptionist and the other patients. Trouble was, panic was flooding my body, like a blush spreading up my neck and face, only this was cold and prickly.

The doctor called me into his surgery with a sympathetic smile. This was it. There'd be no escaping the truth now.

I was pretty sure I had a brain tumour. A late-stage inoperable brain tumour. My mother, on the other hand, did not think I had any kind of brain tumour. She'd dragged me to the doctor so he could convince me of this fact. A few weeks before, it was stomach cancer. Or it could have been a malignant melanoma. Or liver cancer. Or angiosarcoma. My poor mum . . . dealing with a daughter who was obsessed with terminal diseases.

It started when I was eight. Tetanus, lung cancer, leprosy—I had them all, although not necessarily at the same time. When I got older—into double figures—things became a lot worse. My parents had to ban me from watching *Marcus Welby, M.D.* and other medical dramas. Those shows often featured scenes with a young woman lying in a hospital bed, her head swathed in bandages—a young woman with her whole life ahead of her. Ah, but then we'd see the doctors put X-rays up on a lightboard and shake their heads sadly. The tumour was inoperable. The young woman was a goner. For me, medical shows were the equivalent of horror movies.

The human body is an amazing thing, with millions of tiny parts working in harmony. There is comfort in that. Then again, the more you know about the hair-trigger processes involved in survival, the more you could worry about what can go wrong. Every time a cell divides, it could turn nasty on you. And as far as I was concerned, my cells were out to get me.

Feeling any tiny symptom, I would latch onto the rare cancerous possibility. For most people, a runny nose means they have a cold or hay fever. For me, it meant I could have lethal midline granuloma with only months to live. If I found myself with a neurological symptom such as the inability to look down, I would immediately consider Steel-Richardson-Olszewski syndrome. Sure, the odds were laughably small that a thirteen-year-old girl in the suburbs of Sydney would get Steel-Richardson-Olszewski—one chance in several million, probably. But someone gets it. Why should I assume it wouldn't be me?

Even at the time, I knew there was an appalling arrogance to my fears. Seeing myself as special, singled out for tragedy. I knew my hypochondria was self-indulgent. I was deeply ashamed to be fretting about maybes when there were people wrestling with nasty realities. I hated myself for the shame of my countless phantom illnesses knowing there were people facing real ones.

But of course self-loathing and guilt-induced stress have been associated with cancer and auto-immune diseases. So the more guilty I felt, the more blood tests and X-rays I thought I needed.

I knew my fears weren't rational. I would crack jokes about the craziness of my phobia. But in the end the terror was still there, slowly oozing up, like acid in my gullet, until it swamped me.

Nights were always the worst. Every scary thing is scarier at 2 am. My logical self knew that in the morning, things would seem better. But at 2 am, the morning seemed an unbearably long way off.

I'd lie awake, conjuring up the scenes that would torment me most of all. The scene where I was in a hospital bed, dying, saying goodbye. In my head, I've composed dozens of farewell letters to the people I love.

Why was I like this? In the years during and since, I spent many hours trying to figure it out—on my own, in reading and in various kinds of head-shrinkery. Was it a bizarre kind of low self-esteem that made me distrust my own body as a treacherous thing? Was it a form of obsessive-compulsive disorder? Did I have an overheated imagination? Was it some unfathomable quirk of brain wiring or chemistry? Was it evidence of the danger of television (all those medical dramas)? Was I simply a ridiculous attention-seeking drama queen? Or some combination of the above . . .

On those long nights of terror, I wouldn't just think about myself. I'd lie in bed wondering how many other people were awake, too. I knew that somewhere out there, at that exact moment, someone had been told terrible news. Their lover was leaving them, they had a serious illness, their child had been killed—something awful. Someone had had the world snatched out from under their feet. It felt like I was dipping my finger into some deep, constantly flowing channel of pain in the world.

Unfortunately, being a carcinophobic mental case did not let me off the hook of other kinds of adolescent angst.

My first four years of high school were spent at a single-sex private school that I still affectionately refer to as the Academy for Bitches. (Recently I returned to the grounds of that school for a function and was shocked by the jolt of animal hatred for the place that shot through my chest.) Cliques of girls can devise diabolical schemes to torment their 'friends' and I— stupidly—let it get to me. I can remember crying so hard and for so long, my eyelids were too puffed up to open properly for some hours.

Meanwhile, on the romantic front, I was a hopeless case. I didn't have the looks or that astonishing confidence some girls had around boys. Bus-stop flirting was out of the question for me. Dates, pashing and boyfriends belonged in the fabulous parallel universe inhabited by Pretty Girls.

I was the girl who guys confided in about problems with their girlfriends. I knew I'd never be the woman who men fell desperately in love with. My only hope was to put in an undeniably strong application for the job of

Girlfriend. My strategy was to be clever, accomplished, funny, and hang around long enough that eventually I might catch some guy as he stumbled away from heart-break with a pretty princess girl. Unfortunately, this strategy wasn't very successful, so there were many more tears shed on my already salt-encrusted pillow.

But all the time, amid the floods of tears and the obsessive cancer worries, I turned my imagination to another obsession: writing plays. I had started writing plays when I was ten. When I announced to my parents, 'I'm going to be a playwright', they gave me an Olivetti portable typewriter for my birthday. I bashed away on that typewriter for years, piling up pages, sending them off to competitions and theatre companies. I can't believe the gall I must have had back then to think that I could write plays and people might read them. I functioned through those years with an incongruous mixture of excruciating self-hatred and breathtaking boldness.

It's weird to think about all the different teenage girls I was at the same time—the driven junior playwright, the sturdy hockey player, the pimply social cripple, the cancer-obsessed nutcase.

That day in the doctor's surgery, I was examined and reassured that I did not have a brain tumour. As Mum and I walked out into the street, a potent mixture of feel-ings was churning inside me. The diagnosis was like a reprieve from execution, liberating and exhilarating. At the same time, I was dreading the cranky lecture I'd cop from my mother, who was, understandably, worn out by these dramas. I was nauseous with shame that I'd wasted everyone's time and made a fool of myself, yet again. And in the back of my stewed mind was the niggling worry that the doctor had missed something and I might really have a brain tumour.

Of course, the mental squirmings of an able-bodied middle-class girl are nothing compared with teenagers who have to face great struggles like illness, abuse, disability, poverty, wartime tragedy and dislocation.

I don't know why some of us torment ourselves so much over so little. But I do know that most people survive. At least you can try to recycle it into something useful. In my case, friendship and the writing probably saved me. Writing was also handy for converting my agonies into profitable objects—for example, I've written plays about hypochondria and about being a teenage social cripple.

Adolescence can leave scars and odd pathways in your brain. Even now, thirty years later, I notice visceral reactions in myself and I wonder, 'Where does that come from?' and I realise it's a thirteen-year-old girl with low self-esteem who's reacting like that. The 45-year-old happy partner, mother and writer gets cranky for letting that thirteen-year-old girl have any skerrick of brain space.

I don't want to trivialise or romanticise teenage angst, but I do believe it can give us insights, empathy, resilience, a respect for true friendship and other valuable gifts. Every adult I know has been formed by that time and you can see the teenager they were once you scratch the surface a little. In many cases, it's our best qualities—compassion, the ability to laugh at ourselves—which were forged back then.

I hope that if I see a person in mental anguish—like that thirteen-year-old girl in the doctor's waiting room feeling the brain tumour vibrate inside her skull—I won't judge without compassion. I won't ever forget what it's like to be in the clutches of a fear that your rational mind can't defeat. I hope I'll always have space in my imagination and my heart for the messy business of being a human being.

DEBRA OSWALD is a writer for stage and television and an author of children's fiction. Her plays include *Gary's House*, *Mr Bailey's Minder*, *The Peach Season*, *Sweet Road* and *Dags*. Her TV credits range from *Police Rescue* to *Bananas in Pyjamas* to *The Secret Life of Us*. She has written eight books for children, including *Aussie Bites*, and teenage novels.

The Marks of Memory

Tara June Winch

Experience is the word we give to our mistakes.

Oscar Wilde

Sometimes I think that the mistakes I've made outweigh the experiences I've had. And other times I have no regrets about the past, and pack my photographs away in the old navy suitcase in the cupboard. I keep most of my memories crumpled behind doors and in the back of my mind.

Some memories aren't ready to come back yet—I've shut them out for a while longer, maybe until I'm strong enough to face them, knowing that the reaction might mean falling in head-first. Sometimes in my dreams they surface and twist my world back to my childhood, or to my days at school, exposed and frightened. Sometimes I'll remember shards of moments past and I'll be taken aback by how different I am to when I was a teenager, how things that mattered so much then have no grounding any more, no relevance to my life. But in the throes of being a teen I wallowed in the drama and angst.

It seems like an entire lifetime has passed since I was a teenager, but then I remember it was only four years ago; four short years that have lapped against my short life. Teenager. It's funny—if I sum up my experience this far it only really began when I was fifteen. I've only really existed as myself for seven years. I'm still coming into the world.

In some ways, moving from adolescence to adulthood was no great feat. I spent a lot of my adolescence being an adult, performing adult duties—paying rent, looking after myself, cooking meals. I think sometimes that it's as if I'm proficient at being an adult but also still very much performing on a shaky foundation; that the line between adolescence and adulthood is blurred. The adult things that I could do well as an adolescent were often unshaped. I mean I can manage bills, because you realise that if you don't, you eventually get hunted by debt collectors, and I know about safe sex because I've fallen pregnant.

I suppose this is where the mistakes and the experiences merge, that point where there are no longer any excuses. I'm contained in an adult body and should be well adjusted, but I think there's still a huge part of me that's trying to re-learn the proper way of coping and moving within the world. I can't just shove my rucksack of belongings on my back and take off to somewhere else, run away; I've realised it doesn't work anymore.

I'm twenty-two years old. I'm a Wiradjuri woman. I'm a mature-aged tertiary student. I'm a single mother. I'm an author.

As a teenager I felt unsteady on my feet, awkward, even though I look at photographs of me at sixteen and see a beautiful young woman, struggling to understand her body and what it did. I don't really remember any conversations with my mum about sexuality, about respecting my body. I think her approach to my inquisitiveness was to ban me from parties and ignore that I was becoming a woman altogether. I suppose in a lot of ways I thought that all the adult duties I performed meant that I was mature enough to handle the chaos of sex as well—that if I could pay the rent and meet the grocery budget I could just as well fuck whomever I wanted to without the responsibility that comes with it, emotionally and physically. It didn't help that Mum had a string of boyfriends during my teens and I never felt I had a strong father figure in my life. I copied my mother, of course, and had a string of boyfriends who mirrored hers: druggie, drinking pigs. It's funny how women so often become like their mothers, the good bits and the bad.

Maybe I had lots of sex with lots of boys as a way of accepting my body and who I was. Maybe I thought that if they found my body attractive then it could heal my own insecurity. It wasn't a conscious thing—it only really occurred to me once I stopped doing it to heal my wounds or to seek approval, and did it for pleasure and for *love*.

My body now is covered in little silver scars, stretch marks. They're beautiful things, tattoos that only mothers get. They remind me of the tiny glistening shapes in the sand at the beach, when the tide drops off and leaves the snake indents like rivulets, whose salt water catches the shiny sun.

I fell pregnant. I never had a strong idea of contraception, menstruation and intercourse. I never realised that a woman ovulates around the same time of the month and that I could actually fall pregnant. It seems stupid, but some things you never learn until you really learn them.

My stomach felt bloated and it'd been a while since I'd had a period. I got up off the floor where I was crashing at a friend's place in Brisbane and walked, in my pyjamas, down the main street to the chemist, and waited out in the Queensland sun for the 'open' sign to flip over. I bought two instant pregnancy tests and walked back to my friend's house and did them. Both were positive. I knew it was true. In front of the mirror I pushed out my little stomach as far as I could and looked at myself. 'Could I walk around like this?' is what I asked myself. The answer was yes, but was I ready to? I didn't realise what it all meant. Looking back now, though, whether I was twenty-one or forty-one, I would never have understood what I was really in for.

In Brisbane I worked furiously to finish my novel before my baby was due to come into the world. I worked at nights, waitressing in a cafe, and slept in my boss's lounge room. Eventually my stomach ballooned and it was time to prepare for the arrival.

I gave birth naturally to a little girl. A beautiful healthy girl, whom I named Lila. I did it all on my own—I still do it all on my own. Having a baby wasn't in my big plan for my life. Being a mother is a new role I've had to learn by default. But I'm coping. I feel competent in the role, enough to keep striving to be a great person, achieve my goals and give unconditional, wholesome love to the most important person in my life.

People ask me if having Lila has changed the way I write, if it has given me a new insight into love. In some ways it has—in the way that all that beauty and love and happiness is bottled up into one look at her face. But in other ways it hasn't. I spend my days juggling playing blocks and going for big walks to discover the world, and cooking meals and paying bills, and having baths and breastfeeding, with the mere moments at night when I get to write. It's stalled the progress in my life. But I think that at the end of the day, when I'm here bashing out words, I'm stronger for it. The road and I are both worn enough to walk it well.

On these shaken foundations I actually feel confident that we'll both make it through. That while I know life is at its hardest some days, I have hope on my hip, cradled in my arms. That I can't give up—not for the past, not for the wrong or right decisions I've made, but for the future, for our future. Aside from mistakes, at the heart of it all, from the edge of the road looking back, I'll know that my regrets will all still be experiences. And our experiences will strengthen our foundations. And we'll be okay. At the end of these long days, we'll be okay.

TARA JUNE WINCH was born in 1983. She is a Wiradjuri woman. In 2004 she won the David Unaipon Award for Indigenous Writers, for her novel, *Swallow the Air* (UQP). In 2006 she was awarded the Victorian Premier's Literary Award for Indigenous Writing and also nominated for *The Age* Book of the Year Award for Fiction, the Queensland Premier's Literary Award for a Short Story Collection and a Deadly Award. Her work has appeared in *The Best*

Australian Stories 2005. Tara has written and is currently writing for *The Age*, *The Sydney Morning Herald*, *The Bulletin* and *Good Reading* magazine. She lives outside Sydney with her darling daughter, Lila, and their garden.

Confessions of a Drama Queen

Bianca Dye

There's no denying I was a massive drama queen growing up—the attention seeker, the performer, the class clown. It started at age six when, in my Sesame Street cottontails and nothing else but my stepmum Janis's stilettos, I got up on the coffee table at one of Dad's dinner parties and belted out Rod Stewart's 'Do Ya Think I'm Sexy' in front of a bemused crowd of hippies. And it continued right up until I was voted the one with the 'most manipulative personality' in Year 12.

I was always told that I talked too much and that no one really wanted to hear what I had to say. (Ironic, I guess, that I now have a radio show where a lot of people *do* listen to what I say!) I must have been a pain in the arse. I accept that. I'm pretty full-on now as it is, so imagine me as a teenager, when that 'filter' that tells you when you're acting like a tool is only just starting to feel its way around. I must have annoyed the hell out of (but hopefully also amused) most of those around me . . .

Showing off in my house was applauded—my dad is a fabulous performer and always had us laughing with his dry sense of humour. And I guess as the only child of a family where my parents split when I was three and Dad got custody (which was unheard of in those days, let me tell you), I felt I needed to get attention. A lot of it.

I was the girl in Third Class who got in trouble for kissing a boy in the cubbyhouse on the sandpit when everyone else was sipping lukewarm milk and drifting off into baa baa black sheep land . . . I wasn't *trying* to be a 'rebel', I just had that tomboyishness about me that a little girl gets when she's brought up by an outspoken dad whom she worships. I wasn't gonna be a little shy petal now, was I?

I'm positive I pissed a lot of people off when I was a teenager—for starters, Mum. She smoked like a chimney and every time she lit up in the car I'd wind down the window of the little Datsun and pretend I was choking—sound effects and all, coughing and spluttering, half hanging out the door—until Mum, embarrassed by the commotion I'd cause when we stopped at the traffic lights, would butt out the dirty durry, muttering something about wishing abortions had been easier in the '70s (she was kidding—I know!). Poor Mum, I gave her such a hard time! Whenever she had a boyfriend, I was so vocal about how I felt about him—to his face—that I think Mum started to wish that she didn't get to have me every weekend (only on Jewish New Year, perhaps). Later in my life she admitted that I must have had some weird insight as a child into which guys weren't good enough for her because she didn't end up liking them either (especially that weird one who used to lick the crumbs from the cake my nanna baked us off his fingers, one finger at a time—it drove me mental!). Kids have some instinct for that stuff, don't they?

Growing up the child of a '70s TV and music star had some awesome moments—I remember being lifted on stage at the ABBA concert in the early '70s when I was eight to join my dad, who was saying hi to the band after their show. At the time I had no idea who they were, of course, but it made for a fun show-and-tell at school the next day—naturally, no one believed me. And no one in my Year 8 class believed that my auntie (who made most of Olivia Newton-John's clothes) took me to lunch with ONJ herself in Melbourne at the famous Pelligrini's (still my favourite spag bol ever). Olivia signed a picture for me and the next day at school I was again ridiculed, for 'forging' her signature.

I think that sort of stuff at school either makes you shy away from being the kind of person who pushes the boundaries or makes you think 'stuff you' and push them even more. I guess I'm sharing all this because if you're a teen reading this and you feel alienated for whatever reason, I want you to know that it can all work out all right. I love that I'm outspoken now—I love that I am usually the only one who will speak her mind. I'm not saying I like to pick a fight; I actually avoid confrontation—I watched Mum and Dad fight enough to feel the pain of that come stabbing at my heart whenever tempers flare. I just mean that I don't usually have any fear of saying what I am thinking. It has got me into trouble on my radio show, don't you worry! But life's boring without a bit of trouble, right?

Being a bit of a turdburger as a teenager had its fun,

though—I remember when I was eleven running up and down the halls of Channel Nine in Richmond when Dad was filming there and bursting into Bert Newton's dressing room while he was in the make-up chair and yelling 'BOO!' and squealing with laughter and slamming the door and running for my life back down the corridors. I'm surprised Bert agreed to let me interview him for my radio show!

I know what you're thinking—behind every clown, behind every loud mouthed, remotely humorous performer there usually lies a battered, damaged child sucking its thumb, lying in the foetal position and staring into space . . . and I'm no different. I guess as you get older you learn to use the scars not so much as something to hide behind but to show off. To laugh about so that you don't have to face up to any home truths—and there are many home truths, none that I'm too ashamed to admit or explore, but that's all too much for this story. Another time—or over a coffee, perhaps!

Although I did feel most at home being the drama queen, it also created friction with people around me—family and friends. I remember when I broke up with someone I'd thought I was going to be with forever, after finding out that while I had been overseas he had shagged anything that had a heartbeat behind my trusting back . . . I had rung my best friend many times in one day, leaving distressed messages on her phone in the hope of getting her to come over and comfort me, as I was feeling pretty down. In frustration, I rocked up to her apartment—her flatmate was in the shower so I let myself in and found a note on the coffee table that I shall never forget as long as I live. It was from my then best mate to her flatmate and it went along the lines of: 'Good Lord if bloody Bianca rings AGAIN, tell her I've gone out, would you? What a drama queen.' It cut me to the core. I guess I had become the girl who cried wolf—I was so over the top all the time that when I really *was* in pain and needed TLC, even my true mates couldn't see it. I was gutted that day, and my friend and I were never the same after that.

Since that day I made a decision that I would stop apologising for who I am and how loud I am, because along with that loudness comes a passion for life—a love of people and their quirkiness, and a loyalty many can't compete with. I was sick of being 'sorry' for being 'me'. I wanted to be around other passionate (slightly mental but always loving and generous) people who didn't make me feel shit about myself. That's me and I was always going to be this way—my dad is loud, boisterous and passionate and never takes any shit from anyone, my mum is highly outspoken and intelligent, and my stepmum is a colourful lady. What's more, all of them are slightly nutty so there wasn't really much choice for me!

BIANCA DYE is one of Australia's top radio personalities and currently hosts her own 'Drive' show on Nova 96.9. Bianca has won the Australian Best Music Personality Award two years in a row. A regular guest on national TV shows like *Sunrise*, *Today* and *A Current Affair*, she also writes feature articles for national magazines and newspapers. Bianca has just written her first book, *Playing Hard to Get* (Harper-Collins Publishers, 2007), with relationship guru Dr Cindy Pan. Bianca's website is www.biancadye.com.

Fitting In

Di Morrissey

Thirteen. It hovered on the horizon as a magic number. When the date rolled around and I turned thirteen, I knew that everything I'd dreamt of and wanted would come to pass.

'When you're a teenager you can do those things . . .'

'Wait until you're a teenager . . .' It was held up as a turning point. At thirteen I'd join that special tribe.

Exactly what I wanted to come to pass on the morning I woke up to find myself aged thirteen was rather hazy. I didn't know my horizons might be limited. There was never enough money for things about the house, for the small ferryboat my father ran, and especially not for all the books I hankered after on the rare occasion I was near a bookstore. I promised my mother that when I became a teenager I'd make lots of money and buy her beautiful dresses. It was all she seemed to lack in my eyes.

I already thought my life rich and fulfilled in many ways. I mightn't have holidays or fancy toys or a bike or a pile of neighbourhood friends, but even then I knew that I had a pretty special existence. I lived in Pittwater in Sydney, an isolated but beautiful wilderness reached only by boat. I ran barefoot over oyster-studded rocks, rowed my dinghy around the bays, caught fish, lived in shorts, hung out with eccentric and artistic grown-ups who were to influence my life.

When the day finally came it was not as I'd imagined. I felt saddened and saddled with responsibility. My strong and invincible father and my chubby, happy baby brother were gone. Both drowned when my brother Michael fell overboard and my father jumped in to save him. The accident made us objects of pity, sympathy and whispers. Some well-meaning do-gooders made decisions for us, taking control away from my 'poor, grieving' mother as if she had become mentally unstable, when she was not only distraught from loss but also the knowledge that we had no savings, no future. There was no such thing as grief counselling or government assistance, but our good friend, the actor Chips Rafferty, arranged a fund and a collection for us, which was spent on two P&O liner tickets to America for Mum and me, so she could be reunited with her sister, who was married to an English professor who taught Political Science at Berkeley in San Francisco. It was time for Mum to reassess our lives and to bring a little joy to her life. We knew we would not stay for more than a year.

Mum's younger brother Jim, a journalist who'd been running (at age twenty-two) the *Mt Isa Times*, came along with us to spread his wings and expand his credentials. There were drinks in the lounge to see us off as I raced about the alleyways of cabins. Streamers finally snapping, friendly faces fading, we eased away from the dock accompanied by a throaty drone somewhere in the bowels of the great ship. I was so excited, but also fearful and worried about fitting in with new people who seemed to lead such different lives to what I'd known.

But once at sea my world became shipboard life and I rarely thought about what I would face when the journey ended. I only recall certain events of life during these weeks. In New Zealand we sat in a mud bath. It was misty, cold and rainy, the sloppy mud soothing and warm. At the Equator I remember Uncle Jim taking pictures of the crossing-the-line ceremony, where we were anointed with green jelly by King Neptune in a cloak, wig, cardboard crown and sceptre. In Hawaii Jim took a photo of me—dressed to the nines in a good frock and my lace-up school shoes—gazing at Waikiki Beach, so different from the beaches at home. Mum bought me a raffia 'grass' hula skirt, which I treasured.

Mum had been befriended by the star couple on the boat—an American nightclub crooner and his glamorous actress wife. They had a young daughter about five and one night I was asked to babysit when they went to a formal dinner with the Captain.

It was my first job. I lay beside her in the bunk and made up stories for her. Ghost stories. Scary stories. I was so over Goldilocks. It worked, as she fell asleep, only to awaken, screaming with nightmares, as her frantic parents burst into the room. I never babysat again.

Jim got off to start his career and a new phase of his life in Vancouver, the second-to-last port of call. We arrived in San Francisco to be embraced by Auntie Bette and Uncle John and three-year-old Cousin Christine.

I remember the house in Wheeler Street, Berkeley, well. White clapboard, an upstairs, polished wooden floors and what seemed to me the utmost in latest appliances— especially the roaring garbage disposal in the kitchen sink. And glory be, there was a cute young guy living right next door! I was soon invited in to make pull taffy, stretching the sticky toffee the length of the kitchen under his mother's directions. I wrote home to my best friend, Diana, about 'my boyfriend'.

My aunt and uncle obviously talked to Mum about her future—she had no income, how was she to support us? Uncle John suggested she join a TV and film training course that had begun at the university, and he arranged for her to study there. The immediate problem for me was getting into the teen scene—I was scrawny and felt far behind the sophisticated girls my own age around me. A bra appeared in my underwear drawer, together with a book on menstruation (I was a late starter, it seemed). I was more concerned about fitting in with the other girls and longed to own a stiffened horsehair-net petticoat to give the requisite bounce and swirl under my skirts and dresses. A BIG one. I had visions of Scarlett O'Hara's crinolines.

I was enrolled in the local junior high school but the horsehair-net petticoat was banned by my mother for school wear. So, modestly dressed, my hair in braids, I set off with bobbysocks and lace-up shoes, clutching my precious old school case, which I'd brought with me from home.

Oh, the shame. The ignominy of it! I was adrift in a sea of puffed and pushed-out skirts, Mary Jane shoes, lipstick and pink nail polish, and everyone carried their books in their arms or with a strap around them. I was teased about my case—'Going on vacation?'—while curious girls with sharky smiles circled, oohing and aahing over my 'darling accent'. Unconsciously I began to mimic them. I hated being 'different'.

So I entered a teen world of surprise parties, fancy-dress nights (in the hula skirt, of course), sleepovers and cookouts. But the horror party was a 'Come As You Are' occasion. One of the girls in my class rang my aunt's house and, after small talk, asked me what I was wearing at the moment. I should have smelt a rat as I wasn't especially friendly with her. I told her I was wearing pedal pushers and an old blouse. On my feet? Sandshoes—I mean sneakers.

She gave a peal of laughter—'I'm inviting you to a party: come as you are!'

Mum and Auntie Bette tried to curl my hair and jazz me up a bit—lipstick was forbidden—but like a fool off I went in the outfit I'd been 'caught out' wearing. Of course, no one else turned up in old clothes. Everyone looked like they'd just come from one of the big stores like JCPenney or Sears, Roebuck with a brand-new outfit. One saucy girl (there's always one in every class, an outlaw in the sexuality stakes) turned up in baby-doll pyjamas she just 'happened' to be wearing in the middle of the day when invited. Oh, sure. We played Spin the Bottle, but it thankfully never stopped to point at me. The boys were a loud, noisy and slick bunch who stuck together and laughed a lot. And chewed gum. I didn't fancy having to kiss any of them.

For the first time in ages I was part of a family. Uncle John, eccentric by some standards, with his great intellect, sense of humour and fun, and love of music inherited from his English Salvation Army family, opened doors in my mind and expanded my horizons. He told me I had a gift for expressing myself with words, and coming from him it meant a lot to me. I began to think my dream of writing one day might not be an impossibility.

A year later we returned to Sydney, my mother armed with training in film and the new medium of television. We moved into a tiny flat at the back of a rambling old beach house at Mona Vale, a long walk from the main road. Mum got a job in radio while waiting for the big new Artransa Park Film Studios to be built at Frenchs Forest, where she'd been promised a job. She worked at Radio Station 2CH in the AWA Tower in York Street, then the tallest building in Sydney.

I was happy to be back in the less pressured world of Australia, where knowing the latest fad, being the first to wear lipstick, nail polish and earrings, and having a bedroom with frilled curtains, a flounced bed cover, cuddly toys among the pillows and pictures of heart-throbs cut from fan magazines on the walls was *not* the norm. I wandered the length of Mona Vale Beach, explored the 'castle' on Bungan Headland, was given a bike and rode shakily on back roads. I felt happy to be in a natural setting, and while it wasn't the bushland of Pittwater, I loved the beach and the freedom.

I longed for the holidays to be over so I could start at Narrabeen Girls High School. After the competitive dressing of school in America, I was happy to have a blue pleated winter tunic, long-sleeved white blouse, blue and yellow striped tie, short plain white socks and a velour hat, and in summer a simple blue and white checked dress with a straw hat. I was ready to fit in, to be just like every-one else.

But to my dismay I was initially ostracised by everyone except a small group—my best friend Diana, and Margaret, Cynthia and Eileen. Carefully, they broke the news to me that I didn't fit in because I had traces of an American accent, I'd been overseas to school, and I had the mystique of a family tragedy hanging over me. I was *different*.

I handled this exclusion badly. Instead of trying to be as much like everyone else as possible, to conform and kowtow to the bossy girls who were leaders of the cool 'in' group, I did the opposite. To cover my hurt feelings I became more American, loud and boastful. I talked about going to Disneyland—and I had my Annette Funicello Mickey Mouse ears to prove it. One day I wore nail polish and pale lipstick to school—and was sent to Miss Fredericks the Headmistress for a dressing-down.

Eventually the sharp and snarly girls grew tired of baiting me and turned their attention to an unfortunate new arrival from the country.

So I turned my focus to schoolwork. Miss Collins the English teacher, who wore gold studded belts cinched around her tiny waist and dresses that many considered more appropriate for a party than for teaching, was complimentary, critical when needed, but kept an atten-tive eye on my writing, telling me that I 'told a good story'.

America and its memories seemed a world away. And I missed my aunt and uncle. Somewhere there was a niche where I would fit, fulfil my dreams and see my stories between the covers of a book. I had no idea how I was going to achieve this, but the power of dreams, knowing what I wanted to do and encouraged by others, drove me forward.

It took some time, but I got there. And now, looking over my shoulder at those teenage years, I realise they were precious and valuable, and that I was not always the outsider I thought I was.

DI MORRISSEY is Australia's most popular female novelist and one of the most successful writers Australia has ever produced. She is the author of fourteen bestsellers, each novel outselling the last. All have been written in Byron Bay, NSW, where Di has lived for the past sixteen years. Each book is inspired by the Australian landscape and explores an issue or theme while being an entertaining and absorbing read. Di is well known as a former TV presenter on the original current affairs program *Good Morning Australia*, as well as for her environmental work as patron of the Southern Cross University Whale Research Centre and her public service work with several organisations including the National Breast Cancer Centre. Her website is www.dimorrissey.com.

There's Light in the Darkness of Mental Illness

Jessica Rowe

Mental illness. Something that's extremely close to my heart and an issue that affects a lot of women. Something that has an enormous impact on families, particularly children, whose stories often remain forgotten and unheard.

Mental illness is isolating. It leaves people feeling powerless and alone. That's why I'm telling you my story about how mental illness impacted upon my childhood. How it left me feeling helpless and out of control, but how at the same time it gave me strength and courage.

It's not a glamorous topic—there's nothing beautiful about someone suffering a mental illness, and psychiatric hospitals aren't very inspiring places. But one of the most beautiful and inspiring people I know has a mental illness and that person is my mother. Mum sees her illness as just a part of her life. It doesn't define her life. There's no cure, but she makes every day count.

I realised that Mum wasn't like other mothers when I was aged about eight or nine. My bedroom was right next to hers and every night I lay in bed listening to her sobbing herself to sleep. I would creep out, put my head next to her door and listen to her cry. I wasn't sure what to do. Eventually, I would make my way back to bed and curl myself into a tight bundle, but I'd find it impossible to go to sleep until I knew that Mum had stopped crying.

Mum has bipolar disorder. It used to be known as manic depression. Fortunately, it's an episodic illness with periods of remission. So there are times when Mum's well. It's a condition that gives her periods of frantic manic energy. There'd be times when she'd stay up all night cleaning the flat, wearing next to nothing. Another time she became fixated on the idea of making hair clips for my two sisters and me. Not just one or two, but twenty or thirty different designs.

But those periods were very brief. Afterwards, Mum would come crashing down into a deep, dark depression. Her face would look drawn, her eyes would be sunken with big black rings underneath. She existed on no sleep. Her appetite would start to go. She'd lose her sense of smell. Any food in her mouth would make her gag. Any sound around her became amplified. Talking, traffic, music became unbearably loud for her. Gradually, she'd just withdraw, finding it harder to interact with people around her.

I was ten when Mum had her first breakdown. My sisters were aged nine and six. Because Mum went to hospital, we went to stay with my father and my step-mother. At the time, it just seemed like an extended sleepover at their place, and part of the adventure included picking up my sisters from school to visit Mum in the hospital. We'd have to take a bus and a train, and I remember being frightened because I had to ring the bell on the bus, and I had to stand on top of my suitcase to reach it. But, being the eldest, I knew I had to.

From then on, when everyday living became too hard for her, Mum would end up in the psychiatric hospital, sometimes for three months at a time. The trips to the hospital to visit her were very hard. I felt I had to put on a brave face for my mum and my two younger sisters. So early on, as shy as I was, I assumed the job that put enormous pressure on me. My heart used to sink when we'd walk down the hospital corridor approaching Mum's door. I'd be hoping, wondering, praying. What state would I find her in? Would she be silent and sad? Would she just sob or would she also try to be brave? The toughest part for me was seeing her in such a state of despair and feeling powerless to do anything about it.

When Mum was very ill, it just wasn't safe for her to be at home. There were times when she was unwell but still at home, and as I got older I'd notice the warning signs, so I'd do more to help, like organise the cooking and the shopping. Because this crept up on me over time, the added responsibility really didn't seem that unusual. As well, we had beautiful family and friends who'd come by, drop off food, perhaps stay the night.

When I was about twelve I came home from school one day to find Mum upset because she hadn't been able to cross the road on her own. She had become really frightened of the traffic. She'd been stuck in the middle of the road, unable to take one step forward or back. I was determined for her to know that she could do it, so I took her hand, walked back down the hill with her and helped her cross the road.

As a teenager, I felt even more devastated by Mum's illness. I was never embarrassed by it, though. I realised that her depression came in a cycle and her illness left her in hospital once a year. There was a time when I was studying for my HSC and Mum was going downhill very fast. The doctors were trying different medications but nothing was working. I came home from school and I'd forgotten my keys, so I called out for Mum to let me in. She couldn't walk to the front door. She crawled halfway there, becoming more and more upset. She managed to find the keys then threw them at me down the stairs, abusing me. I could see Mum's desperate face through our security screen, and I managed to squeeze my hand through the gaps in the screen to reach the keys and let myself in.

I couldn't believe it. I was so upset. My simple request to be let into the house had made her worse. It was terrifying to have the woman whom I placed on a pedestal, the woman I thought was meant to look after me, disintegrate before my eyes, unable to cope with the simplest of tasks.

A terrible revelation was when Mum told me that she'd thought about suicide on many occasions. But the thought of us, her daughters, stopped her. It gives me some relief to know that, as a family, we gave her a reason to keep living.

The sense of helplessness and powerlessness I feel about Mum's illness hasn't changed, even though I'm older and hopefully a little wiser. I still get anxious when I notice the warning signs. I still feel despair and anger.

A sense of it not being fair. Why did it have to happen to my mum, to me, to my family?

It wasn't easy as a child coping with Mum's illness. It forced me to grow up very, very quickly and I lost a big part of my childhood. But I found support and I've seen counsellors to help me deal with those issues.

So what do I want? Discussion. It's vital for people to realise they're not alone. The more people feel they can openly talk about mental illness, the faster the myths and the stigma about it will disappear.

And I want support, for all those touched by mental illness, both the sufferers and their families. It's essential for people to know that help is there. Because it's possible to use the strength and courage we find within ourselves not only to survive but to thrive and lead a positive and enriching life.

So it's my hope, my wish, my dream that everyone who has a loved one with mental illness receives the help and support they need to find some light in the darkness. Just as I have.

Reproduced with the kind permission of Jackie Frank, editor of marie claire *and the* marie claire *best-selling collection* What Women Want *(Random House, 2002), in which this story originally appeared.*

JESSICA ROWE is a co-host of the *Today* show on Channel Nine. She has always been passionate about news and current affairs and has a degree in Communications from Bathurst's Charles Sturt University and a Masters degree in

International Studies from the University of Sydney. Jessica has co-authored a book with her mother, about their family's experience with mental illness, *The Best of Times, the Worst of Times* (Allen and Unwin, 2005). Jessica loves her family, reading, high heels and her cats, Audrey and Alfie. She's revelling in married life with her husband, journalist, Peter Overton, as they embark on the perilous but joyous journey of parenthood.

First Love

Vanessa Gorman

I fell in love for the first time at fourteen. It was as tender and ecstatic as any teenage romance. I was more girl than woman at that age. Still cheerfully wearing singlets instead of bras, all bony limbs, barely a hip-to-waist ratio to speak of. I was scrubbed clean and open. Just like her. Virginia. Gin.

Those who knew us will know there was nothing sexual about it, about us. In fact, we fell in love over the shared hilarity of everything we didn't know about boys and sex and the churnings of the heart. The comic insecurity of it all. *See you down by the lunch wall*, the note she passed me read. *I saw Gus on the weekend—oh my God!!!* We had a boy to speak about. Too delicious!

I was bound by the insular embrace of a girls boarding school. Country-bred, I was a tomboy struggling to find some feminine essence that might guide me into womanhood. She was city-born, knew Sydney's ways. Where you could slip down one of the Darling Point apartment staircases, walk the harbour pipeline to Double Bay and browse for the morning at Sportsgirl. The kind of place as intimidating and alien to me as a shearing shed was to her.

Visiting her home on weekend release meant an escape from the cold, draughty corridors of the convent, the sandstone castle that kept me prisoner, and waking to sunshine through the windows of a family home in a leafy enclave. Her father would pad about in the morning, serving the entire family tea and toast in bed, a habitual act of grace that left me tongue-tied, mumbling my gratitude. I had lost my own father two years earlier.

Gin's father was a neurosurgeon, a job almost impossible to imagine. Her family hosted French culture evenings for their friends in the elegant living room while we watched *Hawaii Five-0* in the playroom. Dancing like dags to the theme song. *Da da da da daaa daaa, da da da da daaa. Book him, Danno.*

She took me ice-skating at the local rink every weekend I was allowed out. Gus worked there. We knew nothing about him except he was cute. We strapped on our skates and wobbled on rubber matting towards the ice.

'So maybe I could go back in and pretend these aren't the right size and swap them?' she quizzed, blushing at the idea.

'Good one!' I yelled. I was not yet ready to have a crush on a boy but thrilled to witness what it might feel like, how you might navigate the shoals.

'I'll loiter at the back and read the noticeboard,' I suggested.

'Okay, but don't make me laugh.'

She did nothing but exchange the skates for ones that were too large but we grew bold afterwards, finding laughter in the tiniest nuance of the encounter.

'He looked interested.' I grinned.

'I thought he was just about to invite me out, don't ya reckon?' And we fell down on the ice at the stupid fun of it all.

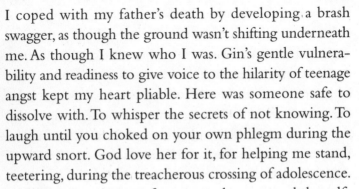

I coped with my father's death by developing a brash swagger, as though the ground wasn't shifting underneath me. As though I knew who I was. Gin's gentle vulnerability and readiness to give voice to the hilarity of teenage angst kept my heart pliable. Here was someone safe to dissolve with. To whisper the secrets of not knowing. To laugh until you choked on your own phlegm during the upward snort. God love her for it, for helping me stand, teetering, during the treacherous crossing of adolescence.

She was a mixture of sunny exuberance and shy self-effacement. But she was not shy with me, and I would come to feel her courage in the face of every fear. I whisked her down to my farm in the holidays so she could share the joy of my thousand-acre playground. Secretly, I wanted her to see my command over this environment. Like any lover, I wanted to impress her.

The sheep's carcass strung up from the rafters dripped a dark slime of blood onto the floorboard, grimy with lanolin. Our manager, Mr Cocking, hacked at another on the table.

'So this is where chops come from,' she marvelled, poking at the ribs.

'Yeah, where did you think?'

'I thought they just, you know, jangled around separately inside the sheep.'

Cocking smiled his wry grin, but I was as delighted as she was by her discovery.

Away from the confines of family and the expectations of a certain code of behaviour, Gin embraced country life and seemed to flower under the wide blue skies. We both relished the wild mayhem of our relatively unsupervised days now my father was gone and my mother worked full-time in the city.

I taught her to drive Beryl, our old bush-bashing station wagon. We would deck out Beryl as a sin bin, adding curtains, cushions and a mattress, for trips to the local drive-in, where every film was accompanied by the soundtrack of a bleating mob of sheep, grazing in the paddock between the parked cars and the giant screen. With my four brothers and sisters and our mob of friends, we drank port by bonfires and lapped the main street of Wagga, driving like maniacs along country roads to be home in time for *Countdown*. We danced like rock-god maniacs with air guitars in the living room.

She lay with my sister and me, outside our tent down by the dam, as we drank in the stars, and gave us the gift of asking about our father. Cried with us in the sadness of all that opened.

I loved every cell of her: the shy, timid ones; those with a howling sense of the absurd. She was compassionate and kind, only bitchy when pushed. She made my days a joy, and everything that happened, I lived to tell her about.

Virginia was shorter than me, brown silky hair to my frizzy mop, full fleshy lips to my hopelessly thin ones.

Her hopelessness may have lain in her freckled skin. Either way, I knew the world would judge neither of us as covergirls but her face was beloved to me. The animation that lit her from within was beyond the definitions of beauty.

Still, it was an immense relief to share the telepathy of insecurity.

'Were you thinking what I was thinking when Ruth was talking about Arthur's nightclub?'

'Oh my God, exactly!'

'How groovy it was, that it was all so brightly lit?'

'Worst nightmare!' we chimed in unison and dissolved again.

She taught me about lip-gloss and eyeliner and that at fifteen, everything you needed to know was in *Dolly* magazine and that laughing at yourself was more fun than laughing at others.

I betrayed her once. We had both been up to some mischief during the school lunch hour; I can't remember now how we had transgressed. But I do remember our formidable Headmistress stopping us on the stairs.

'Virginia,' she said, curtly, her voice a baritone perfectly pitched to strike fear, 'I believe you were seen down by the labs engaged in blah, blah, blah . . .'

'I'll see you later,' I muttered and turned to walk away, thinking I hadn't been spotted in the same enterprise.

'Vanessa!' The baritone went up an octave. 'I believe you, too, were involved?'

The embarrassment of being caught and the deeper

vanessa gorman · 389

shame of my betrayal flooded my face a deep red as I turned back to meet my fate. I came from a family where survival of the fittest was the law of the jungle. You got away with what you could.

'I can't believe you were going to leave me in the shit,' Gin accused later.

I pleaded a pardon for my baser instincts and grovelled an apology, hoping she would not define me by that moment. But the cock had crowed.

I cannot paint her in any entirety. I am leaving out her artistic side, her academic prowess, a thousand things. But if each of us is a many-sided prism, I glimpsed through hers once, to see the full spectrum of the rainbow. And it remains a defining image.

It was at the Boatclub Dance, an institution for the sons and daughters of Riverina graziers and the Wagga elite. Hence the rules that once everyone had arrived, neatly preened and primped, the doors were sealed shut. Fruit punch was served, an array of finger food wilted on trestle tables, and a fairly daggy band was employed to arouse the teenage passions. Although any passions aroused were fairly soon doused by the sizeable contingent of adult chaperones. We suffered the tameness for years and then discovered that the window grate of the women's toilet could be removed, allowing my brothers to pass through alcohol before making a delayed entrance.

That night was our last Boatclub Dance so we didn't care about anything but taking the piss—and drinking a fair slab of it.

We had adorned ourselves in a kooky array of vintage cocktail wear from Vinnies, teamed with ironic statements of hats and gloves. The pursed lips of the chaperones gave us great satisfaction. Gin let loose that night in a display that I had not seen before or ever would again. It was less a dance than mayhem in motion. Designed not to entice, but alarm. With each flailing kick of the legs her dress began to tear, until the skirt resembled a hula skirt of torn lace and silk, and the zip at the back gaped seductively open. Watching her dance, I felt the pride of a mother witnessing her daughter's flowering. I laughed until I was in danger of vomiting, clapping my hands in wild approval of the wacky animal on display. Wishing that they knew what I knew, that tonight she had left the chrysalis, emerging for a brief flight into a halo of unfamiliar light. Whoever she may have been, whoever she was to become, I bowed down to who she was that night on the dancefloor.

Like most women, I could define my life as much through the women I have loved as through the men I have shared a bed with. The intense road of female friendships branches and branches again. I don't see her much anymore. We speak rarely. Not through lack of love, just due to lives gone in different directions, geographical separation.

She made me a cot-sized quilt during my first pregnancy. When my baby daughter died she asked me if it was appropriate to still give it to me. I cried, fingering its handmade love, and stored it with the rest of Layla's things. I nervously took it out two years later when my son was born, wondering if it was too precious to use.

I rang her yesterday, to tell her I was writing this story. Like most mothers on the phone, we were multi-tasking. I was nursing my sick little girl over my shoulder and stirring the pasta sauce. I could hear her lifting her eight-year-old son into a billycart as her other boy yelled something from the background. 'Happy hour' for those with kids was just beginning, so we didn't speak for long. But I felt, from a thousand miles away, the familiar ease of her warmth. We talked a little of her mother's difficult illness, how the children were. And no, Gin told me, she didn't need to read the story beforehand. She trusted me. I wasn't sure if the years had left me with that same amount of trust in the world.

I now lay that precious quilt each night over another unspeakably precious gift, my son. And finger the stitching as I stroke his hair, remembering the bond of that one safe harbour and the first girlfriend, whom I trusted with my heart.

VANESSA GORMAN is a documentary filmmaker and writer. She has worked for many years for ABC TV, most notably on its prestigious biographical series, *Australian Story*. In 2001, the ABC aired Vanessa's video diary documentary, *Losing Layla*, about the death of her baby daughter. Her memoir, *Layla's Story* (Penguin), was published in 2005. She lives with her two small children in northern NSW.

A Black and White Picture

Belinda Alexandra

When I look at a picture of myself at fourteen now, I see a fresh-faced, pretty girl, rather Slavic in appearance, with high cheekbones and angular features. My dark brown eyes, however, are deep-set and sad. My lips are rosy and my teeth are white and straight, but my smile is hesitant compared with the unrestrained beams of the other fourteen-year-olds who had their pictures taken that day. Their faces are vacant, while the slight pinch between my brows suggests that I already know the weight of history. My school uniform is a nondescript check pattern with buttons down the front, but the blue colour is striking. It is the colour of the sun-bright sky in Australia and the summer sky that serves as a backdrop to the onion domes of my mother's homeland, Russia.

That picture of me may be in vivid colour, but when I think of my teenage years—in particular, my time at school—there is no blue uniform, no rose colour in my lips and cheeks. Everything turns to black and white and my heart becomes heavy. The problem was, I was never really part of things back then. I never belonged.

School doesn't work for everybody. It didn't for me. I was taunted daily with remarks like 'ugly!', 'pimple-face!', 'hag!' You hear a lot about the nastiness of teenage girls, but these comments were made by boys. I was a sensitive child and the taunts did affect me. By the time I was fourteen, I had covered all the mirrors in my room, would turn away from my reflection in public bathrooms and sat with a book in front of my face in class. The way I was treated and the way I reacted are puzzling to me now. I look again at my 'European' features in that photograph. I didn't really have pimples that were noticeable enough to be teased about and I certainly wasn't ugly. I was different, perhaps. My cheekbones are prominent in a way that never shows on the fleshy faces of Anglo-Saxons and my wavy hair falls in exaggerated curves around my high forehead. Were the taunts because I didn't look 'Aussie' enough?

I went to school on Sydney's affluent North Shore and most of my classmates were fourth- or fifth-generation Australians. Those who were children of migrants tended to have parents of British stock whose fathers had been transferred to Australia on business and decided to stay. There were a number of Dutch–Indonesians, a couple of Australian–Chinese kids with broad accents, and a few Greeks and Italians. The British migrants had large houses and were looked up to by the Australian parents as having come from some mysterious place still referred to as 'home'. The Dutch–Indonesians were also wealthy and fastidiously neat, and there were enough of them to mingle with one another. The Australian–

Chinese kids were all good at sport and studies, and were generally treated as equals—unless they beat an Australian at something, which then brought on an onslaught of abuse that included words like 'slanty-eyes' and 'chong'. The few Greek and Italian migrants lived above their family businesses and kept to themselves.

My mother wasn't a *migrant*. She was a *refugee*: a White Russian who had fled China as a child with her mother when the communists took over. For her, Australia represented the end of a long journey spent escaping an enemy. My grandparents had fled Russia after the Revolution and settled in the Chinese city of Harbin, where they lived peacefully for a few years before the Japanese army invaded and my grandfather was killed. My grandmother left her house and belongings behind and took my mother to Shanghai, where she met a kind Russian man who became stepfather to my young mother, but he died a short time later.

My father, an Australian of Irish–English descent, had lost his family to various tragedies in childhood. It was something he never liked to talk about. He met my mother at a combined YMCA and YWCA meeting, and they grew successively closer over musical appreciation evenings, bicycle rides in the park and dances. They loved each other faithfully for more than forty years, two lost souls who were lucky to have found each other in their youth.

While my classmates talked about weekends with 'Nanna and Pop', with their legions of aunts and uncles and cousins, for family I only had my mother's photograph album with the engraved Chinese dragon on the cover. It contained sepia pictures of smoky-eyed women and handsome men in fur hats whom I would never know: they had met their ends early in front of Stalin's firing squads or in countries far from their homes long before I had been born.

I think this family background does in part account for the feelings I had of being separate in outlook to my classmates. While they talked excitedly of visits to country relations, cricket and picnics with their extended families (*'Don't you have an aunty or uncle? No cousins?'*), I sometimes felt as if I were going to school with the weight of revolutions and early twentieth-century epidemics on my back.

Not that my parents were morbid about their past. Both of them had a great sense of humour, and my happiest memories are of the stories and anecdotes told at the dinner table. In a strange way, this turbulent family history enriched me as a person and gave me the insight I needed to become a writer. It did, in many ways, make me mature for my years. But for everyday life, and certainly for my adolescence, it put me somewhere on the outskirts of normal suburban reality.

When I used to tell my mother about how the boys teased me, she would say that they were just jealous and trying to get my attention. As an adult, I understand that anybody who taunts other people doesn't like themselves much. But as a young girl, I could only accept that on an intellectual level—I didn't have the life experience to let that fact sink in emotionally. My tormentors were my peers, and when you're a teenager that's who you listen to for acknowledging your place in the world, not your inner self. I was a bird being pecked to death for being perceived as weak by the others in the flock. My peers had judged me worthless and I accepted that there must be some sort of truth in it.

What is interesting to me now is that at some level even then I recognised that my life would have been easier if I had freckles across my nose, straight hair and tanned legs, but I was never very attracted to being what was thought of as a 'true Australian'. Part of me longed for that mysterious essence I saw in the faces of those deceased relatives in my mother's photograph album, despite the tragedies and terrors that littered their lives and their deaths. I wanted their culture, their ability with foreign languages—which they picked up out of necessity as much as interest—their intellect, their connection with great music and literature. They seemed more alive to me than the healthy children of my suburb with their neat parents who mowed lawns and washed cars on Saturdays and sat down to lamb roasts on Sundays.

I'm not sure I could have survived these conflicting pressures—between the life I was supposed to want and the life I had and the life I really wanted—if my world outside of school had not been so full of colour and possibility. My mother's Russian girlfriends, most of them refugees like her, used to include me in their lunches and afternoon teas, where I learnt to cook blinis and came to understand that time spent with a friend was of more importance than getting the laundry done. While my schoolfriends' mothers had accounts with Farmers department store, my mother and her friends scouted St Vincent de Paul shops for quality clothes they could send to poor children overseas. My mother passed away suddenly a few years ago, and her open-hearted generosity to disadvantaged children is my proudest memory of her.

My father seemed to gather eccentric friends of his own, who would bring us spicy delicacies to eat and treat us to slide shows of their treks through India and Nepal long before such trips were fashionable. In fact, my whole family was a source of support. I had two older brothers who were my playmates even when the other kids were mean. Chris and Paul were always good to me. The first serious story I ever wrote was about a dove trapped in a cage. Chris loved it so much that he photocopied it several times so I could give it as a Christmas present to some of my friends.

During the wonderfully long school holidays, I was free from the taunts for weeks on end and could choose to spend time with friends from school whom I liked and who were kind to me. There was time, too, to wander through the bushland that wove its way through my suburb with my brothers for company. Our family cats and the possums, birds and blue-tongue lizards who visited our leafy garden gave me a lifelong love of animals that even now makes me view any garden that has only pavers, lawn and topiary roses as dead.

I was also involved in community groups, where there were girls older than me by a few years. They offered me an insight into a young person's life outside of school. Being with them gave me the hope that perhaps school was indeed just a passing phase. I longed to be independent like them: to drive a car, make my own money, choose my own clothes. It helped me to see that there was a life beyond that of days divided into forty-minute periods by the ring of a bell. Those girls were fun and gave me a sense of self-worth I couldn't get from my peers at school.

And despite the daily litany of derision those boys dished out to me, I had a flame somewhere inside that made me believe I would amount to something one day. That light was sparked by my mother. She always told me that I was beautiful and bright, and she was interested in every success I had with my studies. There wasn't always a lot of spare cash around when I was growing up, but if something was going to benefit my education or make me a happier person, my mother would always find the money to provide it.

The year I turned fifteen, I made a conscious decision that I was not going to let my tormentors destroy me. Whatever they said, however often they said it, I was going to shut them out of my mind and do well at school. I was going to get through it. I had been lucky because I found my source of strength in older women. I may not have had grandmothers and aunties, but my mother's friends became my surrogate family. I could talk to them about things that I couldn't talk about with my mother because she was so protective. If I told my mother about what some of those boys at school did to me— filling my school case with water and ruining my books, spitting on my shoes—she would have turned up at the school and flattened them. Her friends were a step removed and even though—compared with what they had lived through—my stories of my struggles at school must have seemed petty, they were always there to listen. I think I will always have a special affection for older women, who have been so kind to me. Even now, I have many good friends who are twenty or thirty years older than me.

Looking back, I start to understand that photograph of myself at fourteen better—the sad eyes, the hesitant smile. Things may have been different if I had gone to school with the children of other migrants, people who struggled to make a new life in this country—like my husband's parents, who came from the north of Italy after the war. My father-in-law, a well-educated man with a white-collar job in his home village, undertook backbreaking manual work on the Snowy Mountains Scheme to make a new life for his family. I don't have to explain to Mauro what it's like to have had parents who 'did it tough'.

Or they may not have been so bad if I hadn't allowed myself to be treated that way. Why didn't I stand up for myself? The people who taunted me weren't exactly at the top of the pile themselves. My best friend was sent off to kindergarten with these words of advice from her mother: 'If anyone hits you, make sure you hit them back.' Why didn't I turn around and answer, 'Yeah? Well, look at you! You're fat!'? Would that have stopped the tormenting or just escalated the situation? I don't know. In a way, I'm glad I didn't stoop to that level. I've never gotten any pleasure out of being nasty.

If school doesn't work for one, I think the secret is to create a world outside of it that is full and happy and that does provide self-esteem and pleasure. No matter what kind of school teenage girls go to, they are going to be surrounded by other teenagers who are struggling with their own issues—and who, because of that, can be cruel. Bullying is now being addressed in schools with a view of zero tolerance. I think that's essential because I am convinced that bullying can force a teenager to suicide if they don't have enough support systems outside of school. I wish I could tell teenagers I know who are suffering to take heart, to focus on what they want to get out of school and then do things outside of it that they enjoy.

Many of my friends and colleagues have noted that the popular kids who were considered beautiful, bright and glorious at school flounder after it's over without the protective cocoon of institutionalism. They can't compete in the real world. Conversely, it's the guy at school with the lisp who becomes a sports star, the hirsute girl who becomes a successful businesswoman, the overweight girl with braces who becomes the movie star. I saw this kind of coming to life among the kids in my year. Those who had suffered at school blossomed afterwards. The others are still running around with pictures of their glory days. Few of the late bloomers kept their photographs. Why would they? A friend told me about one of her year's beauty queens treating her to an entire afternoon of school photos after she happened to bump into her one day. 'T's life stopped the day she received her HSC,' my friend told me. Now, that's sad.

I came to life the day school was over for good. My life now feels bright and full of colour, but high school for me will always be a black and white memory. I have no desire to attend reunions, although I wish everybody I went to school with the best in life. I've forgiven the people who bullied me because I understand now that they weren't in a good place themselves. I have moved on and created a life of fulfilled dreams. Perhaps my experiences at school made me tougher in the end. I am a successful writer, I have two university degrees, I've travelled the world and met all sorts of interesting people. I married the love of my life and now have thirty-six cousins in Italy. I don't need to stare at pictures from my past to try to work out who I am. I'd rather live in the present, where life is in full colour.

BELINDA ALEXANDRA'S novels, *White Gardenia* and *Wild Lavender*, have been published to wide acclaim in Australia, New Zealand, the UK, France, Germany, Holland, Poland, Norway and Greece. An intrepid traveller, Belinda has a love of other languages and cultures that is matched only by her enthusiasm for her home country, Australia, where she is a volunteer rescuer and carer for the NSW Wildlife Information and Rescue Service (WIRES). She is currently working on her third novel, *Silver Wattle* (Harper-Collins, 2007), which is set in Sydney in the 1920s.

Argentina

Sarah Armstrong

I pretend to be asleep, my eyes open just enough for me to watch her getting ready for school. She is blurry in the dim early morning light, fastening her bra, buttoning her shirt. But I can see her hands making the sign of the cross, over and over. Thirty times, forty times. I lose count of that swift, intimate touching of her own body.

There's a rap on the bedroom door. '¡*Marilena!*' The driver, Alfredo, is waiting in the courtyard outside our room. He is muttering and stamping his feet in the cool air and his cigarette smoke drifts under the door. Marilena continues brushing her long black hair.

'¿*Marilena?* ¿*Está lista?* Are you ready?' His impatience is clear. I hear him go back inside and his voice rumbles from the kitchen as he talks to Celia, the maid. Then there is silence and I imagine he is drinking a cup of bitter maté tea.

'*Aí voy.*' Marilena moves to the door with her school bag. She once confessed to me—late at night, as we lay in the dark—that she hates attending the nearly all-boy technical high school. But she said her mother would not forgive her if she were to leave the school where her dead brother once studied.

She opens the door to the pale morning and sounds from the street wash in—car tyres thrumming down the hill, banging and hammering from a nearby construction site, the world outside gathering speed for the day ahead.

I know Marilena will make the sign of the cross at least a dozen times as she and Alfredo travel across town in the immaculate car. Everywhere in Argentina I see Jesus stretched out, bleeding on the cross. In that moment, as she closes the door behind her, leaving me to get ready for school, I am fascinated by and almost envious of her intimate dialogue with God. In time, though, I will realise that my host sister is simply pleading with God for help.

It takes me a couple of months to learn that I have walked into a house of secrets, a house of ghosts.

I barely speak Spanish when I arrive. *¿Como está?* I can say. *¿Dónde está el baño? Muchas gracias.* But it is not my meagre Spanish that keeps me from noticing the currents flowing and curling through that big white house on the hill. I have carried with me a template of my own family and I try to lay it down upon this one. I am seeing these people through my own, utterly mismatched prism.

It is siesta time. I am learning to lie in a darkened room for an hour after lunch, while Marilena sleeps on her bed an arm's length away. From the kitchen there is the rattle of crockery and the sound of Celia talking to someone as she washes up. Dubbed Brazilian soap operas burble from the master bedroom where my host parents are propped side by side, drinking maté. Outside on the quiet, abandoned street, two boys walk by and I can hear every incomprehensible word.

I am floating in a sea of Spanish. *La mar* and *el mar*. The sea is both feminine and masculine. Every night and every afternoon, I lie with my eyes closed, floating, trying to hold on to the day's new words. I am completely surrounded by this sea of otherness. And I want it. I have so wanted this year away, to become independent, separate from my parents, separate from my country. I am fifteen and desperate to hurry into maturity, to lose my virginity, become a woman.

Four-year-old Emilio appears beside my bed with that wide shining smile. He whispers, '*Venga, Sarita.*' I follow him and we stand together in the dining room, on the cool polished tiles, looking up at the small shrine to his brother, a glowing red lamp that is never extinguished. We stand there, wordless, and I wait for Emilio to indicate when we can go.

After siesta, my host mother, Lila, sits me at the round kitchen table and lays out her dead son's diaries—thick notebooks of drawings and jottings. She asks me to translate fragments of English and I am confused until I realise he has copied song lyrics: 'Michelle, ma belle, these are words that go together well. I love you, I love you, I love you.' I flick back and forth through my dictionary, trying to find the right words.

She moves the tray of sugar and jams and powdered milk to one side and spreads newspaper clippings over the table, indicating that I should read them. I decipher the journalists' graphic descriptions of how Dante was dragged under a truck, riding his motorbike home from school.

His broad smiling face has been reduced to small grey dots of newspaper print, the paper soft and felty between my fingers. My Spanish does not yet extend to expressing subtleties of regret and condolence. *Lo siento. Lo siento.* 'I am sorry,' or, more literally, 'I feel it. I feel it.'

'I see him,' she tells me. 'Sometimes I see him turning the corner in the street. *Mi hijo, Dante.*' Dead barely one year.

Alfredo picks me up from school and we drive across to Emilio's school, where we park in the shade of a big tree. Alfredo smokes and I write a letter to my parents.

'*Sarita*, little Sarah,' he says, 'I am going to tell you some words. Don't let anyone teach you these words.' His long dark face is serious and he directs a stream of smoke out the window. 'I tell you these so no one will trick you.' And he repeats them slowly, syllable by syllable, his eyes averted. *Pel-o-tud-o. Bol-ud-o.*

But already I know the awful weight of these words. Lila's grief and anger spill in one direction only: onto Marilena, who stands mute, her black eyes on the floor, her nostrils flaring as these words drop on her, like rocks, like anvils.

I don't tell Alfredo that I first heard these words spoken mother to daughter. I don't tell anyone, I don't even write in my diary about the times I have seen Lila stand in the dining room, in the bedroom, in the hall—wearing her heels and her tight-fitting woollen skirt— words of hate slipping easily from between her beautiful lips.

It shakes me that it is possible for a mother to speak to a daughter like this. It means that nothing is safe, nothing can be trusted, after all.

Mi amor. Lila is loving, too, and kind and funny. '*Mi amor.* My love,' she says to Marilena, to all of us. And Marilena crosses herself in every private moment. An urgent tracing of the crucifix upon her body.

Celia finishes brushing bleach onto Lila's dark roots and we sit in the kitchen waiting for it to fade her natural brown. I carry boiling water from the stove to replenish the maté pot. Lila sits straight-backed, a towel around her shoulders, reading a magazine and sucking the tea through a metal straw.

'Ana used to do this with me,' she says. Ana, the daughter my age who is on exchange in Europe. I will meet her for only a few weeks at the end of my stay. She is another ghost in this house.

'Ana sets the table. She cooks when the maid is away at her village. She is so kind, so helpful,' Lila says. I hear the real meaning: Marilena is none of these things. And I wonder if Ana is able to protect Marilena as I am not.

Lila squeezes honey into the maté pot and tells me how her first husband—Marilena's, Ana's and Dante's father—beat her with a leather belt until she ended up in hospital. Her tone is matter-of-fact. 'I thanked God when he left because I could not leave him. That's the way it is here. It's not possible for a woman to leave a man, you know, Sarita.' She and my host father, Carlos, married in Brazil and it pains her to know that the Pope would not accept their marriage.

She checks that Celia is busy in the laundry and leans over to pull a glossy catalogue from her handbag. 'See this? She chose this perfume.' She points with a long burgundy fingernail. 'I found it in his glove box. He is buying her this.'

A line of blue pen makes a loose circle around a photo of French perfume. Lila thinks Carlos is having an affair.

'I won't confront him yet,' she says and refolds the catalogue. 'I'll wait for him to make a mistake.'

I think she is paranoid and that it can't possibly be true but I nod and pour more hot water into the maté pot. Not long after I fly back to Australia, he will leave them for another woman. Whose name is also Lila.

I wake disoriented. I have dreamt in Spanish for the first time. At the breakfast table, I recount my dream and they are all delighted.

'Que fantástico, Gringa,' says Carlos and smiles across at me. He stands and gathers his papers; as ever, dressed in suit pants and a crisp shirt, his black springy hair oiled and combed back.

He is the only one in the house who seems to understand me, but I don't tell him how much I hate it that my English is slipping away from me. I am losing words daily, the Spanish pushing them out, like a cuckoo chick ejecting the rightful egg from the nest. In letters home, my sentences are strangely structured and basic words misspelt. I read and reread novels in English, seeking nuance and subtlety, but soon I will speak two languages imperfectly, my English no longer sophisticated and my Spanish bald.

Even if I had the words in either language, I would not speak to anyone of my desperate homesickness. It's something I keep close to me, a shameful secret, that this experience is not the exciting adventure I wanted. That I am not so mature after all. I count the days on the calendar inside my school folder, crossing them off, one line in the morning and one at night. Day by day. *Dia por dia.*

One day Marilena notices me doing it. '*¿Cuentas las dias hasta que vuelvas?* Are you counting the days until you go back?'

'No. No,' I say.

But I see that she is not fooled.

Andrea has come to live with us while she finishes the school year. She is the teenage daughter of family friends. She and I walk back from school together most days and stop at the gelato stand. Forty flavours. I am eating my way to comfort. Trying to anchor myself in the familiar language of food. I know well the subtle grammar of sugar and cream, hazelnut and cherry. After we eat our gelato at one of the small tables on the pavement, Andrea and I walk home, arm in arm, or with my arm slung around her shoulders. We are in rhythm. It is easy, intimate, the way women walk here. The way I will walk with lovers in the future.

At home I crave little cakes made with *dulce de leche*, caramelised condensed milk. And thick tortillas from the store on the corner, dry flaky layers of bread. I lie on my bed during siesta and rest my hands on my body. My jeans don't fit anymore, nor do my T-shirts. Letters from other female exchange students tell me they have put on four kilos. Seven kilos. Ten kilos.

I find a way to reverse the awful momentum. I try to stop the gagging sound of fingers down my throat. I hate the watering eyes and pounding heart. But it gets easier. Too easy. The shame is no worse than that which seems to surround me in this house, and now I have a secret too. Secrets are all that stir the air here.

He is the most handsome in the group of exchange students and later I hear that he's aiming to tally more than 100 conquests during his year in Argentina. One in the back of a bus. One at the side of a shop. In bedrooms. In hotels. And in someone's front garden.

We are in a city in the south, walking home from a restaurant with a group of other exchange students. He leads me off the footpath into someone's park-like garden—'Come this way.' I can hear the smile in his voice. His hand is firm on mine and I let myself be led. I want this.

It is late—well after midnight—but there is a light on inside the house and as I follow him into a small clearing and lie beside him on the cool grass, I picture a woman sitting up, reading in an armchair.

I don't tell him it is my first time. It is cold and I am wearing a borrowed yellow sweatshirt with 'hot-dog' written on the front. When he stands up afterwards and leans against a tree trunk, he is just another shape—along with the trees and bushes—silhouetted against the night sky.

I don't know what I expected to feel—but not the restlessness and disappointment that eddies around us in that dark garden. It will be much later that I am sad to be number fifty-six or seventy-eight or whatever I am on his list. I can't see his face until he lights a cigarette and then there is a snapshot of it, startlingly beautiful. He passes me the cigarette then lights another and takes my hand, and we walk through the bushes to the road. I look back and the light inside the house has been turned off.

We spend a lot of time driving around in Lila's old Renault, between our various schools and the shops, Lila at the wheel, smoking, gossiping, chiding, cajoling. I examine her profile from the back seat—her aquiline nose and the way her nostrils lift slightly as she laughs, her elegant fingers waving a cigarette in its long filter. She manoeuvres us through the narrow streets, which are as I imagine European streets to be, narrow, cobbled, opening into small plazas and triangles of park.

Every time we pass a church or shrine to a saint, there is a fluttering of hands in the car—all of them making the sign of the cross. 'We are paying respects,' Lila tells me. The crosses mark our progress across the city. Flutter, flutter.

The Andes rise high over the terracotta roofs of the town, great triangular cliffs of orange rock. The air is thin up here in the foothills and the light blue of the sky looks strained and gauzy.

For months Marilena crosses herself when we pass the Seventh Day Adventist Church near home until Lila admonishes her, 'It's not a real church, Marilena!' Their crossing is habitual, automatic, and they keep chatting as their hands touch the points of their body, except when we pass the place where Dante died. We go that way infrequently, that stretch of four-lane, bland cement road. Lila slows the car and closes her eyes as she makes a cross and doesn't open them until Marilena calls out, '¡Mamá! Mamá!'

❧

I am on my knees, rubbing at the satiny clay floor tiles with my Minnie Mouse nightdress. My feet have left marks on the floor, damp telltale signs that I have been downstairs, scouting. 'You're not to walk with bare feet on the tiles,' I've been told. 'You'll get cold and sick and it leaves marks.' I want to tell Lila how I spend my life back home barefoot, inside and out—the summer's goal to toughen my soles until I can walk over bindies and hot sand.

I rub at the footprints and retreat upstairs. Something has happened in the night—there is a full ashtray in the living room and a makeshift bed on the couch.

At breakfast Carlos has already left for work. As she chain-smokes, Lila tells us that in the night Andrea accused Carlos of touching her while she slept. Today Lila says she believes Andrea. The next day she will not.

Although my Spanish is fluent now, I make Andrea repeat the story of what happened. I don't want to believe her and, to my shame, I ask her again and again if she is sure it really happened. '*¿Estás segura? ¿Estás segura?*'

Her eyes full of tears, she nods. She is sure. So sure that she got up just minutes afterwards and banged on Lila and Carlos's locked bedroom door with her fist. She shows me how she pointed that long slender finger of accusation at him. Arrangements are made for her to leave as soon as possible.

In front of the bathroom mirror, I practise making the sign of the cross. There is a satisfying symmetry to the action. It feels like calligraphy, like painting a seal upon my body. Sealing in God.

'Do you believe in God?' Lila had asked me the first week I arrived.

'Yes.' I was lying. I knew my god was not their God.

'Ahh.' She had sighed and offered a relieved smile.

I watch myself in the mirror. There is a borrowed comfort in the slow, steady cross I make.

In that year, far from home, I discovered that adulthood was not the next destination, after all. Losing my virginity and holding my own in a foreign land did not ease me over the threshold into womanhood. Instead, I learnt silent endurance and the language of secrets.

I spoke to Marilena on the phone several years later

when she was in her early twenties. She was married, with a newborn baby, and she refused to let her mother see the baby or know where she lived.

'You know why,' she said to me down the echoing phone line. 'You know my mother.'

'Yes, I know why.'

Again and again I have pulled out the photo that arrived in the mail a week before I flew across the Pacific to spend that year with them. They are sitting on the front steps, strangers smiling and squinting into the sun, the maid standing just off to one side. Part of the house is visible behind them—a slice of white stucco wall and black cast-iron gate. It's a simple photo of a family called together for a moment on a bright Saturday morning, and I have examined it, looking for some hint of what was to come. Something in their faces, in the way they are sitting, the way their hands fall into their laps. There is nothing to see.

Sarah Armstrong's first novel, *Salt Rain* (Allen & Unwin), was short-listed for the 2005 Miles Franklin Literary Award, the Nita Dobbie Literary Award and the Queensland Premier's Literary Award. Sarah lives on the north coast of NSW, where she teaches writing workshops and retreats. Her website is www.sarah-armstrong.com.

Old School Ties

Lisa Wilkinson

'So, what school did you go to?'

It was a weird question and I heard it constantly. Weird because, to me, the answer seemed obvious once the new acquaintance had already established the name of the small town on Sydney's western outskirts in which I'd grown up.

The pity on their faces when they realised I was from somewhere that wasn't east, or even *north*, of the city was palpable. Hence the follow-up question about the school I'd attended, almost as if there was still hope for me if my parents had somehow seen the error of their outer-suburban ways and sent me somewhere, well, more appropriate, for my education. But there was no saving me. It was the local government high school. Wilkinson ... sorted ... shuffled to the bottom of the deck ... NEXT!

I was first asked the question at the age of eighteen on day one of a secretarial course I was doing after achieving what could only be described as a supremely mediocre pass in the HSC. Journalism was my hoped-for career destination, and with a stunning lack of interest in the hard slog of a four-year communications degree—and no parental expectations that '*of course* you'll go to university'—I figured that shorthand and typing just might give me the learn-as-you-go back door into the media I needed.

But first I had to survive the rather stuffy surrounds of the inner-city 'business college for ladies' I'd somehow settled upon. The place was, almost without exception, populated by a sort of 'society girl' I'd never before encountered—the kind who 'do' ski seasons and deportment courses, and whose parents had decided that secretarial training would give them something suitable to occupy themselves with until they found a sober-suited male protector and provider . . . preferably of the privileged variety.

At lunchtime the girls' talk was of B&S balls, the family beach house at 'Palmie', and chums called 'Dee' and 'Bin' and 'Boo'. Their cardigans were cashmere, and their nails were always remarkably neat and shiny, just like the brand new Celicas they'd been given by Daddy for their 18th. And, oh yes, all of them were private-school educated. But of course.

Me? I'd gone to the local public school three blocks from home. Infants, primary, secondary. In our town there was only one high school, so there was no decision to be made. Unless, of course, you were Catholic. But our family wasn't, and when I saw the immensely sensible brown shoes that were strict standard issue with the local Catholic girls' high school uniform, I was very pleased that we weren't.

At my government school, the dress rules were a little

more relaxed. We hitched our skirts and ditched our blazers, and even though the Headmaster frowned, no one took his threats of detention seriously. He must have decided there were bigger issues to a worthwhile education. Such as encouraging good teachers—like Miss Jackson, my Year 9 English teacher. Miss Jackson was brilliant, and rebellious, and nurturing, and I'm sure, working in a government school, incredibly underpaid. But she gave me, and no doubt many others before and since, a deep love of the written word, and was the one who inspired me to follow journalism. I remember asking her once why she didn't become a famous writer instead, because even through a fourteen-year-old's eyes, I could see that the job of teaching was often a thankless task. She assured me it wasn't.

As a school, we were proud of our tight-knit community. '*Viribus Unitus*, we a–chieve suc-cess through u-ni-ty,' went the school song. As a bunch, we grew up just streets away from each other, and for thirteen years shared everything from our first teary, front-toothless days of kindergarten to the sick-making silence that filled our school hall as we turned over our first English paper of the HSC.

And I do mean sick-making. In the years since (and there have been plenty), the HSC and my complete lack of serious study for it, have haunted my dreams. Even today, I know I am under stress if I wake up having had The Exam Nightmare. (Don't worry, I know, Freud would have a field day.)

Scholastically, our collective wash-up wasn't bad, but probably no better or worse than any random sample you'd care to take of the population. And despite a personal HSC result that had been too often predicted in my school reports (*Can do better!*), I wouldn't change a second of my simple, suburban public schooling for anything.

Neither would my husband, Pete. He, too, went to the local public primary school, just down the road from the modest orange farm in the bush where he grew up. But high school was going to be a different story. When the time came, he pulled up his socks and headed off to the same elite private boys' boarding school in the city that his father, three older brothers, all his male cousins and every one of his uncles had attended.

It wasn't easy, though—the farm was far from a financial fountain. Help came in the form of a small inheritance left by his grandfather that had been put aside, and every cent of it went to his secondary schooling and that of his six siblings.

'You only get one shot at education' was his family's belief, and once food and shelter were covered, anything left over should go straight towards making sure your children got the best possible start in life. An admirable dictum and one that is difficult to argue against.

But was his school better than mine? It depends, of course, on how you want to define 'better'. Both our schools were around a century old, but where his buildings had sandstone, mine had bricks and weatherboard. Where he had the choice of eight perfectly manicured sporting ovals, our lone playing field was somewhat hampered by the creek that ran along its border and regularly flooded. While we sat in demountables during scripture class, he had his own chapel. And as we bussed it to the public pool fifteen minutes away, he popped into the school's twenty-five-metre indoor facility, summer or winter (it was heated, of course).

In terms of friends though, my life couldn't have been richer. Michelle, Sue, Christine, Julie, and Lisa P. were a constant source of joy, with sleepovers providing the weekend glue that meant we were rarely out of each other's sight. Such gatherings were always fuelled by Lolly Gobble Bliss Bombs, Wagon Wheels, and the latest copy of *Dolly*.

Ah, *Dolly*. Our guide to life, boys, striped over-the-knee socks and, most importantly, how to wear the latest shade of Yardley Pot O' Gloss on our eyes, lips and cheeks. All at once. And we did. Because *Dolly* said.

Dolly was our collective bible, and I never ever threw my copies out. Instead they were carefully filed under my bed in chronological order. (Another one for Freud no doubt.) After all, you just never knew when one of those *Dolly* Doctor or What Should I Do? problems would apply, so best to keep them near. I had the only complete set among my group, and so sleepovers were often at my place as a result.

Christine, though, had the coolest destination on Saturday nights. The times, they were a-changin', and Chris's mum Lillian, as she insisted we call her, was newly divorced. She would help us dye our hair with Magic Silver White, ignore our giggles and whispers well into the wee hours, and happily let us play our records— basically anything currently making the Countdown Top Ten—at full volume on the three-in-one stereo. But the ultimate indicator that Lillian was part of a new breed of mum? *Her* bible of choice was *Cleo*. Now I didn't read *Cleo*. I couldn't; my mother wouldn't let me. It did, after

all, have that naked male centrefold. And when I discovered an issue among Lillian's stash that contained
five fold-out pages of Skyhooks in all their naked, hairy,
rebellious glory, I decided this magazine just wasn't for
me. It wasn't just the fact that Red Symonds had chosen
to cup his genitals in a gas mask for said photo that
helped me come to this decision. Back then, the teen
population of Australia was split into two sharply divided
groups ... those who followed Skyhooks and those who
worshipped Sherbet. I was one of the latter, and most
tragic, kind. It was a Daryl Braithwaite thing. And *Dolly*
featured them regularly.

Well may you wonder what all this had to do with
my schooling. Heaven knows my geography teacher,
Miss Coleman, certainly did. It was always in her class—
first period, third Tuesday of every month, when I was
supposed to be immersed in the prime export figures of
Papua New Guinea or somesuch—that my hot-off-the-
press, just purchased issue of *Dolly* would be confiscated.
Of course, if I'd known then what I know now, I could
have simply pointed out that I was studying for my career.

For some reason Miss Coleman always gave *Dolly* back
at the end of class, but I have little doubt that no such
tolerance would have been extended at my husband's
school. The culture there was one where the expectation
of high achievement in all things was enormous, and the
fact that the children of people in high-salaried professions—doctors, barristers and the like—went, after
studying in those same hallowed halls, in large numbers
into those same high-salaried professions isn't surprising.

As to my own post-school life, a huge desire to wipe
the slate clean and finally apply myself, mixed with a

massive dose of right-time/right-place luck saw me answer a tiny three line ad in the *Sydney Morning Herald* just a few weeks after I left college. I was nineteen. It was for the job of receptionist at *Dolly*. 'Girl Friday who is prepared to do absolutely anything' was the exact wording. And I was. Those back-issues, now dusty but still under my bed, still in chronological order, if a little dog-eared, had come home to roost. All those missed geography lessons, justified. The fact that I hadn't gone to a private school didn't seem to hinder me at all. In the interview it didn't even come up. Indeed, I can't help wondering now if, instead of choosing the post-HSC secretarial course I did, private school would have just about ensured four years of university, making me miss that ad completely. And, with all those years of uni study under my belt, would I have been happy to become a Girl Friday? I'll never know.

Either way, that job proved to be the opportunity of a lifetime, and two years later, clearly trying to make up for years of 'can do better' report cards, I had become *Dolly*'s editor.

In the years since, I've often been asked whether I knew someone to get that magazine job. Or if I'd called on the old school tie (a term that amused me, since the only old school tie I knew of was the one I'd ditched along with my high-school blazer). Surely, they thought, I must have done at least a little 'networking'. Or known someone whose dad was on the company board. But here's the thing: I think if I'd realised that such a powerful force as 'who-you-know' could prejudice appointments made in the business world, I probably would have been too intimidated to put my hand up for the job in the first place. In many ways, I was too far out of the 'network' loop to know what I didn't know . . . if you know what I mean.

So here Pete and I are, over two decades on, with three young children, and making decisions about their futures in a climate where our federal government has never been less interested in public education. Meanwhile, there simply aren't enough private schools to meet the ever-growing demand.

What have we chosen for our kids? So far, we're united in the belief that the local public school will be their home for the first seven years of their education. Just two blocks from where we live, it offers them a sense of the local community, plenty of sleepover pals who live nearby, a band of dedicated teachers and a terrific Principal.

Our hope is that our children will see from the various working bees, fetes, gardening days and car-boot-sale fundraisers, that mucking in and being part of a committed, if a little cash-strapped, school community is a good thing. And at the very least they will understand that things like the computers they work on and the books they read don't just magically appear out of thin, privileged air.

Where will they go in their senior years? This is still under discussion. Pete is quite firm in his view that our two boys should attend his old school, and I have to admit that the facilities it offers and academic results it achieves do seem impressive. Against this, I worry about producing young ones who might take privilege as the norm. Who go on to pigeonhole others according to the school they did or didn't attend. Just like those girls back at secretarial college.

In the end, there can never be a definitive answer as to what's best. Ultimately, the sort of adult your child becomes is dependent on an almost limitless number of factors, many of which are outside your control. But the ones you can influence, the qualities I will look for in my own children when they graduate, should never be the sole burden of the school you choose, public or private . . . Qualities such as a sense of personal responsibility, tolerance, generosity, a love of learning, respect for the environment, and a natural curiosity. They are the true mark of the person you send out into the world.

And then of course, whatever school we choose, there is still that whole other issue of single-sex versus co-ed. But that's another story . . .

LISA WILKINSON was appointed editor of teen magazine *Dolly* at age 21. It was here that she discovered a totally unknown redhead by the name of Nicole Kidman and put her on the cover of the magazine. Rumour has it that she has been on a few magazine covers since. (Nicole, not Lisa.) Four years later, after almost tripling *Dolly*'s circulation, Kerry Packer personally headhunted her (Lisa, not Nicole) to become the editor of *Cleo*. Over the next decade, after getting rid of the centrefold (please forgive her—her best friend almost has), and starting the magazine's now infamous list of Australia's 50 Most Eligible Bachelors, Lisa oversaw *Cleo*'s biggest-ever circulation surge, taking it to the unprecedented position of number one selling women's lifestyle magazine, per capita, in the world, and going on herself to become *Cleo*'s International Editor-in-Chief, also running editions in New Zealand, Singapore, Malaysia and

Thailand. Lisa then spent six years as Editor At Large of *The Australian Women's Weekly*, and most recently, as Executive Editor, helped devise and launch *Madison*.

Today, as well as being co-host of Channel 7's top-rating *Weekend Sunrise*, and a regular on Sydney radio's 2UE, she is one of Australia's busiest female corporate speakers and presenters, and runs her own international magazine consultancy business, with many of her initiatives receiving industry awards both here and overseas.

Lisa is also an ambassador for Barnardo's Children's Charity, the National Breast Cancer Foundation and Cure Cancer Australia. She is married to former rugby player, fellow journalist, broadcaster and author Peter FitzSimons and together they have three young children.

But she still has nightmares about sitting the HSC.

The Magic of Dance

Cindy Pan

Like many young Australians, I first became a teenager at the age of thirteen, an unlucky number, and for me, and I suspect many others, an unlucky age. All my life I had loved ballet. Even thinking about ballet now brings a tear to my eye if I think about it too long. Because I was destined, you see, to become the world's greatest ballerina, only no one else knew. Only me.

There were other troubling matters too. I was frustrated. I couldn't speak. I couldn't be heard above the din of everyone else. I was shy and retiring although internally highly argumentative. I didn't know how to stand up for myself. I didn't know how to swing things my way. I just stood by and stared and then looked away.

But I loved ballet. I loved dancing. I loved poring over ballet books and watching ballet shows on TV or really anything with dancing. I was good at dancing. I loved being on stage flooded by the lights and lost in my imaginings. I enjoyed the rush of hearing my music and knowing when to run on and start my dance. Just thinking about it makes me smile. If life could be a ballet or even a ballet concert, I would know how to live. You wouldn't have to talk. Everyone would just know when to come on and dance and then come off still beaming and get ready for their next number. What a pity life's not a ballet. Wouldn't it be wonderful if all you had to do every day was dance?

When I was a teenager, dancing was not all I thought about but whatever else I thought about, dancing was in there too. Whatever I was doing, I was thinking about dancing. Whatever I was thinking, it would be in relation to dancing. It was wonderful to have a focal point for everything. People talk about obsession as if it is a bad thing. But it's not. It's great. I think I was a more focused person with a better sense of direction and a clearer sense of who I was and what I wanted when I was a teenager because it was simple. I didn't want everything. I didn't want to be everything. There was no need to balance or juggle or compensate. I just wanted to dance and to be a dancer. Everything else was secondary, in the background, easily falling away when I stood up to dance.

I knew my parents would not let me leave school to do ballet full time. My dad said 'Do you see any Chinese people in the Australian Ballet?' My mum said 'You'll waste your brain.' I argued with them about it but I knew it would be useless. I wasted my breath and my tears. I knew it was a waste but I did it anyway. It was part of my dance, I suppose.

I didn't tell anyone else that I had been thwarted. I never told anyone that I wanted to be a ballerina. I never discussed the issue with anyone at school or even at ballet. Not my fellow students, not my teachers.

No one. I couldn't see the point. It wasn't part of my dance, I suppose.

I kept dancing but I was sadder and sadder about it and it began to seem rather useless and pointless. I thought it would lead nowhere or at least not where I wanted it to.

I danced last night in the moonlight under the stars across yellow painted markings in an empty asphalt car park. We had just had dinner at the local Chinese and my three-year-old Anton wanted me to gallop. So I galloped and leapt and polkaed in my jeans and thongs like an easy breeze, fast-flowing, unfettered and floating on a melody of stars and lightning and galaxies, while Anton cavorted jerkily beside me in his boots. My husband Andrew stood by the car boot holding Jeremy, our nine-month-old, who looked on curiously. Andrew shook his head and said, 'We just don't understand, do we Jeremy?'

I felt so happy. So light and full of light. Radiant, so startlingly glittering and flittering. Like a beautiful lightning bolt scattering blooms of rainbow hues with wild eyes, wild hair, wild limbs and a wild, whole, unfettered heart.

I have loved ballet all my life. I love it more than anything I can think of. I have given it more energy and it has brought me more joy than any other activity. Thinking about it stirs more emotion than any other thing. There are tears rolling down my cheeks and dripping all over my folder right now. I don't know why. Nothing else makes me feel this way. Like a teenager again.

Just the word ballet reminds me of when I first saw it and wondered why it looked like it should be pronounced the same as 'ballot'. It seems most things that have a Frenchy pronunciation turn out to be pretty cool things. Things I'll like, even if only conceptually. Such as lingerie. Or champagne. I don't drink but I like the look of it. And champagne glasses are gorgeous. Not the flutes; I mean those shallow wide-mouthed ones. So impractical. So lush.

I remember I actually argued with my parents about the word ballet. I was sure they were wrong. I said I thought ballet was spelt B-A-L-L-E-Y. It seemed more logical. I was usually right about things like spelling. But in this case my mum said 'No I'm pretty sure it's a T'. I had drawn a picture of a beautiful ballerina and written the words 'I LOVE BALLEY' above and below it in fancy script. I eventually conceded that I might have been wrong but I didn't spoil the image by changing it. As the song says 'I did it myyyyyyy way.'

I remember hearing Margot Fonteyn on *The Magic of Dance*, her TV show. She said ballet like 'bally' as in 'ballyhoo'. Just listening to it in my head still makes me chortle inside. How funny that the Dame herself pronounced it in such a funny way. Maybe she also thought it should be spelt with a 'y'.

I loved ballet and somewhere in my teens I gave my heart to ballet and somewhere in my teens I broke my heart over ballet and it still breaks every time I think too much about it. I think having something you love or want or prize or care about so intensely it makes you cry and leap for joy and laugh and dance in the moonlight is what life is all about. People talk about values. I value all the things that ballet means to me: life, love, freedom, artistry, beauty, music, energy, romance, that feeling of bursting . . . pure joy. I discovered this when I was a teenager.

When you love something, you will waste your breath and your tears and break your heart and your voice and tear yourself apart over it even though it's not worth it in any practical way. You have no choice because it is part of your dance. And when that part of your dance is over, you'll dance a different dance and it will be all the richer and more joyous for all the sorrow that has gone before. It might be in a car park. You might be wearing thongs. Maybe no one is watching and no one understands. But just the memory of it will make you cry. And you feel so happy. Just like a teenager: happy, crying and intensely alive.

CINDY PAN, MBBS, FRACGP, is a doctor who works in the media. She has many years of experience working in general practice as well as sexual health and women's medicine. She is the author of the best-selling *Pandora's Box—Lifting the Lid on Life's Little Nasties* (HarperCollins Publishers), a funny, information-packed book on health, relationships, sex and drugs. She writes a weekly health column for Sunday papers all over Australia, including *The Sunday Telegraph*, and has a regular column on relationships in *The Women's Weekly* in Singapore and Malaysia. Cindy has danced and acted on stage and screen, and was principal dancer in the Australian tour of *The King and I* in 1991–92 with Hayley Mills. She has appeared on a number of television shows, including *The Glass House*, *Sunrise*, *The Panel* and *Beauty and the Beast*. Cindy's new book, *Playing Hard to Get* (HarperCollins Publishers), co-authored with Bianca Dye, is due for release in 2007. Cindy's website is www.cindypan.com.au.

I Was a Teenage Misfit

Kim Wilkins

I grew up in a rough area and went to a rough school. To say I didn't fit in is an understatement. I was bookish and hopelessly daggy: I had to wear a plate with a rubber band for my teeth; I had bad skin and stringy hair; my parents wouldn't let me wear my hemline an inch below my knickers like all the other girls; and, worst of all perhaps, I was smart.

My small group of so-called friends were quick to turn on me and ridicule me for their own self-preservation. I remember one time in Year 9, I had won an academic award and had to go up on stage in assembly to accept it. At lunchtime afterwards, my friends took great delight in impersonating my self-conscious, staring-at-shoes walk, over and over, for the amusement of three of the tough girls who sat nearby.

The days I was ridiculed were largely the good ones—some days, I just got beaten up. I always sat in the front row of Maths class, and usually nobody sat next to me.

But there was one girl, one of the popular crowd, who would occasionally slide into the next seat at the start of class. If she did this, I knew I was in for a bad day. Every time the teacher turned around to write something on the board, she would punch my upper arm, really really hard. My response was to keep perfectly silent, so that the teacher wouldn't know and the girl wouldn't get in trouble (you couldn't get a reputation as a dobber). She thought it was a great game. For one six-week period in Year 9, I had a permanent bruise on my left arm.

By my fifteenth birthday, I only had one friend left at school, and she was just as unpopular as me because she belonged to some weird cult that didn't do Christmas. At least she had God to comfort her. My alcoholic dad was an atheist, and fond of telling me that when I died I'd be 'worm tucker'. Not very reassuring. Eventually, my odd religious friend left school too, and I didn't really have anyone.

I disappeared, as I always had, into books. I loved *The Lord of the Rings* and any other fantasy or ghost stories. I spent a lot of time in the library on my lunch breaks, reading by myself, and then writing stories about a girl just like me (except with better teeth) who had interesting friends and went on fantastic adventures. The library was a haven. It was the place where my imagination was free to roam. While other girls were cheering on the football team or gossiping about boys behind A Block, I was off in the magical land of Antara, where I was responsible for the fate of the whole human race. An evil queen had taken over, and kidnapped my best friend too. My journey through the forests and wastelands was epic.

I gathered a ragtag mob of friends on the way, each one of them a misfit like me, each one of them willing to risk everything to help me.

The tough girls never found me and beat me up in the library—I doubt they'd ever been near a book. The toilets were where I was in most danger: either I'd be coerced, under threat of having my head flushed, into watching at the door for the arrival of a teacher while they smoked in the end cubicle, or I'd end up the butt of some joke. One afternoon, I walked around for two hours with the sticker from a sanitary-disposal unit on my back. I had no idea it was there. Not even my teachers bothered to tell me.

I couldn't really turn to my parents for help. My dad was in the middle of a grand descent into alcoholism, which eventually killed him, and my mum was dealing with his terrifying mood swings, his infidelities, and his inability to earn anything more than sickness benefits. She was being so strong, holding the family together, so whenever she asked how things were at school I'd just say 'fine' because I didn't want to worry her. Beyond that, I was young: I didn't really have enough experience of the world to know that there were things I could do to make my life better; I didn't know my own strengths because they'd never been tested; and so I just coped—one day at a time—and hoped that I could get through school without being crushed by the pressure.

Then, about halfway through Year 10, a new girl started at school, and the teacher sat her next to me in Maths class. I was frightened of her at first. She was very sophisticated, very self-possessed and extremely pretty. She dyed her hair black and everyone said she had a boyfriend with a motorbike. She seemed far too cool for me, but we had to work together and found we had precisely the same sense of humour. I made a crack one time about the teacher's hair, and that set her off laughing so hard that she couldn't stop. Then, of course, because we weren't supposed to be laughing, we laughed even harder until we both got hot-faced and hysterical and the teacher made us stand outside until we calmed down.

Nobody was more surprised than me when she began to walk with me from Maths class to morning tea, and seemed very comfortable to sit with me and trade more jokes. Looking back now, I guess she was new and looking for a friend, and she probably came from a school with a very different culture to mine. She listened to punk music and said she didn't care what anyone thought of her. Not only did she like the same books as me, but she seemed to be really interested in what I did and said. She thought being smart was cool, and when I confessed one day that I liked to write stories, she thought that was cool too. We immediately embarked on writing a science fiction story together.

Oh, the relief! Someone was interested in what I thought. I didn't have to second-guess everything I said in case it invited ridicule. At the start of Year 11, another new girl arrived, and we recognised a kindred spirit in her straightaway (maybe it was the enormous fantasy novel she was reading under D Block one morning that tipped us off). Pretty soon, there were six of us, all sitting in the library courtyard at lunchtime and writing crazy science fiction, fantasy and ghost stories. We embarked on a mad round-robin story in which we were all characters on a spaceship heading for an outer colony of the solar system. It was forty per cent soap opera, forty per cent wicked in-jokes about our enemies, and twenty per cent sheer magic. As time went by, my teeth got straighter, my skin got better and, thanks to a group of girls who cared about me, I even sorted out my hair (and started dying it blue!). I blossomed, I no longer cared what the popular girls thought of me; I thought so much less of them.

They say the best revenge is living well, and I believe it. I once ran into one of the girls who victimised me at school, and she'd married and had babies too young, was now divorced, unhappy and living a life of quiet desperation. Everything about me that made me daggy and unpopular has turned out to be a blessing. I was naive, so I bloomed later, made the right decisions about men, and ended up in a wonderful relationship that has endured. I was smart, so I've managed to do well in my studies and in my career; I even have a PhD now. I was creative, so I wrote books. But most of all, through being a misfit I've learnt how important it is *not* to fit in all the time. Fitting in sometimes means compromising yourself, losing a little piece of your identity that you might never find again. That road leads to unhappiness that lasts forever. Always, always be yourself.

KIM WILKINS was born in London but grew up in a seaside town north of Brisbane. She has a PhD from the University of Queensland, and her books have won numerous awards and are sold all over the world. Her works include the supernatural thrillers *Rosa and the Veil of Gold* and *Giants of the Frost*, as well as the Gina Champion detective series for young adults and the Sunken Kingdom fantasy series for children.

Summer Lovin'

Tara Moss

I found my first glimpse of love during the long sunny days of an Indian summer in the quiet suburbs of the Canadian town of my birth.

It was 1986, and the world as I knew it was an idyllic paradise. The air was clean, the trees had not been cut down, and there was no such thing as September 11, AIDS, spam, mobile phones, the war in Iraq or Paris Hilton. I was blissfully unaware of the issues of debt and poverty, so much so that in a school essay that year I described my lower-middle-class family as being wealthy, much to the horror of my mother, who tried to explain that she did the after-hours stocktaking at cut-rate department store Zellers and my sister and I wore hand-me-down clothes with patches on the knees and elbows precisely because we were not what people called 'wealthy'. I had no idea that in some other place people might have more than we did or, in fact, much less. It seemed there was not a care in the world.

Then I had to go and discover boys.

I was one of those girls who did everything early. By

all accounts, I was born with a full head of hair and legs that hung over the edge of the bed in the maternity ward, pretty much fully formed into my current self, probably with a martini in one hand. I took my first steps at nine months, was a connoisseur of Stephen King horror novels by ten years, and stole a *Playgirl* magazine and taped the centrefold up in the girls' toilets at eleven. I guess it was no surprise, then, that I first fell in love at twelve—or, more accurately, fell in puppy love.

In the summer of 1986, my best friends were Theresa, Dahlia and a tall, freckly, red-haired boy named Benjamin. We all lived within four leafy suburban blocks of one another and we were inseparable. We rode banana-seat bicycles, built a go-kart, discovered roller-skates you could strap onto your high-top runners, and climbed the cliffs around the rocky Canadian beaches like billygoats. Time stretched on in a way I have not since been able to emulate, no matter how much I manipulate the clock. Blissful afternoons dissolved into long sunny evenings. Days melted one into the next. There were no school-books or teachers, responsibilities or cares. Being three tomboyish girls and one boy, we were delightfully unaware of the implications of relationships, gender and sex, let alone our own heartaches to come. And then one evening, after running around like puppies until we fell exhausted into a heap on the grass of the school field, the four of us gazed at the cloud formations in the orange and purple sunset, panting. And, with no real warning, Benjamin and I kissed.

It was a kiss on the lips—spontaneous, but still quite unmistakably a kiss.

The jolt of unfamiliar intimacy was disorienting.

We pulled away seconds later, but everything had already changed. The two of us stared at our feet and blushed wildly, and if Ben and I were shell-shocked by this occurrence, we weren't the only ones. Dahlia and Theresa had seen what had happened. Not so long before, such an encounter would have evoked cries of 'boy's germs!' But not now.

Without saying a word, we all just pretended that nothing had happened.

But that wasn't the end of it. The next afternoon, the four of us lay on the soft green front lawn at Dahlia's parents' place after skateboarding up and down the street all day, and Ben and I found ourselves holding hands and grinning stupidly. A strange euphoria came over me. I no longer thought of him as Ben, the geeky friend of mine, but rather as BEN—in capital letters and with hearts around his name. Before long, he was making cassettes of Air Supply ballads for me, and I was drawing dragons for him with little love poems and slipping them into his parents' mailbox. We stopped staring at the moving clouds the way we always had, and started staring into each other's eyes with lovesick intensity instead. We were infatuated.

Disaster could not be far behind.

One day Ben and I were holding hands, and most probably not paying nearly enough attention to our two other friends, when Theresa burst into tears and ran into her house. Dahlia had to explain that Theresa had a crush on Ben, but had failed to mention said crush to me, or to him. In retrospect, it seems inevitable. It was the first summer our hormones had started to get the better of us, and with Ben being the one male among three female friends, someone was bound to harbour curious feelings. How could our little group survive our sexes now that we were on the cusp of becoming teenagers?

Sadly, it couldn't. Bryan Adams' 'Summer of '69' was still being sung by teenagers everywhere while our own summer break of '86 came to an end, and the tensions in our young changing lives pulled us slowly apart. Dahlia soon dropped out of school just as her brothers had, and we didn't see her much. Theresa's family moved, and only four years later young Theresa was a single mother living on what the Canadian government could provide. Two summers on, I was already thrust into the adult world of work and responsibility as I negotiated an early modelling career in Milan. And Ben—well, I don't know what happened to Ben. I never saw him again after that first, failed summer of love.

I knew nothing about love at the time, but then again I was only twelve. Twenty years later, I am not sure I have any excuses . . .

TARA MOSS has made the transition from international top model to international crime-writing success as the author of the best-selling novels *Fetish*, *Split*, *Covet* and *Hit*. Tara has enjoyed writing stories since the age of ten. She earned a Diploma from the Australian College of Journalism in 1997, and in 1998 won the Scarlet Stiletto Young Writers' Award for her short story 'Psycho Magnet'. Her novels have been nominated for both the Davitt and Ned Kelly awards, and are published in ten countries and six languages. Her in-depth writing research has seen her tour the FBI Academy in Quantico, Virginia, and spend time in squad cars, courtrooms, morgues and criminology conferences around the world. Tara has also taken polygraph tests, shot guns with the LAPD and flown with the RAAF Roulettes. She is currently in the process of getting her private investigator's licence. Tara immigrated to Australia in 1996 and is a proud Australian–Canadian dual citizen. Her website is www.taramoss.com.

To . . .

Grace Whiting

I want to . . .

- ❤ sleep until I'm no longer tired
- ❤ trust someone with my deepest secrets
- ❤ learn the meaning of a new word every day
- ❤ peel back the layers of my subconscious to discover who I truly am
- ❤ make my father proud
- ❤ speak another language
- ❤ work in a job that doesn't destroy my soul
- ❤ fall in love with someone who knows me better than I know myself
- ❤ live where no one knows me and reinvent myself without the limitations of friends or familiarity
- ❤ hold beliefs so passionate I'll put my life on the line to defend them
- ❤ watch sunsets over foreign shores and collect stamps in my passport
- ❤ write words that resonate within the souls of strangers
- ❤ fly

❤ grow old gracefully
❤ die in the knowledge that someone else's life has been touched by my existence
❤ be remembered.

I believe that SISTER2sister means something different to everybody and that no two girls will ever take away the same things. Life is a patchwork of experience and inspiration and I, for one, am proud to say that SISTER2sister has a permanent place in mine.

GRACE WHITING, a Little Sister in the 2006 SISTER2sister Program, has just completed Year 12 and plans to study Media and Communications at university in 2007. Grace is passionate about writing and has an insatiable appetite for the written word. This, combined with a deep desire to keep learning and a sense that there are many stories to be told, is what drives Grace towards her goal of becoming a journalist. In the meantime, she will try to accomplish as many things from that list of aspirations as she can—no doubt, she will find herself forever adding new tasks.